POWER UNLIMITED

(शक्त अनन्त)

Relation of Man with God

POWER UNLIMITED

(शक्ति अनन्त)

Relation of Man with God

D.N. Saraf

ABHINAV PUBLICATIONS

abhinav publications

First published in India 1996

Publishers
Shakti Malik
Abhinav Publications
E-37 Hauz Khas
New Delhi - 110016

ISBN 81-7017-333-7

Phototypeset in Platino 11pt by
Tara Chand Sons
Naraina, New Delhi

Printed at
D.K. Fine Art Press Pvt. Ltd.
Ashok Vihar
Delhi

Hymn to the Guru

Gurur Brahma gurur vishnuh gurur devo mahesvara,
Guruh saakshaath para-brahma tasmai sri guravey namah.

The preceptor as Brahma,
The preceptor as Vishnu,
The preceptor as divine Mahesvara;
The preceptor as soul-witness
to the final Path; to that preceptor
Reverence.

Ajnaana timiraandhasya chalaakaya
Chakshurun-meelitham yeyna tasmai sri guravey namah.

Through whom — eyes blinded
with the darkness of unknowing
are anointed with knowledge,
and opened, to such a preceptor,
Reverence.

Om namah sivaaya guravey satchidananda murthaye Nishprapanchaaya shaanthaaya niraalambayaaya thejasey ('ey' to be pronounced as in 'they').

Aum: Reverence to the Siva,
to the preceptor,
to the image of Truth-Awareness and pure Joy,
to the Manifest, to the Serene,
to that which transcends Causation,
to energy, in its brilliance.

About the Satguru

India is, and has been, a land of seers since the beginning of history. Mahatma Mangat Ram stands in this great tradition connecting the past with our present, and with the future of mankind. He was one of the greatest saints of the 20th century and the most profound exponent of "*Samata*" — "Sameness". His teachings are the quintessence of Samata. He taught nothing that he did not practise to perfection. It was my great good luck to be initiated by the Satguru in August, 1952 at Srinagar (Kashmir).

An unusual child, blessed by God from his infancy, Mangat Ram attained self-realization at the age of 13. He led an ascetic life of intense unremitting contemplation. The high mountains, deep forests, lonely spots and open sky remained his night companions for life. A wandering *faqir* with no possessions but a love of God, his living was startlingly simple.

Revelatory verses welled up from the depth of his *samadhi* and spilled over for hours on end. Bhagat Banarsi Das, who served at the Master's feet for 15 years, collected as many of these as he could and compiled them into Granth Samata Prakash. The prose sayings on questions of applied *Dharma* and the way to right living are conserved in Granth Samata Vilas. Revelation and doctrine converged on a single focus: *Samata* where differences and duality drop; a state where finite melts into infinite, where being thunders into its ultimate. Beyond space. Beyond time.

SATGURU

MAHATMA MANGAT RAM JI

MAHARAJ

(1903-1954)

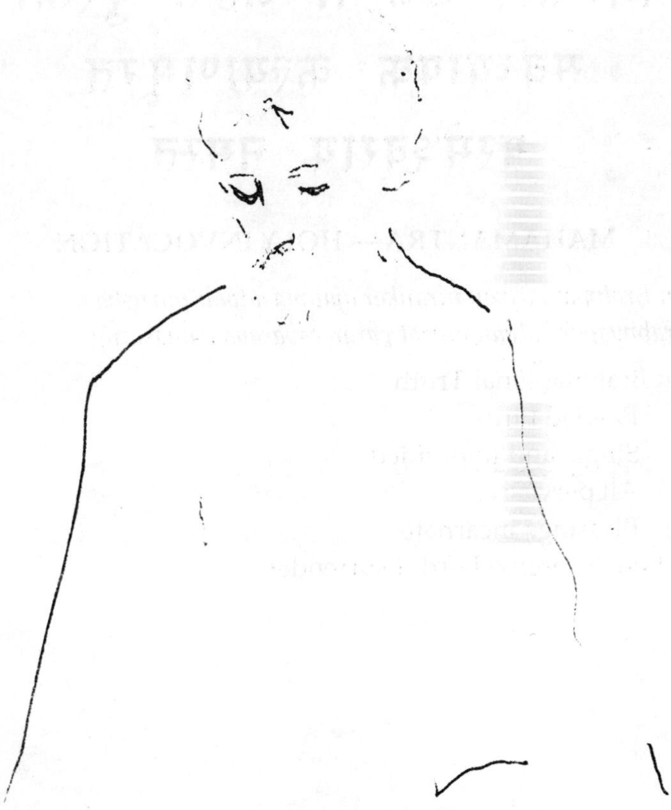

In dedication to him

गुर की सीख ने कियो निहाल।
सरन पाई प्रभ दीन दयाल।।

'To "the Lord of the Lowly": *Din Dayal*!
With the Master's teaching I am replete,
Now I seek refuge at your feet.'

ॐ

ब्रह्म सत्यं
निरंकार अजन्मा अद्वैत पुरखा
सर्वव्यापक कल्याणमूरत
परमेश्वराय नमस्तं

MAHAMANTRA — HOLY INVOCATION

Om Brahma Satyam nirankar ajanma advait purusha
Sarabvyapak kalyan murat paramesvaraya namastang

Om Brahma, Final Truth
Beyond birth
Single and undivided
All pervasive
Blessings incarnate
To you, Supreme Lord, I surrender.

समता
अपार शक्ति

'SAMATA' — THE INFINITE POWER

'सत सरुप शक्त अपार'
(Sat Swarup Shakta Apar)
Your real self is Power Unlimited

(Mangat)

निमख निमख अराधिए, एको नाम भगवन्त।
"मंगत" भरमन सब मिटे, घर परसें शक्त अनन्त।।

Worship, from moment to moment,
One Supreme Being,
Free from all delusion,
You will experience within
The 'Power Unlimited' says "Mangat".

।। मङ्गलाचरण ।।

नारायण पद बंदिए ताप तपन होये दूर।
नमो नमो नित चरण को जो सरब आधार हजूर।।
हिरदे सिमरो नाम को नित चरणी करो डण्डोत।
सत शरधा से पूजिये रख सत्गुर की ओट।।
दुविधा मिटे मंगल होये जो चरण कंवल चित धार।
रिद्ध सिद्ध आवे घर माहीं पावें जय जय कार।।
साचा ठाकुर सरब समराथा अपरम शक्त अपार।
"मंगत" कीजे वन्दना नित चरणी बलिहार।।
सत मारग सोझी मिली तन मन भया निहाल।
गवन मिटी संसार की सत्गुरु मिले दयाल।।
बार बार करूँ बन्दना सत्गुरु चरणी माहीं।
"मंगत" सत्गुरु भेंट से फेर गर्भ नहीं आई।।

MANGALACHARAN — BENEDICTION

1. Surrender to Narayana's feet
That the heat of anguish may retreat.
Bow always to his feet — the Lord
in whom the world finds its support.

2. Deep in your heart hold to his Name
May your ways be ruled always by the same.
With faith worship One — the true
Take refuge in your Satguru.

3. Doubts effaced, contained be —
In spirit at his Lotus-feet.
If wealth and fulfilment visit one:
Thank Him from whom all blessings come.

4. The Lord of Truth's an emperor
   A limitless, an endless power.
   "Mangat: The Mendicant" worshipped Him, he
   Sacrificed self to Eternity.

5. The true route's the direct route, once this is met
   Bodily fears and mental fears — these are laid to rest.
   The wiping out of worldliness, once this is begun —
   you'll receive the Satguru's compassion.

6. Again and again I surrender to
   The sacred feet of my Satguru
   By the gift of Mangat's example may
   Release — not rebirth, be my way.

(Translated by
Priya Devi)

Contents

Introduction

In my early thirties, while working in the Department of Industries, Kashmir, I heard a saying from a colleague of mine: "You and God can do anything and you are not alone." Little did I then understand its full implication. But after initiation by Mahatma Mangat Ram Ji (1952), and with a degree of effort towards self-realization, I can now say how true the saying is. It dawned on me how unaware we are of the remarkable potentialities which are within us, and that to make life's most exciting and constructive discovery was to know our real self and our own latent self-worth. This journey into self-discovery has been the sum of my studies and the story of my struggle for over half a century.

With economics as my subject in university, marketing as my special discipline and development of handicrafts as my profession, I had all along an innate urge of self-enquiry, a quest of spirit, a search into the hidden layers of my own being. Relationship of matter and spirit in practical life has intrigued as well as encouraged me to understand that life has a purpose, it could not be compartmentalised as material or spiritual. However, it could be a full life. Glorifying the outer manifestations of life by the light of the inner-self — as a practical and desirable combination — this has been almost an obsession with me. I continue to study, contemplate and try to apply these precepts.

The reason in putting together material for this book is basically my own continuing interest in this subject as an aspirant. I am writing primarily for the simple joy of self-communion. At the same time I have a call of conscience to share with the modern youth some thoughts on the spirit, on meditation and allied subjects, which are wrongly considered the preoccupation of the old and retired people. Often people have not been exposed to considerations of the spirit. We must know that it is very much a part of life. And, it is this life which holds so much for each one of us if we believe in and actually experience the presence of divinity in us — that power which sustains all life.

The younger generation may regard religion as representing fads and decadent dogmas, and rituals which are not compatible with the present-day realities, not even with the real science of the spirit. Most of them seem the opposite to spirituality. At the same time nothing is more barren than to be obsessed with the present and forget the past with its meaningful values and traditions. It is important that old scriptures should be reviewed, rediscovered and re-interpreted.

Side by side, as a result of disillusionment with and reaction to the supposed pre-eminence of materialistic rationalism which more or less dominated the intellectual horizon of the so-called enlightened world, from the 19th century till about the middle of the 20th, a desire for rediscovery and re-interpretation of mankind has now become a universal phenomenon. With our material development, unfortunately regression appears to have overtaken progress in areas of integrity, ethics, spiritual compassion and altruistic feelings for others.

It is, however, now being increasingly realized that it is the Supreme Life that shines in and through all life. Believing in the Supreme Being, and experiencing His presence within us could convince anybody that matter and spirit are two parts of an integral life; they are not separate. And, we can with perfect confidence build up an inner life which would enable us to live in constant communication with the spiritual realm, understanding and following the all powerful — 'Overself, Teacher and Guide' in us — while pursuing our normal worldly activity. Understanding our real-self, our full and complete self, enables one to act in the world from a deep sense of inward peace and fulfilment. Self-knowledge transforms human motivations.

Everyone of us, more particularly young people, face in life crisis of one type or the other. How to overcome a crisis? A spiritually-oriented person will draw strength from within to overcome or endure any type of crisis. Adversity and suffering may sometimes turn out to be the greatest help and purifier of the soul; surprisingly very often they turn out to be opportunities in disguise. If even a great calamity overtakes us we should remain still and remember God, says Mahatma Mangat Ram. Remaining still with trust in God's will does not imply the helpless stillness of inertia which heralds dissolution, but the stillness of assured sovereignty which commands the harmony of life. The attitude of equality, sameness — Samata (this concept has been fairly explained in the book) transforms consideration of all things. Here both success and failure lose their apparent meaning and the soul takes an equal passive or active composure in all happenings as the steps and formulations of the divine will. Everything depends on the inner condition and the outward condition is useful only as a means and a help for expressing or confirming the inner state and making it dynamic and effective.

The book talks of certain tools for the development of greater potential for the benefit of those who wish to give time and effort to discover the latent power that is inherent within them and who are willing to cooperate with the law of evolution as it pertains to each one. I have tried to traverse a middle path practical for people like me, aspirants who are householders or career persons; individuals who want to pursue higher values in life without abandoning the pursuit of right worldly responsibilities. This path is different from that of the renunciate who gives up many of the worldly activities and interests in order to devote more time and energy to the goal of complete liberation.

The title of the book may sound slightly ambitious. It need not be so. It only points to a reality to which we shut ourselves. The reference is to the vast untapped potential in us, the power of the spirit. In choosing this title and writing this book, I have been intensely inspired, more than I can say, by the teachings of my spiritual master Mahatma Mangat Ram. To quote one of his many inspired verses:

> अनन्त शक्त सत रूप को, बारम बार चितार।
> "मंगत" सो निज रूप है जल थल में भ्रतार।।
>
> *Ananta Shakta 'SAT ROOP' ko barambar chitar*
> *"Mangat" so nij roop hai jal thal mein bhartar*
>
> 'Unlimited energy is one's true form. Recall this again and again. This, Mangat's own true form, roams at will both earth and ocean.'

These are the words of one of the greatest saints of the 20th century. I have quoted him time and again in this book, though it is like picking up only a few pearls from the great ocean of his teachings as given in two great works — Granth Samata Prakash and Granth Samata Vilas. The master always advised that we should listen to prophets and founders of all religions. The sermons though delivered centuries ago — for instance by Krishna, Buddha, Christ, Muhammad — are so universal in character and so potent that no length of time can ever make them irrelevant or obsolete. They will shed light through ages to come. In fact these become more radiant and shine today like beacons. The Buddha's unique message of love and lasting peace, perhaps, is needed even more today in a world which has begun realizing the damage that destructive technology can do.

However, we must bear in mind that 'Mere celebration of the greatness of prophets will not save man. For that end, he will have to live the righteous life and follow the noble principles that those prophets revealed unto mankind!' Without purification there can be no illumination. 'An ethical mode of life is the most important and basic ingredient for a spiritual form of life' (Samata Vilas).

We would do well in listening to all good and blessed people. In this spirit I have drawn upon the works of many saints, sages and philosophers more particularly of recent times. I have also availed myself of the publications of many prominent writers, who too have referred to the power of prayer and spirit for being successful in the modern world. We may profitably ponder over many of such words of wisdom as have an aura of power, splendour and vitality around them. Readers will find them both in the main body of the book and the annexures.

I have absolutely no desire to propagate personally any radically new moral attitudes, or express views more lofty than those which can be applied to practice. It would be too presumptuous on my part to put on the robe of a thinker, or a guise that is not my own. I am, however, an incorrigible but conscientious collector of good thoughts, and am fond of fitting ideas together, as coherent and convincing statements, not as judgements. As Rig Veda implores: 'Let good thoughts come to us from every side.' Openmindedness is certainly good for spiritual health, as Mahatma Mangat Ram also advises.

In the modern age when science too is recognizing the existence and importance of the spirit, our idea need not necessarily be that state of spirituality which withdraws from life, but believes in the conquest of life by the Spirit. Spirituality is really song of the soul while science is song of nature. The two supplement, not contradict, each other. In fact the great seers as Indian Rishis have also been 'the great scientists of life'. This book attempts to consider a unified view of God, Life and Man.

The world even though described as an illusion by some philosophers is the creative manifestation of the Lord. Let us accept the reality of the world as it is, with all its happiness and pain, its beauty and ugliness and see how we can make it a better place for us to live in and for those who will follow us.

We are living in a world of astonishingly diverse cultures, where political ideologies have reached a dead-end. Economic disparities are increasing; social egalitarianism is waning. The progress of physical and biological sciences has advanced human comforts and conveniences considerably. Today we see a humanity fairly satiated but not really satisfied by 'victorious analysis of the externalities of Nature'.

As Mahatma Mangat Ram says: 'Research on outside elements in pursuit of sensual pleasures will lead to more and more unrest and fear, instead of bringing peace. No doubt about it.' 'Let man side by side investigate into life force, for peace within and peace without', he advises.

The world cannot be made a better and safer place by legislation or merely by a new economic order. The metamorphosis can only be achieved by each individual improving his own inner personality — discovering freedom and strength of spirit — and joyously striving to be of service to entire universe.

This book does not talk of an ideal which worldly men are not prepared to accept. It attempts to bring out the values of humanity, self-sacrifice and love which are common in the spirit and character of all mankind. It also seeks to make us aware of the tremendous power of the spirit for personal bliss and worldly progress, lasting peace within us as individuals and peace in the society and the world we constitute. Self-knowledge, self-reverence and self-control—these three will lead man to sovereign power.

Spiritual life is not just a conglomerate of fantasy, mythology and allegorical romanticism, as many fake spiritual teachers would make us believe. True spirituality embraces the whole of life — health of physical body, the mind and the life energies. It accepts life, seeks to improve and perfect it, not to reject it. This positive note should appeal to the rising generations. Spirituality suggests: Let each of us try to fulfil all our obligatory duties as best as we can, in a spirit of detachment, joy and dedication. The more we work in this attitude, the more we are released from our inhibitions, repressions and other emotional entanglements.

However, there are realized souls who can show the way to the Good, the True and the Beautiful — to peace, happiness and well-being of all. I have tried to act as an interpreter between the seers of ancient wisdom and the seekers of modern knowledge. It is not, however, an easy task. To interpret and evaluate the substance of the Vedas, the Upanishads and other ancient scriptures, as quoted here and there, we need a powerful imagination and intellectual elasticity that can jump over the tremendous space that divides the beliefs, aspirations and psychologies of modern life from those of a long-past age.

As said in the beginning, I have collected quite a few 'priceless pearls' (that is how I regard them) — quotes of some of the highly enlightened souls, of profound knowledge and experience. After going through them, it should not be enough for us to say that these sayings are true and beautiful. Generally we know truth, but are not truthful. We do appreciate love, but hardly live in love. We give the most beautiful discourses upon the divine qualities of our higher nature, and yet in our everyday life we act as though we remain preposterous, irredeemable animals. After all our studies we only acquire that which we put into practice as Goethe put it.

If the readers find any merit in the ideas and experiences put together, the credit goes entirely to those who have inspired me — the chief among them being Satguru

Mahatma Mangat Ram (briefly mentioned as Mangat, Gurudev, Gurudeva, Satguru at places, in the book). Any weakness or flaws in them are my own.

Many friends have provided valuable guidance and assistance; too many to be listed. I thank them for their help, frank criticism and warm encouragement. I would like to end this introduction on a hopeful note that young people, in particular, may find the book fairly friendly, interesting and educative.

D.N. Saraf

Note: When you read this book, please read as if the author was talking to you. Underscore sentences, quotes and words that are meaningful to you. Memorise self-motivators so that these become part of your subconsciousness.

CHAPTER 1

The Purpose of Life

जीवन की ये सार है। जो जीवन रूप लखाई।
"मगंत" विरले हरजन, पाई निर्मल ये बड़याई।।

'The essence of living is to understand the Reality of life (the Power of Existence). It is only rare godly people who avail of this propitious privilege', says Mangat. He implies: 'Recognize life in life. It is through inward contemplation that the book of life is known...Blessed is that human life which has experienced that power of *life* by the power of which life exists.'

Why am I born? An interesting question for anyone to ask but not so easy to answer. Am I merely a wave in the ocean of life, as some put it symbolically, or am I a result of my actions (*karmas*) in the past life as certain ancient philosophies believe. The fact of life and the answer to the question 'What is it all about' is still a puzzle for most people.

कहां से आया, कहां नर जाएं। कौन तेरा मुकाम।
"मंगत" सार विचारना, मानुष जनम का काम।।

Where have you come from? Where would you go? What is your destination? To ponder over these questions rightly is the purpose of human life, according to "Mangat"

What is the purpose of life? This query generally crops up when we are facing a catastrophe, when we see someone whom we love die or when we find ourselves in particularly painful and difficult circumstances. Again, there can be possibly as many answers as the questioners according to individual thinking, precepts or assumptions. For some life is a burden, to others an opportunity. Individuals react differently. Some feel submerged in the ocean of life, while others keep gracefully afloat. Literally life is not a play-ground but a medium of growth and learning.

Perpetual happiness:

What does an individual want? One thing seems common—happiness; each one of us wants a state of continued happiness, and tries to seek it in physical objects, the external resources available. Most of us must have experienced that material objects—and there is tremendous growth of them in modern times—do give us comfort and joy limited in time and scale. We try to seek more and more objects in the hope that these would make us happy or happier. But does mere satiation of wants, though necessary and important upto a point, really satisfy us in the sense of providing sustained happiness to our souls? Experience would suggest it does not. Where there is limitation there is no lasting happiness; Unlimited alone is bliss.

What constitutes happiness is yet a matter of dispute. People generally identify it with some obvious and visible good, such as pleasure or wealth or honour. Some say one thing, some another and the same person would say different things at different times; when he is sick he thinks health is happiness, when he is poor, wealth.

Here is a small Sanskrit story: A king asked his Prime Minister what constituted a really happy life. The reply was:

Arth a gam, nityam arogita, priyasch bhariya, priya badinisch, bashius putra, arthkarisch vidya khat jivalokasya sukhani Rajan!

Material gain (income), continued good health, a loving wife, also one who speaks sweetly, an obedient son and productive education, these are the six things, O! King, which make life happy.

It is not a bad listing, for a happy worldly life, but it falls short of that state of happiness which knows no fear. Here again, Mahatma Mangat Ram observes:

'The purpose of human life is to realize the fearless state of peace, that is, a state of peace that suffers not from any lack or modification. The realization of this state of peace is possible only when real investigation is made concerning nature of body, and effort is made to discover that power in the body that keeps it alive.'

Dharma, Artha, Kama, Moksha:

The aim of life, according to traditional Hindu society, is based on:

Dharma : related to ethics; legal and moral duty; the right law of life.

Artha : represented wealth creating; economic and material gain.

Kama : covered material needs and desires, which within certain limits were never looked down upon.

Moksha : meant release, emancipation, liberation.

These premises have to be accepted and put in order, for the natural, practical life must be lived and the forces it evolves in the human being must be brought to fulness. Indian culture gave a large recognition to the primary turn of human actions — 'Artha' and 'Kama' but this element must be kept from making any too unbridled claim or heading furiously towards its satisfaction; only so it can get its full result without disaster. Wealth in hands of unprepared intellects and uncultured hearts is not only suicidal to themselves but it is a threat to the very stability of society. Wealth must fulfil some missions: the rich are the trustees of the poor and the needy.

'Dharma' enjoins that a life governed in any absolute or excessive degree by self-will, passion, sense attraction and desire cannot be the natural whole of human existence. Indian culture raised the crude animal life of desire, of self-interest and satisfied propensity to a noble, self exceeding shapeliness by infusing into it the order and high aim of 'Dharma'.

But its profounder characteristic or aim was to raise the nobler life too of the self-perfecting human being to the great aim of spiritual liberation and perfection—*moksha, mukti.* The entire life of an individual was ennobled by this aim. The great freedom—called *moksha* (in the East) freedom from body, freedom from mind, from any kind of chains around—just pure consciousness—what a wonderful state it can be! As an ideal it is most inspiring, even if we cannot reach it.

Bondage to freedom:

Freedom is true nature of our spirit. The right objective of life is to be free from bondage. Christ calls it salvation. What binds us? Evidently our unrestrained desires. Life of bondage is characterised by desire, whereas that of freedom is characterised by desirelessness. It is desire in the form of ignorance which tethers the individual to the wheel of becoming. 'Spirit is free being, and its life consists in breaking away from conventions and penetrating into being', says Dr. S. Radhakrishnan, an acknowledged expert of his time on Oriental and Eastern philosophies. 'He who has seen the real is lifted above all narrowness, relativities and contingencies.

When we are anchored in the spirit we are released from the multitude of opinions. Authority is no longer binding and ritual is no longer a support.'

What is it that gives dignity to man?

Self knowledge, the knowledge of what you are. Knowledge is the straight and simple path of *moksha* (salvation). Just as we cannot cook without fire, the same way we cannot attain *moksha* without knowledge of *atman*, says Shankaracharya. He adds: Ignorance of our reality binds us. Its knowledge releases from bondage. Salvation is not just freedom from birth and death. Body is subject to these two, not the *atman* which is immortal. When we realize our reality as *atman*, we are free from birth and death, hell or heaven, virtue and sin.

Indeed, freedom is the first condition of man's perfection, as the wise say.

Let us not make the mistake of looking for this freedom away from the present life. Freedom, indeed, is life. And as Mahatma Mangat Ram defines freedom: 'Only such person is inwardly free who is established firmly and resolutely in the Absolute...The ultimate meaning of life in the world is to gain freedom from bondage. They gain freedom from bondage who extinguish, through waters of renunciation, the flames of desires. It is necessary, therefore, to cultivate an attitude of selfless service through word and deed. Pure is the journey of life that seeks not self-interest...Liberation or freedom denotes, in fact, the state of total desirelessness. Few fortunate ones alone can attain it...The desire for liberation is not everyone's cup of tea nor does everybody feel the need of it. Only few exceptional souls seek it, very few of them endeavour for it, and fewer still attain it.'

But all of us can live a life of duties well performed (as instruments of the Lord and remembering Him all the time): life which seeks not only its own good but sacrifices comforts for the amelioration of others in utter humility.

Here is a highly practical dictum of Gurudev (my spiritual master):

> हर सिमरण निरमान सुभाओ, सत सेवा चित पेख।
> आज्ञा प्रभ में विचरिये, सुन जीवन मुक्त का लेख।।

> God-remembrance, humility, selfless service, conscientiously undertaken—and carrying out the will of the Lord. These, in brief, lead to an emancipated life.

There is another aspect of freedom: We must endeavour 'to live free, moment to moment—fresh, innocent, alive'. Lives based on having are less free than lives based on doing or being. What we have or collect is not so important as what we are and what we do for others. 'Life's goal should not be to acquire and possess and keep and enjoy for yourself but (to see) how much you're giving to society. Riches themselves bring no happiness. It is in sharing what you have that brings real joy and peace, says Mahatma Mangat Ram. He emphasises: 'One who wishes well of others is really happy.' He also advises us that one must not depend on others for one's living; honest work and honest earning is necessary. That is also an angle of freedom.

Cognition of our divinity:

It is the paramount duty of every thoughtful person to think seriously of the meaning of life; to consciously, deliberately evolve towards a wider, more liberated and luminous state of being. It is to realize Divinity of human soul—the blessed state of love, fearlessness and desirelessness. Let us endeavour living continuously in the consciousness of the Divine and the Supreme, the True and the Eternal. The realization of the Divine spirit within can only come from a pure and courageous heart, focussed resolutely on the Eternal. With continuous cognition of our Divine nature, we can act in the world without any hindrance, and thereby 'add a glow to our achievements, and soften the reactions of any disappointments that we might meet with in life's pilgrimage', in the words of Swami Chinmayananda.

> 'Merely to know is not enough to escape from the tangle of illusion. Faith and discipline of life are necessary. The illusion arises not so much from ignorance as from attachments.' (Kathopanishad)

All existence is but an expression of God's own being. The desire for union with the Divine is an inborn necessity of all life. No life can find purpose and lead to inner fulfilment unless it enters into communion with its source.

Human birth is meant for seeking Truth. All the great religions of the world agree that it is possible to know the Divine in us — the Brahm, to identify the Reality, to realize that wonderful state. In the words of Charles Morgan 'To be aware within oneself of the secret, the unrecorded, the unobserved, of the scent of woods unvisited, the beauty no one saw and the music no one heard is an enablement of man's interior life.'

Aldous Huxley (reference his Introduction to Bhagavad Gita translated in English by Swami Prabhavananda and Christopher Isherwood) writes:

> 'Man's life on earth has only one end and purpose: to identify himself with his esteemed Self and so to come to unitive knowledge of the Divine Ground (the Spirit)...'

God is that which cannot be seen with the eyes but that by which the eyes have the sight. That power dwells in every creature, but we very often fail to realize its presence because desires would not allow us to concentrate on it; they continuously distract away our attention from it.

The power pervades the body and the world, bestowing blessedness on all. It cannot shut off its own benevolence, protection and love; it is a constant flow. God does not withhold help, support or peace from anyone. But you and I can block it ourselves, by our excessive or misdirected ego which prevents us from becoming Divine. The realization of the Divine is the one thing needful. It is not merely an intellectual conception or the psychological experience. It is making real to our lives and in ourselves the transcendent and universal Divine and view in that light all aspects of our worldly existence.

Life indeed is the greatest adventure imaginable. Although some lives are without much interest and excitement, others are full of extraordinary experience. We should not permit ourselves to lose interest in life. 'Man with intelligence knows how to protect himself against outside attack but he must also know how to protect himself against his own bad habits and evil ways.'

The best way to be successful in the adventure of life is to be your own friend. As Krishna said in Bhagavadgita (VI:6), 'The Self is the friend of the (transformed) self, but the enemy of the unregenerate self.' Mahatma Mangat Ram suggests: 'Right endeavour constitutes the good of life.' He adds, 'the aim of human life is to know the right principle of life in the world. It is not the goal of life to be enslaved to conventions and traditions.'

Let us determine our priorities and know what our major motivations are, in relation to how we live our lives. All we have to do is to become clearly aware of what we think about all day long, and what we do with the major portion of our time and energy. This will easily reveal to us what things we consider to be important in our lives.

Life is nothing but constant activity; and cessation of activity is synonymous with death. Because we live in this material world, we naturally have obligations and duties relating to it. We have to do our duty as a citizen, as a husband, as a wife, a son, a brother and a friend but we should not be so obsessed by these duties and relationships that we forget we also have a higher duty, one which is of prime importance. If we respond to it correctly, we can rest assured that all things we do will be done correctly. This higher duty we have is to learn about and experience the reality of God and to live in harmony with nature's laws.

The human destiny and the purpose of human life have been seldom correctly interpreted. Modern science makes comfort and care of the living body almost the end-all and be-all of life. Some of the major faiths of our times make happiness in the other world the goal of human existence. For others detachment from the world and self-denial are the most desirable targets to be achieved in life. 'It is generally ignored that life, of course, is activity — the activity that reveals the nature of all things, including the Creative Spirit, God...Life is the activity of God', as Aurobindo put it.

We surely have a master purpose in life, and that is to be our Self; the Self we are created to be. We live in a purposeful universe. Every atom and organism in the universe bears witness to a design and purpose which determine their make-up, function and role. In our present state of understanding, we are unable to see the whole purpose of even the smallest item in the universe, but through faith and intuition we feel that there must be a universal purpose in all creations — that the Creative Spirit, whatever its ultimate nature, must have some reason for all that exists. So too, each person must have a purpose built into the very fabric of his being. Otherwise we would not ask in moments of self-analysis such questions as Who am I? What am I? What am I doing? Where am I going? Why am I here?

'Arise, awake and stop not till the goal of right knowledge is reached', says the Kathopanishad.

That knowledge is the knowledge of Atman — our inner Being. In the words of Swami Vivekananda who has also echoed the above message emphatically: 'My Atman itself is the final goal, its realization is the greatest goal.'

Peace of Mind:

इस तृखावान संसार में सत शान्ति को प्राप्त करना ही असली जीवन का ध्येय है।

The real purpose of life in this world of wants is to attain true peace of mind.

(Mangat)

The goal of human life, let us reiterate, is to realize the fearless state of peace, that is a state of joy which is not subject to variation. Not just the fleeting joy which material things provide us. 'Wealth, power and efficiency are the appurtenances of life and not the real life itself', as Dr. S. Radhakrishnan aptly puts it. To quote Mahatma Mangat Ram again:

मानुश जनम इस खातिर है कि जीव अपने असली धाम समता आनन्द को प्राप्त हो जावे।

'The (true) purpose of human life is that embodied soul is able to achieve its real abode of Samata Anand, unison with the Supreme Being. A peace which suffers not from fear of change.' Sai Baba equates the Supreme Being to LOVE and says: 'Understand that the purpose of life is to know the Embodiment of Love, namely, God.' 'Love and demonstrate through your own love that you have known Him', he advises.

Dr. Paul Brunton says in his book 'Quest of the Overself': 'We live only when we touch our perennial source, otherwise we exist.' 'One must', he suggests, 'begin to acquire a new way of viewing things and a new habit; that of timeless inner repose. One must learn to distinguish between ephemeral sensations and enduring life even while both coexist within us.' Further, 'one must learn to live in the eternal, that inward serenity unaffected by vicissitudes, perpetual underlying steadiness at the centre of one's conscious being.' That is the state of Samata — sameness, inner peace under all outer circumstances. 'Human life is an opportunity to reach that state of Samata, where opposites get reconciled and conflicts get composed absolutely and irrevocably', says Mahatma Mangat Ram.

Everywhere you see people pushing, striving and worrying and making life a game of acquiring possessions and special status, rather than inner satisfaction. Here it would be pertinent to quote Dr. Wayne Dyer who says in his 'The Sky's the Limit':

> 'If you have bought as the purpose of life prestige, money, awards, recognition or any of the multitudes of what I call 'external rewards' that society certainly tries to sell you, you are stuck on the treadmill of after-chasing for success — which, practically speaking, entails all the modern neurotic ailments including high anxiety, stress, hypertension, ulcers, depressions, worries, headaches, cramps, twitches, heart disease and emotional traumas such as unsatisfactory family relationships, a flabby life-style, a lack of love in life and so on ad nauseam.'

Basically each one of us wants to be happy and comfortable. For this, undoubtedly certain minimum material objects and facilities are necessary. There is however a limit to one's needs but not to one's greed. Those who have made their life's goal merely collecting money and all the worldly goods are not aware of the Truth which has the power to bestow upon them the showers of imperishable peace. Again as Gurudev observes: 'The unbridled hedonistic extravagance and indulgence — extreme attachment to the pleasure of the body — leads to destruction. Blinded by addiction to sense pleasures people grope in darkness.'

Darkness to Light:

'Lead us from darkness to light' is a common prayer

most of us make. Mostly it is mere repetition of words, without intensity of feelings. If one really means to move from darkness to light nothing can stop him. God is the Light! What is needed is honest and strong determination and unwavering action, a firm-footed movement. 'Cry to the Lord with an intensely yearning heart and you will certainly see Him', advises Sri Ramakrishna. To quote St. Augustine: 'Our whole business in life is to restore to health the eye of the heart whereby God may be seen.'

According to Upanishads — the epitome of the wisdom of ancient Indian sages — there are two paths — the path of the good and the path of evil. The former leads to prosperity and happiness and the latter to adversity and suffering. We must also distinguish between the path of the good from the path of the pleasant. Swami Rama has thus translated an Upanishadic statement: 'That which is pleasant is not necessarily good and that which is good may not be necessarily pleasant.' When a discriminating person is aware of his or her goal of life, he or she chooses to follow the path of the good in the external world, which is practically the first step in the ladder of enlightenment. This helps one to take the next step which leads to the spiritual dimension of life.

Unfortunately in the hurry and scurry of modern life we are not given to exploring the great bliss of the Being that is our own essential nature. 'The Kingdom of God is within you', Christ said. Vedas teach this since time immemorial. Gita teaches this. Islam teaches this. Buddha teaches this fundamental experience. Mahatma Mangat Ram observes: 'The founders of all religions the world over had only one aim — to enable man to realize the peace that is true and real. They had only one message to deliver (to mortal man) that he see, in this very frame of flesh, the Lord of the entire Universe.'

The Tao of the Chinese — the Brahman of the Hindus — the Law of the Buddhists — the Good of Hermes — that which cannot be named, according to the ancient Jewish tradition—the God of the Christians—the Allah of the Muslims—the Justice, the Truth of the materialists, all proclaim profundity of one Universal Truth.

The purpose of man's life is to become conscious of That. His mission is to manifest it. *Tat Twam Asi* — you are That, declares the Chandogya Upanishad.

All religions, all the teachings of all the sages are nothing other than methods to reach this goal. The keynote of religion lies in the reaffirmation of the divinity inherent in man and the validity of the individual spiritual quest. 'With the Divine is peace and certitude and even the solution of all difficulties.'

Hence the man of wisdom, an intelligent person, should earnestly set about knowing, through serious earnest self-enquiry, the true nature of the self -- the Infinite, eternal and pure, free from sorrow, attachment, malice and fear, pain and desire, changeless and formless. To realize our Reality, our eternal identity is, indeed, the purpose of life.

Matter revealing Spirit:

Saints describe man as an evolving spirit, capable of Godhood. He has the spiritual capacity to pass to a supreme and extraordinary pith of manhood. Released into the cosmic consciousness his spirit can become one with God; his nature merging with universal nature can become one dynamic power. 'Man in the Indian idea is a spirit veiled in the works of energy moving to self-discovery, capable of Godhood' (Aurobindo).

As Dr. Karan Singh, who has deeply studied Aurobindo philosophy, says: 'Each individual has a spark of divinity that permeates the entire cosmos. The goal of human existence is to fan the spark into the flame of spiritual realization.'

The world is indeed a manifestation of Divine Reality, the matter and spirit are not two opposite entities. They are rather complementary. In the words of Mahatma Mangat Ram: 'One who engages himself in the tasks of the world with a vigorous discipline as well as follows the path of the spirit is blessed with the awareness of fearlessness.'

A question is asked 'how to be in the field of relative (worldly) existence yet established in that field of eternal existence, never-changing Being? How to live a life of practical experience and activity yet engaged in that state of eternal Being? The answer is that introduction of spiritual values in all walks of life can make it really meaningful, full of extraordinary energy and intelligence, and beautifully balanced, with love, beauty and harmony. The quest for self-realization can and should go hand in hand with bold heroic action. Here is the advice given to Rama (the Lord of Ramayana Epic) by his preceptor, the Sage Vasistha:

> "Holding firmly at heart to the truth of your being, play like a hero your part on the world-stage, inwardly calm and detached, but assuming zeal and joy, stirrings and aversions, initiative and efforts, and performing outward actions appropriate to your particular role in various situations."

What a practical advice for everyone and for all times!

Having attained a human body — lucky as we are to have achieved that state of evolution — we must ever strive to gain the knowledge of the Truth. Human life is the greatest thing known in the world. It is no vile or unworthy existence as some cynical philosophers make it to be.

This wonderful world:

'We live in a wonderful world that is full of beauty and charm and adventure...I am interested in this world, in this life, not some other world or future life', said Jawaharlal Nehru, the first Prime Minister of independent India. Let us not make life complicated. You know when you want to see a beautiful view, you just look at it and it is there. Many people would see only the negativity or problems in their life. Negative attitude has often resulted in insensitivity towards the duties and relationships of the world. Hendrik Willem Van Loon, a great Dutch writer with refreshing humour, writes: 'I remember at least two missionaries who did not insult the Almighty by speaking in a contemptuous fashion of this utterly lovely planet which has so generously been bestowed upon us as our temporary place of abode and which is capable of so much beauty and joy that we could establish our paradise right here on this earth...'

There is nothing more dehumanising than being in a state of ever-recurring pessimism. The clouds of despair must move away from the horizon of mind. Let the sunshine of a new hope reveal to us fresh vistas of meaning of life. In fact, meaningfulness is whole life. It is in the human body that the spirit can proceed to self-discovery. 'Let us inquire of the Inmost, the One, in us, the secrets which it holds for us, through the ages.' This life is so great and beautiful when seen with a truer eye. 'Paradoxically the human spirit possesses in itself the revelation it seeks.' Life is so much that we go on exploring it but we cannot exhaust it. The mystery is timeless. And, as Albert Einstein said so beautifully: 'The most beautiful thing we can experience is the mysterious. It is source of all true art and sciences.'

'Whatever good act has to be done, it must be done during one's independent life journey, for one knows not when this body would come to an end' (Samata Vilas).

Our life is what we make it by our own thoughts and actions. The greatest use of life is to live in the present and to spend it for something that will outlast it. The ability to live in the present is essentially an attitudinal skill. A strong sense of purpose gives meaning to life and lends creative movement to it. To say as some do that all existence is mere illusion — is rather ungenerous. Stillness and movement both have place in our life — inner stillness and outer activity. If the external activity disturbs the inner peace, surely there is something wrong somewhere with us.

A Sanskrit saying—*Sariram khalu dharmasadhanam*—suggests that body is our means for fulfilling *'dharma'*, the Godward law of our being. Our physical, emotional and aesthetic parts have to be developed; by their growth, subtlety, flexibility, power and intensity, we are able to come nearer to the Divine Reality. Spirituality takes them all and gives them greater, diviner and intimate sense.

'Spirituality is an awakening to the inner reality of our being, an attempt to know and live in the highest self, being aware of another consciousness than the ego.' Calm awareness is spirituality; dwelling in illumined awareness.

Spirituality is not intellectuality, not idealism, not religiosity or an ardent emotional fervour. It is the leading motive and determining power of life. It is inner life of man, founded in the consciousness of his true, his innermost, highest and largest self and spirit. Spirituality is most intelligent way of living. It does not flourish in the void; it lends stupendous vitality and unlimited power to life.

Living a spiritual life means the awareness of the Divine Presence in all things and always. Spirituality is an active path. We become more involved in the betterment of the world. Spiritual aspirants should learn how to develop noble human values that will transform and enrich their lives enabling them to make positive contributions to the world.

Let us aim at gaining personal excitement and ecstasy for ourselves combined with a genuine sense of purpose and mission. Let us pretend that the real purpose of life is to journey through life seeking and manifesting divine, the truth, the real happiness in us; being at peace with ourselves, being natural, helping as many as we can, victimising none, and undertaking tasks that will make this planet a better place to be on for everyone now living and those who will live here, after we leave. Thus seeking our individual salvation, we would have done our duty towards the society, in a spirit of selfless service. That should be a life with a purpose, a life well lived and resulting in a well deserved liberation and real freedom from our apparent bondage.

Liberation and Life Divine:

Describing the Nature of Life Divine, Mahatma Mangat Ram says:

> 'Truly is that life divine which is dedicated to God alone, and which free from selfish motives seeks nothing but good of others, by following the will of the Lord. Adherers of the life divine free themselves from the illusory whirlpool of the world to the extent their life in the Lord is deepened. Liberation is the peace that comes from this state of life divine.'

'A prevalent idea would persuade us that the sole aim of liberation is to secure for the individual soul freedom from physical rebirth in the unstable life of the universe...the aim of escape from rebirth has long been fixed in the Indian mentality as the highest object of the soul. Many religions have fixed in the mentality of the devout the enjoyment of a heaven beyond. Indian religion has also partly, especially among the dualists, kept up the idea of '*swarga*' (heaven) as part of their spiritual motive.'

'Undoubtedly', adds Aurobindo, 'a release from the limitations of the mind and body into eternal peace, rest, silence of the Spirit, makes a higher appeal than the offer of a heaven of a mental joy or eternalised physical pleasure, but this too after all is a lure. The desire of personal salvation (in a sense) is also an outcome of ego. We should seek Divine for the sake of divine and for nothing else, because, that is the supreme call of our being, the deepest truth of the spirit... That gets us close to the Absolute and its supreme values which are the absolutes of all things. Perfection has to be worked out, harmony has to be accomplished. Imperfection, limitation, death, grief, ignorance, matter, are only the first terms of the formula — unintelligible till we have worked out the wider terms and reinterpreted the formulary; they are initial discords of the musician's tuning. Out of imperfection we have to construct perfection, out of limitation to discover infinity, out of death to find immortality, out of grief to recover divine bliss, out of ignorance to rescue divine self-knowledge, out of matter to reveal spirit.'

While we strive diligently for the inner experience, we can and should cultivate ideal relationship with the world around us, relating ourselves to all beings with nobility, sympathy, kindness, love and selfless service. 'We can experience the sweetness of life in self-giving, in wiping out the tears of the suffering brethren! This would help us, as well, in checking growing violence, increasing fractionalism, expanding adolescents' confusion and revolt, thus enabling us to contribute to making this world a better place to live in. God who has created us has also gifted us in so many ways and life gives abundantly; one just has to be the recipient' (Swami Chinmayananda).

After having talked of the 'Purpose of Life' may we end this chapter with four quotations one each from Gita, the Bible, the Quran and Samata Prakash each advising us broadly about life and living:

> 'You may move among sense-objects but without attraction or repulsion for them.'
>
> (Gita)

> 'Life not centred on God is purposeless and meaningless. Without Him, nothing else can satisfy. With Him, all of life and His other good gifts are to be gratefully received and used and enjoyed to the full.'
>
> (Bible)

'Those who believe, and do right, joy is for them and bliss their journey's end.'

(Quran)

हर हालत में ऐसा जीवन धारन करना चाहिए जो संसार में विचरते हुए संसार से अन्तर में निर्लपता प्राप्त हो जाए।

'Lead life, under all circumstances, in such a way that while moving in the world, you remain uninvolved in the world, from within.'

(Samata Vilas)

CHAPTER 2
The Reality We Are

अरूप त्याग, सरूप सम्भाल। साध-जनों की कीरत नित भाल।।

Give up the assumed notion of yourself,
Know and hold to the Reality you are!
Be this your search — and tribute — always
to the truly realized souls and saints.

(Mangat)

Self-realization:

Self-realization or *atmansakshatkar* is the *summum bonum* of life.

SAT (It is) - *CHIT* (It knows) - *ANAND* (It is bliss). These three great words, put together called *Sachchidananda* — Being, Awareness and Bliss — are three attributes or qualifications of the Reality, the Divinity in us, which we are prone to forget for lack of realization. And, if we do remember, it is merely on the mental level and seldom as a living reality.

सच्चदानन्द चेतन परगासी। आत्म खोज पुरख अबनासी।।

Probe into the Atman and find there the Immortal Being — *Sachchidananda,* the effulgent consciousness.

(Mangat)

Everybody knows that he or she is not just the body. There is something within me which makes me live. Let us call it the life-element force or principle (the Power of Existence). If one has a will, an aspiration, a faith and a need in the heart to know what is this life-principle, one can possibly find an answer. 'The principle which gives life, dwells in us and without us, is undying and eternally beneficent, is not heard or seen or smelt (by external senses) but is perceived by the man who desires perception' (Aurobindo). That is the Divine or the Reality in us.

'God is near me (rather in me), and yet I may be away from God, because I may be away from my own Self', said C.E. Bolt. According to the Mother (of Pondicherry): 'If one did not carry the Divine oneself, in the essence of one's being, one could never become aware of the Divine; it would be an impossible venture. And then if we reverse the problem, the moment we conceive and feel in some way or the other, or even to begin with, admit that the Divine is in us, as well as we are in the Divine, then already this opens the door to realization, just a little. Not much — slightly ajar. Then if later the aspiration comes, the intense need to know and to be, then that intense need widens the opening until one can creep in. Then when one has crept in, one becomes aware of what he is. And that's exactly what Sri Aurobindo says, that one has forgotten, that due to this separation of *Sat, Chit, Anand,* forgetfulness comes, forgetfulness of what one is.'

Kabir, the mystic saint of 15th century, has a nice parable on this sort of forgetfulness:

The musk-deer carries the *Kastoori* (a highly fragrant substance) in its own abdomen. When it is ripened it smells sweet; and the deer sniffs at it in the blowing air of the woods and wanders all over, little knowing that the *Kastoori* is in its own abdomen.

It is said that when we see the Lord within, we see Him everywhere. He is not confined to the body — He is everywhere — but we have to reach that particular level of consciousness to see Him first within, and then we see Him everywhere, outside in the world.

Swami Chinmayananda has a vivid view on the sort of enlightenment or realization we are talking about. He says:

> 'When mind is absolutely pure, it is no more mind. It emerges to be the Self. The delusion is ended. Enlightenment has come. This realization is not the vision of something different, but it is seeing everything differently.'

We may go to Gita, to understand the relationship between the Self and the body. It says:

> "*Atman*, the Self, is the sustainer or the ruler of the body, and is internal; the body is the ruled, and is external. *Atman* is all consciousness and holy, the body is all flesh, blood and the rest of it. *Atman* is eternal, since it is Existence itself, the body is transient, as it is subject to decay and death. And, yet people see these two — body and *Atman* — as one. What else can be called ignorance but this?"

Mahatma Mangat Ram says:

> आत्म तत्व अनुभव से, काल करम दुख जाये।
> "मंगत" नित आनन्द में, मन तन शान्त समाये।।

> On realizing the Atman, all agonies of time and action vanish
> Mind and body then rest in continued bliss.

One wonders sometimes, what is 'real' and what is 'unreal'. The following statement by a co-disciple friend of mine provides some clarity:

> 'The unreal is called *maya,* ignorance, mind, ego or appearance. The real is called *Brahman*, God, *Purusha, Atman.* In the Islamic tradition, it is called the supreme reality; in the Christian, the Father. The devotees call it

> the Lord and the Yogis, the Word. From the point of view of epistemology, it is reality and from that of life, salvation.'

According to Gita again, man is a complex being with numerous dimensions. He is composed of elements of matter, life, consciousness, intelligence, but above all he carries in him 'a spark of Divinity'— the *Atman*, very subtle, subtler than the subtlest. It is not recognizable by the senses. We should not separate our being from Being. How can we? Each one of us is a drop in the ocean. And ocean is in the drop — the latter being its miniature.

'Divine radiance is present in everyone', says Mahatma Mangat Ram. With a little effort but deep interest one can achieve that state of radiance, solitude and bliss within oneself. But there are some qualifications necessary for it.

> 'Only such a person achieves the state of transcendental solitude and remains ever in the blissful state who has definitely arrived at the knowledge that body is perishable and the Atman is imperishable, who is firmly established in the contemplation of Reality, who moves in the world with dispassion and non-attachment, who expresses his acts in the service of all creatures, who, whatever he does, leaves the fruit of action unto God, who remains equal to body pain and comfort, and who constantly worships and recollects the Name of the Lord.'
>
> (Samata Vilas)

'To become ourselves is the one thing to be done; but the true ourselves is that which is within us, and to exceed our outer self of the body, life and mind is the condition for the highest being, which is our true and divine being, to become self-revealed and active. It is only by going within and being within that we can find it...This then is the first necessity, that the individual, each individual shall discover the Spirit, the divine reality within him and express that in all his being and living' (Aurobindo).

I am reminded of a couplet which, I think, would appropriately fit here:

محروم حقیقت ہیں ساحل کے تماشائی
ہم ڈوب کے سمجھے ہیں دریاؤں کی گہرائی

> *Mehroomay haqiqat hain sahil kay tamashaie,*
> *Ham doob kay samajhay hain daryaoon ki gehrai!*
>
> 'Devoid of truth are the onlookers at the shore. We learnt about the depth, after diving deep into the depths of the rivers.'

Yes, we have to dive deep into ourselves to know and experience the truth of our divinity — our true Self. In the words of Gurudev: 'Truth alone is God.' Truth is also the Reality in us. Here is how Gurudev describes the true Self:

> सत सरूप अपार अनामी । अच्छर, अवगत सरब अन्तरयामी ।।
> युग युग आध आप बिसमादी । नित सम रूप अगम अगाधी ।।
>
> 'The true Self is limitless, without any specific name, indestructible, all-knowing, omniscient, primordial, splendorous, ever the same (in constant state of equilibrium), incomprehensible, unfathomable.'

Intellectual conception not enough:

While we shall go through several statements of saints and philosophers, sometimes slightly variant with each other, it is not enough — not even absolutely necessary — to reach an intellectual understanding of the Divine. This may lead us to know all that has been thought, said or written about the Divine, and yet we may not know Him at all. Reading and pondering over what saints and sages have said about the Divine, and its awareness, that is just the first step.

'The essential thing is a call from the soul, an aspiration accompanied by a strong will and unwavering faith' (The Mother).

I would like to recall here a bold and forthright statement by Swami Vivekananda:

> "We can talk and reason all our lives, but we shall not understand a word of truth, until we experience it ourselves. You cannot hope to make a man a surgeon by simply giving him a few books. You cannot satisfy my curiosity to see a country by showing me a map; I must have actual experience. Maps can only create curiosity in us to get more perfect knowledge. Beyond that, they have no value whatever...Was there ever a more horrible blasphemy than the statement that all knowledge of God is confined to this or that book. How dare men call God infinite and yet try to compress him within the covers of a little book?"

Mere philosophical intellect ends in abstraction. The heart and life...cannot live with abstraction. They can find their satisfaction only in things concrete or those which can be made sizable whether physically, mentally or spiritually...Therefore, when the heart and life turn towards the highest and the Infinity, they strive at a conscious being — a *Sat Purusha*, a *Chaitanya Purusha*, an *Anandmaya Purusha*. They must insist on all three in one. Then the soul rests in its native state of communion with the divine — *Sat-Chit-Anand*.

About knowledge Mahatma Mangat Ram says:

ज्ञान सो ही जो मन तृखा विनासे। सत सरूप में लिये निवासे।।

The real knowledge is that which makes mind free of desires, thus enabling one to live one's true self. He further says:

सार ज्ञान ये ही है मीत। सरजनहार को राखो चीत।।

Oh friend! the essence of gnosis (knowledge of truth) is that we keep in mind our Creator.

Two questions were put to Gurudev regarding knowledge and his replies are:

Q: What is the form of gnosis (knowledge)?

Ans: By itself knowledge/gnosis is nothing. That is a statement of a reality. When reality is known, knowledge is out. Then reality only remains. No duality. Who will ask, who will reply whom then?

Q: How long or what period of time shall it take to attain the knowledge of the Self?

Ans: A mind that is fully concentrated shall attain the divine state of the Self within a period of a week or fortnight. What, however, is needed is the right endeavour.

As Dhammapada puts it:

'Rouse thyself by thyself — examine thyself by thyself, thus self protected and attentive wilt thou live happily. For Self is the Lord of the self, Self is the refuge of the self, therefore, curb thyself...'

The above ancient advice may be compared with the lines of Abu-al-Farid (1182-1235) a great Muslim sufi who wrote in his poem 'Ta-iyya':

'But when I cleared the film from me, I saw myself restored to consciousness, and mine eye was refreshed by the Divine Essence...'

We put veil after veil between splendour — our self — existent being — and ourselves, says Sai Baba. The thing to do, he suggests, is to remove the curtains, to take them all away, to go through and find oneself in the presence of the splendour. The will to discover and realize is most important. Knowledge of self alone, asserts Sai Baba, can quench the thirst of man.

Realizing the self is only letting go the non-self, advises Ramana Maharishi. He quotes the well-known saying of Christ: 'The kingdom of heaven is within you.' And, says further:

> 'All men are realized. Everyone is already realized and ever-realized. One thinks one is bound because one mistakes the body for the Self which is Infinite, pure awareness. What we call realization consists in getting rid of the wrong idea that one is not realized. Realization is not something newly got. It is only the elimination of ignorance, *avidyanasa. Avidya* is the sense of separateness. There is one Self. Limited, it is the ego; unlimited it is the infinite Self, the sole reality. Egos are different and numerous, like bubbles; the Self is one alone, like the ocean. Accept your identity with the real; be the water not the bubble. Dive in.'

Could there be a simpler and a more direct approach to knowing the Reality in us? No intricate maze of philosophy! The Self is obvious and ever present. Let us ponder over it and give it a practical trial.

Sachchidananda:

Coming back to the three main attributes of our internal, pure and perennial Being: *Sat* (Truth), *Chit* (Consciousness) and *Anand* (Bliss), let us briefly discuss them. But before we do that we may as well understand that Sachchidananda is the One with triple aspects. In the Supreme the three are not three but one — truth or existence is consciousness, consciousness is bliss — and they are thus inseparable, not only inseparable but so much each other that they are not distinct at all.

> 'Though we mention separately
> Sat and Chit and Ananda,
> The three are one in lived experience,

As water pure, that peerless drink,
Proves liquid, sweet and cold at once.'

Truth:

'Truth is one although the wise may perceive it in different ways' (Rig Veda).

'Truth alone wins, never untruth. The path leading to the Divine is paved by truth' (Mandukya Upanishad).

'Truth', as Mahatma Mangat Ram says, 'is that which abides for ever.' 'The search for Truth', he emphatically states, 'is not limited to any particular religious frame or pattern, for Nature ever gives mute intimation of Truth to every mortal in the depth of his heart. It is truth alone that needs to be known and worshipped.'

सत की खोज से बंधन नासे, मन पावे विसरामा।
सत ध्यान परम पद देवे, विरत होए निश्कामा।।

Truth, when investigated, frees one and sets the mind at rest. Contemplation of Truth exalts one and induces selflessness.

सत ही केवल रूप पहचाने, तन मन तिस में वारे।
दुर्लभ देह मानुष की होई, साचा कियो ब्योहारे।।

Recognizing Truth as one's real self, body and mind be totally devoted to it. Such a person would be truthful in behaviour and dealings.

'God is Truth and Truth is God.' The intellect in its pure state can perceive the supreme Truth right within the body. But intellect will never become pure, unless the mind is directed and fixed on Truth.

According to Yajurveda: 'By self-dedication one obtains consecration; by consecration one obtains grace, by grace one obtains faith and by faith is Truth obtained.' The Truth is described as limitless, without any specific name, indestructible, all powerful, primordial, splendorous.

The ultimate Truth is the Truth of the spirit — most

fundamental and most effective, powerfully creative of the inner, also reformative of the outer life. Good life is the effect, God-realization is the cause.

'Truthfulness (in behaviour) implies that one be always truthful in speech, honest and straightforward in actions, free from simulation or sin. To communicate in any form what one truly knows, feels or believes about any person or event — that is being honest' (Samata Vilas).

To play the game of clever ideas and words has become more important these days than the simple observance and the humble acceptance of obvious truths. However attractive the clever ideas and the worldly goods may be from the material point of view of our outer worldly life, their importance fades when the longing for the highest Truth animates us.

सत करनी, सत रहनी, सत में जीवन त्याग।
"मंगत" सूरा जगत में, कोई आया ले बढभाग।।

True in action, true in conduct, life dedicated to truth—
rarely is born such a brave and lucky one, in the world,
says Mangat.

Gurudev has quoted some instances of saints and prophets who sacrificed their lives for truth:

Believing in Truth Socrates drank poison. So did Meera (a 16th century princess) take poison, given to her, as nectar. Christ lived in Truth and happily suffered on the Cross for the sake of Truth. Mansur too gladly went to gallows for Truth. Ibrahim believed in Truth, sat calmly in the fire (with full faith in Allah).

Gurudev used to tell us often: 'Yeh mun, budhi se pare ka mamla hai' (Awareness of Truth is beyond the range of the mind and the intellect).

Truth is pathless land and each has to be light unto himself.

In his characteristic spontaneous style, J. Krishnamurti speaks of direct perception of Truth. 'There are no footholds to truth, no steps, no levels', he observes.

'Truth', says Swami Chinmayananda, 'is not a theme that can be reached or understood by a play of the intellect. Mere reasoning can cover only the frontiers of the world of objects. The land of Truth lies extended beyond the frontiers of the intellect and the mind. The Reality in us or the Self is cognized only when we transcend the mind and the intellect.' Here is an interesting Urdu couplet:

نکل جا عقل سے آگے کہ یہ نور
نشانِ راہ ہے منزل نہیں ہے

Nikal ja aqal se agey ki yeh noor,
nishane rah hai manzal nahin hai.

'Go beyond the intellect, though it is in the nature of light, but only the wayside light, not the destination.'

Says Satya Sai Baba: 'Believe that there is nothing greater than Truth, nothing more precious, nothing sweeter and nothing more lasting.' The most revered Shirdi Sai Baba used to say in his most simple words but based on his deep personal experience: 'See the Truth inside you.'

Truth is one—
Revealing itself
countlessly
As the thousand petalled
Lotus
of
Understanding.

'Truth will alone set you free', observes Swami Purna (he has authored a book thus titled, printed in Britain). .

Truth will also make one fearless as Gurudev observes:

निर्भय होय जीव तब, जब सत्सार कमाए।
"मंगत" अन्तरगत माहीं, सत ठाकुर दरसाए।।

Truth makes one fearless;
The Lord is seen within, says Mangat.

The Truth if understood and followed honestly would also create the love, the harmony and justice which is so much lacking in the world today.

'Merge in Truth and come out only to express its glory and its dynamic divinity', advises Swami Chinmayananda.

Mahatma Gandhi said:

> 'My experience has convinced me that there is no other God than Truth...To see the universal and all-pervading Spirit of Truth face to face one must be able to love the meanest of creation as oneself. And a man who aspires that cannot afford to keep out of any field of life. That is why my devotion to Truth has drawn me into the field of politics; and I can say without the slightest hesitation, and yet in all humility, that those who say that religion has nothing to do with politics do not know what religion means.'

Consciousness:

जड देही को करे सरजीत। सोही तेरा रूप पुनीत।।

> The One that bestows consciousness to your gross material body is the Divine — Your very sublime Self.
>
> (Mangat)

Consciousness is our very nature. It is an incorporeal energy. The awakening of human consciousness is the chief marvel of creation. Life is Brahman, Brahman is Truth (*Sat*). It is the subtle centre of our existence that is Consciousness (*Chit*) and also ultimate joy and Bliss (*Anand*).

There is a sentence in the Hebrew Bible where the Lord answers Moses, saying: "I AM THAT I AM: I AM THAT."

Rajneesh describes 'consciousness' as 'a comprehension of totality, a perception of completeness', and advises 'Just hold it. It is like a perfume, it is there.'

Shankaracharya says: 'I am undecaying, I am imperishable, I am the Lord, I am the consciousness of the Inner self,

I am full of supreme bliss, I am the supreme self (*Param Siva*), I am the infinite.' Here 'I' means any person. Each one of us can aspire to lay claim to that state which has been described in Hindu scriptures by the following phrases:

अहंब्रह्मस्मि	AHAM BRAHMASMI I am Brahm
शिवोहं	SHIVOHAM I am all beautiful
सोहं	SOHAM I am that
तत्त्वमसि	TATTVAMASI That you are

Mahatma Mangat Ram strikes a note of caution. Says he: 'Without realization, mere utterance of the words such as 'I am Brahm' leads to ego.'

'The only truth which becomes falsehood when expressed is Aham Brahmasmi or Shivoham' (Ramana Maharishi).

We may go over some more striking statements by Shankaracharya on this subject:

> 'I am body' — this feeling is ignorance, which covers the self-reality.
>
> 'I am sat-chit-anand' — this is true knowledge.
>
> With this knowledge what we regarded as world and its fear, turn into *Brahman* — our own self. Fear turns into love; all dualities dissolve then.
>
> Everything, every being arises out of the universal consciousness, like bubbles in water. They form, stay temporarily and then dissolve in the universal consciousness, as the bubbles behave in the water.
>
> Like all trees, whatever their form, shape, size and name, are the same principle.
>
> Just as gold is one and numerous ornaments are made out of it. But all remain essentially gold.

Ordinary consciousness is that in which one knows things only or mainly by the intellect, the mind and the senses:

प्रकृति की गिरफ्तारी में जो चेतन भासता है, उसी का नाम जीव है।।

> 'Eternal consciousness that appears to be in the grip of everchanging gross matter, is called *jiv* (living being) — embodied soul.' (Samata Vilas)

Referring to ordinary individual consciousness, it is experienced that when our mind becomes tense we begin to feel bad and everything around feels bad. We meditate and feel good, and everything around feels good. So it is the state of consciousness. That is, if our consciousness is pure and is in tune with purity of life which is pure intelligence, we are able to create more, understand more, enjoy more. 'Low consciousness means...we fail to understand, we fail to produce. Productivity becomes less, creativity becomes less, understanding becomes less and the capacity to enjoy becomes less. That is why we meditate and make our consciousness purer and thereby gain more ability to enjoy everything', says Mahesh Yogi (of Transcendental Meditation Movement). (We may not totally agree with him if the joy is limited to things material.)

David Cohen has studied individual consciousness from another angle. He says:

> 'The ideas that individual consciousness springs from a primordial all-encompassing human consciousness, is shared by every society. Mythologies, beliefs, customs and symbols used in rites of passage in astonishingly diverse cultures, throughout the world, reflect common human consciousness.'

The spiritual consciousness is stated to be that in which we enter with the awareness of the Self, the divine — and are able to see in all things their essential Reality.

The cosmic consciousness is described as that in which the limits of personal ego — that of mind and body — disappear and one becomes aware of the cosmic vastness.

A concentration which culminates in a living realization and the constant sense of presence of the Divine in ourselves and in all of which we are aware is — as saints say from their actual experience — true Knowledge — Awareness or Consciousness. '*Jnana* (spiritual knowledge)', says Ramana Maharishi, 'is not perceiving something. It is the extreme enjoyment and exercise of one's whole being as awareness.'

To quote Shankaracharya again, in each one of us the 'Chit' or Pure Awareness is devoid of any modification of Self, is incomparable, one indivisible whole, without any parts or limbs. He further says that consciousness, which is of the nature of Bliss, Absolute knowledge, Awareness as one indivisible whole, without a second, 'marries' as it were the Matter (consisting of earth, fire, water, air and sky). The 'Jeeva' (embodied consciousness) then gets drowned in the ocean of becoming, utterly confused and deluded (forgetting its reality).

According to Aurobindo consciousness is not a single uniform reality...It is multi-dimensional. On the highest peak is the Supreme and in the lowest depth is matter; and there is an infinite gradation of levels of consciousness between the lowest depth and the highest height.

Aurobindo has another pertinent point on consciousness and force. He says: 'To be conscious does not only mean to be aware: Consciousness also holds within it power or will and force...As the consciousness is, so will the Force be. Where the Consciousness is infinite, as is the consciousness of Sachchidananda, so will be the Force infinite in its scope.'

'Where the whole nature of consciousness is One knowing itself as the Many and the Many knowing themselves as the One—"Unity in diversity"— there the Force will also be of the same nature. It would be a life that consciously obeys the law of Unity and yet fulfils each thing in the diversity, according to its proper role and function.'

Let us reiterate the fundamental truth — the One that bestows consciousness to our body is our Divine Self. And, that divinity pervades all over. According to Gita: 'One who is united in identity with all the prevailing consciousness and sees unity everywhere, beholds the Self present in all beings and all beings as assumed in the Self.' Entire creation then becomes a beautiful language. We must listen to it. We must understand it.

We can and should actually move from mere head-learning to soul-realization, the state of universal consciousness, all-encompassing and ever-constant awareness, remembering the difference between intellectual conception and actual experience.

"Until you wake up to what you really are
You'll be like the man who searches whole jungle
for a jewel that hangs at his throat."

"Oil, wick, and fire: until they mingle in cruse
they scarcely produce any light,
So how can you expect to dissipate the darkness
simply by talking about lamps?"

(Surdas)

Bliss:

Bliss is the very nature of the Self.
Self is the infinitude of bliss
All Being is but bliss
Knowing this firmly, in the Self
Abide, enjoying bliss for ever.

Eternal bliss is the goal of life. It is the state of our being which knows no separation; that essence of ours which bears no splitting of awareness.

Bliss is uninvolved, extremely independent and self-existent. God is the fountain-head of bliss. How do we reach this state? Mahatma Mangat Ram says that bliss is attained by realizing that Power, by the power of which this perishable body remains alive. It glows within every creature.

सब में रमया आनन्द प्रगासा। सरब अतीत सो पुरख निर्वासा।।

The radiant bliss (life force) permeates one and all.
Yet is completely uninvolved and desireless.

Some of his further observations on 'bliss' are:

आनन्द सरूप का खोज निधान। मिटे द्वन्द परम दुख खान।।

Find out the treasure of bliss within.
This will dissolve all delusion.

आतम तत्त में जब लीन समाई। आनन्द सरूप तब परमगत पाई।।

On merging with Atman,
One realizes the sublime state of bliss.

आनन्द सरूप तब अनुभव होई। सकल भरांत जीव ये खोई।।

On experiencing state of bliss
One is redeemed of all delusion.

आनन्द का सागर अन्तर पेखा। जग का ठाकुर अन्तर देखा।।

(On absorption in Atman) experienced the ocean of bliss within; also saw the Lord of the Universe.

In that state no interference of transient joy or sorrow takes place.

In answer to a question: 'What, Sir, is the real bliss?' Gurudev replies:

'The entire theme, dear one, may be expressed in one sentence. Abandon the (excessive) desire of the body and of the body-related objects; you shall come to know the real nature of bliss by itself when on giving up all kinds of desires, contentment seizes you. The mystery of it is beyond words.'

Baba Farid, another great Indian saint, has also suggested a simple way in his characteristically simple style:

'God says: If you ennoble yourself
O, Man you shall meet me:
And on meeting Me, you shall have eternal Bliss
the whole world shall belong to you.'

What can be a higher state, a higher achievement than that!

Most important thing is to 'ennoble' ourselves; to purify our inner self completely. Without that state we would miss 'bliss'. The bliss presumes innocent purity. The following quotation makes this point strikingly clear:

> 'So long as you can't be in joy, a constant, a calm, peaceful, luminous, invariable joy, well, it means that you have still to work to purify yourself.'
>
> (The Mother)

Saints endowed with highest vision of life in every age of human history, have borne witness to this fact — that of 'Bliss' being the very nature of our real being. In the adventure of our own spiritual life we should try to test this and taste it — for this conviction, this experience is itself bliss.

Guru Nanak correlates Name (of God) with Bliss. He says:

'They who are imbued with Name
Remain intoxicated with bliss night and day
Whosoever searches joy eternal, let him seek that in All-pervading Spirit.'

In a village of old Kathiawad State of India, there was a young person Sri Rajchandra (born in 1924 and died young at the age of 34) whose influence on Mahatma Gandhi is said to be much deeper than even that of Tolstoy and Ruskin. I would like to mention a little about him and some of his observations. A respectable, honest Gujarati businessman in outward life, his inner life was of a saint. His conscious attentiveness was eager to flow in the self, even in the midst of big business transactions. About happiness he says, in very simple words:

'Happiness is not a thing to be achieved. It is a thing to be experienced. Where is the question of attaining it when the soul itself is happiness? Why should one be anxious in attaining happiness? There is no happiness in anxiousness. So also why should one desire to be happy. The desire itself is full of unhappiness.'

'The Self is pure, enlightened, consciousness in core, self-illumination, the abode of bliss. How much be said? If you contemplate over this, you will realize such Self', says Rajchandra.

Temporary happiness:

The pleasures of the senses are both limited in their range as well as relative in their scope. They soon satiate and very often they can change into painful experience. In contrast to this the spiritual bliss is both unlimited and absolute. It suffers no satiety or decline. It has the character of permanence in it. The experience is marked by a sense of supreme value. (It gives one the realization that he has attained the ultimate Truth.)

Temporary happiness which we find when we get possession of the things we seek after is a flicker or spark only from the fire of basic happiness of the spirit. The real pleasure as even a short-lived experience would show, is not in desires, but in desirelessness. We normally experience joy on the satisfaction of a desire for a thing; we are then led to 'thinglessness', a sort of desirelessness which continues for a while before we strive for fulfilment of another desire. And, thus the cycle goes on. Here the reference is to desires limited to one's self-interest. Desire to serve others, to make their lives happy, falls in another category — *Parmarth* (good of others) as against *Swarth* (merely one's own interest).

If we learn to live not to ourselves in the ego, but for God in ourselves, and for God in man — nay in all living beings— and in the integral harmony of the One Universal Spirit, we come to possess Sachchidananda — in ourselves and the expression of it in the Universe: Sat (Truth), Chit (Consciousness), Anand (Bliss). Albert Einstein was surely hinting at something like this universal 'three-in-one' when he said:

> 'The ideals which have always shone before me and filled me with joy of living are goodness, beauty and truth.'

Satyam, Sivam, Sundaram:

Sai Baba has equated the three terms — Sat, Chit, Anand — with Satyam, Sivam, Sundaram, respectively standing for:

Satyam—Truth, the substance
Sivam—Awareness, consciousness
Sundaram—Light, splendour, Ananda

Sundaram is beauty. This applies to everything created by nature, beauty of human beings, of animals, of birds, plants, flowers, mountains, running water, and so on.

We must learn to admire the wonderful works of the Creator even in most insignificant creatures.

'Beauty is Nature's signature upon a thing', says Tagore.

Beauty in manifestation:

God is beauty or beauty is God. As Emil Ludwig says beautifully in one of his poems, God can be seen in the iridescent wings of a butterfly, in the early morning frost, in the pleading look of a dog, in the playful kitten, in the master hands of a great painter like Leonard.

How many of us look at the beauty of the stars, and admire each morning the glory of the rising sun? Too familiar natural phenomena dulls our own sense of beauty—though it should not. It is Ralph Waldo Emerson who said that if the stars came out but once a year, we would all rush out into the streets to marvel at them. We would all be awestruck at the impressive celestial display. What if the sun rose but once a calendar? Wouldn't we gather in the streets and on the hills and—yes, wonder at this miracle? It is as close to visually witnessing God itself as most of us are likely to experience: the majesty, the magnificence, the overwhelming beauty of the golden sunrise!

J. Krishnamurti deplores that man lacks a sense of beauty — beauty as sensitivity not only physically, but also of the heart and mind. To be sensitive is to be intelligent. Can one be aware of the extraordinary beauty of the earth, the richness of a rice field, the beauty of a face, of a smile and the sadness of the tears? he asks. He also says: Thought is totally absent when you see something extraordinarily beautiful (you get absorbed in it).

Mahatma Mangat Ram has also an observation on beauty, much deeper and profound. He says:

> 'Real beauty is that which is unchanging. And which makes even ugly things look beautiful. That is the Atman; life-force in every being. It is that which lights up even inanimate objects. That is real beauty, the great light and the precious treasure of joy.'

In this context, I am reminded of two Urdu verses of my dear friend, late Gumnam Sahib:

تیرا جلوہ ہر جگہ مجھکو نظر آنے لگا
جلوہ کیا جلوے میں جلوہ گر نظر آنے لگا

Tera jalwa her jaghe mujhko nazar ane laga;
Jalwa kya jalwe mein Jalwagar nazar ane laga.

I begin to see (Oh God!) your manifestation
(Oh) what a manifestation!
Behind the manifestation I see
The One who manifests.

جس کے دیکھے سے میرے ہوش خرد جاتے رہے
پردہ میں پوشیدہ خود حاضر نظر آنے لگا

Jis ke dekhe say merey hosho-khirad jate rahey,
Parde mein poshida khud hazir nazar ane laga.

On seeing Him, my senses are stunned,
He who was hidden
behind the curtain,
becomes visible to me.

Blessed indeed is such a state of ecstasy in which one has direct vision of the Creator in His manifestation!

Here are more beautiful words from The Mother on Beauty:

'Let Beauty be your constant ideal
The Beauty of sentiments
The Beauty of thoughts
The Beauty of the action
The Beauty of the work
so that nothing comes out of your hands which is not expression of pure harmonious beauty. And the Divine help shall always be with you.'

She further says that on the physical plane the Divine expresses himself through beauty, on the mental plane through knowledge, on the vital plane through power and on the psychic plane through love.

When we rise high enough we discover that these four aspects unite with each other in a single consciousness, full of love, luminous, powerful, beautiful, containing all, pervading all, she adds.

We owe it to the world:

While recounting the glories of universal consciousness as above, the Mother also reminds us not to forget the debt we owe to the world. She says:

"The usual *sadhanas* (spiritual practices) have for aim the union with the Supreme Consciousness (Sat-Chit-Anand). And those who reach there are satisfied with their own liberation and leave the world to its unhappy plight. Once the union with the Supreme is realized one must bring down that realization to the exterior world and change the condition of life upon the earth for its total transformation."

Swami Chinmayananda has also thus explained the concept of Sachchidananda and its extension to relative existence:

> 'As pointed out by Vedas and Puranas the goal is that Purana Purusa whose nature is Satchitananda:
>
> Sat — Pure existence
> Chit — Pure knowledge
> Anand — Pure bliss
>
> And this was further indicated to be my very Swarupa (real self), my innermost spiritual nature. Thus it would mean that one has to tackle one's own spiritual potential. This can be achieved by a conscious extension of the Satchitananda Swarupa into the grosser realms of relative existence, implying, primarily, that man should seek to protect life and not destroy it; save life because it is the nature of Sat or existence. Next would be the Chit or knowledge aspect, i.e. man should strive to dispel ignorance, his own and his neighbour's and spread the one True knowledge of the basic oneness of all beings. Then what would naturally follow would be the Ananda aspect, that is, man should, as a consequence of this knowledge or understanding, kindled in his bosom, strive to alleviate the suffering and misery of his brethren and unfold the One Love that permeates this entire universe. Thus he verily becomes a dynamic centre radiating the light of Knowledge, and Love, a spark of Divine Essence.'

Self realization—as Sat + Chit + Anand — is, no doubt, an entry into 'the Kingdom of Heaven' within. Referring to this inner illumination some critics have held that if it does not take note of the outer life, it is of no great use, for it leaves the world as it is. This is what has generally happened till now. 'Even those who had very great and powerful realization withdrew from the world to live undisturbed in inner quiet and peace, the world was left to its ways, misery and stupidity', says Aurobindo. But Mahatma Mangat Ram was not 'a saint of the caves'. He moved among people, even when he was a fully realized soul — quiet, self-effacing and humble. Several thousand people met this saint and listened to his illuminating discourses. These people included professors, teachers, lawyers, doctors, government officials, businessmen, as well as traders, farmers, and labourers. They discussed with the saint various problems — spiritual, religious, and social, and got simple, succinct, convincing answers from him. He helped and guided so many! In a sense he was a great crusader being vehemently against wrong religious notions, beliefs and superstitions. (Please see Annexure I for some of his progressive views. Also Annexure II: 'A student of philosophy meets Mahatma Mangat Ram'.)

CHAPTER 3

Our Constituents and Their Care

Man is a multi-fold entity, comprising basically body, mind, intellect and soul. Deep within is the Self, the Atman, the Divine in all. God intends that man harmoniously develop these constituents to their fullest potential, that on earth, as God's child, he may be good, experience good and do good.

Kathopanishad gives us an imagery which is well worth noticing:

> आत्मानं रथिनं विद्धि शरीरं रथमेव तु।
> बुद्धिं तु सारथिं विद्धि मनः प्रग्रहमेव च।।
> इन्द्रियाणि हयानाहुविषयांस्तेषु गोचरान्।
> आत्मेन्द्रियमनोयुक्तं भोक्तेत्याहर्मनीषिणः।।

> 'Know the body to be the chariot; the intellect to be the charioteer; the mind to be the reins; the senses to be the horses; and the sense objects to be the highway. But know the self to be master of the chariot.'

Life is a pilgrimage. The bodies are the midway houses to be lived in for some time and forsaken when the time comes. While alive the chariot of body, mind and intellect is to be employed to progress. The horses must be controlled to high purpose and with courage.

"May we be granted the boon of a pure intellect
the able charioteer endowed with an excellent
vehicle and a group of well-disciplined
carriers — the senses and the mind."

(Taru Manjari)

Mahatma Mangat Ram refers to body as a vehicle or temple or abode of its Creator. To quote a couple of his sayings:

काया कोट अजब हे साजा। जिस में साहब आप विराजा।।

Wondrous is the structure of the body fort; the Creator is Himself seated in it.

पांच तत्त देही का कोट। तिस में पेख एक निर्मल जोत।।

The body is made up of five elements. Perceive in it the presence of a pure Light.

देह के भीतर निर देह लखाई। काल के भीतर अकाल समाई।।

The formless (life-force) is perceptible within the body. The never-changing permeates the mortal ever-changing body.

Our amazing body and the universe:

Our body is sublime handiwork of Divine Power. The basis of all life on earth, as we know, is the cell. The process of evolution has developed this single little cell into a bewildering range of complex forms, the most amazing and complex of all is the human body, which contains approximately 60,000 miles of arteries, veins and capillaries. The average developed adult is stated to be made up of 80 trillion electrical cells. Cells measure in the order of thousandth of an inch.

The human form is a mass of individual cells, all working together in gigantic coordination. Each cell is a microscopic complete unit consisting of cytoplasm and nucleus, surrounded by a thin flexible membrane, which is porous enough for the easy passage of nutrition and waste which passes continuously in and out. The nucleus of the cell contains very small but sophisticated particles called chromosomes, DNA molecules and genes. The cell is fed and cleansed by the functions of the blood-stream.

There are 72,000 *nadis* (astral nerves) in the human body. The all-important brain, an electrical marvel, is the executive director of the central nervous system. Billions of nerve cells called neurons make up the system — there are over 10 billion in the brain alone, any one of which can be related to as many as 25,000 for a number of possible associations. It is the most highly organized approximately three pounds of matter we know.

We have briefly talked above of our micro-world. Vastness and dimension of the Universe are beyond human comprehension. Judge it from the fact that light takes billions of years to reach us from the distant nebula and stars; and light travels at 18,60,000 miles per second.

As regards our macro-world, our sun 8,64,000 miles in diameter with its internal temperature of 18 million C revolves around our galaxy at a speed of 160 miles per second, about 23 times the speed the rocket must attain to escape from earth's surface. At this speed it takes the sun approximately 240 million years to complete a single rotation. And our own galaxy according to the scientists is one among estimated billions. Along with its quantitative revelations science has discovered nature's elegance too. And also perhaps proved that man who is behind itself, is the most elegant manifestation of nature.

Referring to vastness of Universe, saints have described it broadly. Here are a few lines from Samata Prakash (Mahatma Mangat Ram's God-inspired verses):

अरबां दिवस रेन पख मास। अरबां वरख करें विलास।।
अरबां रवीचन्दर प्रगासे। अरबां इन्धर राज विलासे।।

अचरज रचना जगत की, अलख, अभेद अपार।
अरबां तारा मंडल आकास। अरबां पवन पानी विलास।।
"मंगत" गिन्ती न आवे जुग जुग करूं शुमार।।

There are billions of days, nights, seasons, months and years (of different durations); billions of suns and moons shedding their light, billions are their presiding deities. Billions are shining galaxies and skies; so also there are countless dancing winds and waters. This Universe is simply wondrous, indescribable, impenetrable, limitless! "Mangat" says, the wonders of nature could not be counted, through the ages and epochs.

Reverting to ourselves again: man possesses a) five organs of knowledge or perception and b) five organs of action. These are respectively:

a)	b)
Skin (touch)	Speech
Tongue (taste)	Hands
Eyes (sight)	Legs
Nose (smell)	Anus
Ears (hearing)	Genitals

Our consciousness is overlaid by three bodies — physical, subtle, causative or astral and five sheaths.

The physical body is formed of five elements, namely:

the sky (space) or ether — present in and outside our bodies

the wind — permeates our nerves, veins etc.

the fire — present as essential heat in our system

the water — represents blood, urine, perspiration etc.

the earth — makes bones, flesh, skin etc.

A descriptive note on further subdivision of these elements, their functions, attribution in relationship to five organs each of perception and action is given in Annexure III.

The subtle body is formed of 5 *pranas* (described in this chapter), 10 powers operating behind 5 organs of perception and action each, plus mind, and intellect — these make 17 constituents. Some have added in their listing memory and ego to mind and intellect, and these four are termed as *Antakarn* (the understanding, the soul).

The third is the causative/astral body. This represents the seed principle, creating the other two bodies. Just as in dream, so much is created but without any substances; so the causative body, as seed thought, creates the other two bodies.

The reality — the consciousness — is above all the three bodies. On its realization, the three become non-entities.

Panchkoshas: The five *koshas* (sheaths or screens or grades) of higher and higher energies and functions of the body as described in old Indian books are:

1) *Annamaya kosha* (physical or the food sheath) means the physical body nourished by food (Anna).

2) *Pranamaya kosha* (vital or the sheath of the potential and kinetic energy) —*prana* in the body. Scientific researches have proved that there is an electro'structure surrounding every cell and organ of the body. Possibly this approximates to *Pranamaya kosha* sometimes displayed by the human aura, proved to exist (even photographically by eminent radiologists).

3) *Manomaya kosha* (the mental sheath) includes all lower mental faculties of man.

4) *Vijnanmaya kosha* (supramental or the knowledge sheath) covers all the higher intellectual, intuitive and extra-sensory faculties occasionally displayed by the gifted sensitivities.

5) *Anandamaya kosha* (spiritual or the bliss sheath) refers to the blissful state in ecstasy or *Samadhi* when communion with God or Over-soul is established.

The five sheaths are experienced by one and all. These are in full play during waking state. Nos. 2 to 5 are active in dream state and No. 5 alone is active in dreamless sleep. The Annamaya kosha is less subtle than the Pranamaya kosha and the Anandamaya kosha is the subtlest of all koshas. The intermediate ones are located in the order of subtlety.

Right use and care of the body:

Right use of the body is what all religions enjoin on mankind. Lost in the never-ending and ever-increasing distractions and sensual excitement of modern living, man is abusing his senses far beyond their normal capacity and then complaining that they begin to lose their efficiency long before the normal fading-out of old age.

Man cannot renew his organs of sense, but once convinced of the futility of their further abuse and inevitable weakening, he can reduce unnatural living habits and begin to recover a little of their intended power: flexibility and usefulness, by exercising lazy muscles. 'Overstimulation of senses devitalizes the will, so do not create an unnatural craving for anything', advises Swami Chinmayananda.

First we have to be good animal. The question each one of us should ask of oneself: 'Am I at peace with my body, knowing no shame about my animal qualities?'

I wonder sometimes why we always consider ourselves superior to animals; in some respects we behave worse. I am inclined to agree with Walt Whitman who says in his book 'Leaves of Grass': 'I think I could turn and live with animals, they are so placid and self contained.' Look at ourselves; we are often too turbulent and always wanting more and more of material things and comforts.

As far as our animal nature is concerned we have nothing to be ashamed about, but much to rejoice, only if we know how to use our senses rightly. Steadily but surely, we can replace 'the beast in us with the best in us'. For the period we are here on this planet, admittedly we are our body and all that it encompasses.

Body has been aptly described as the temple of God — *dehvo devalaya*. The Supreme Self (Atman) dwells in our own inner being. One has only to make it pure and spiritual, so that it serves as an aid of the spirit and not as hindrance on its way. 'It is in the human body that the spirit can proceed to self-discovery — the fountain of infinite power within the cosmic consciousness.' The body is, indeed, a vehicle for the transmutation of the total being.

Body is meant for righteous conduct, the essence of all religions; it should, therefore, be well preserved and protected. As the mountain is the source of water, so is body that of *dharma*. By its very nature it is a docile and faithful servant. It obeys the mind and the vital. The mind with its dogmas, its rigid and arbitrary principles and the vital with its passions, its excesses and dissipations, soon destroy the natural balance of the body and create in it fatigue, exhaustion and disease. Scriptures advise us to have a robust physical body, to have an ideal moral life and to know our own Self and to know God.

Krishna says in Gita:

> 'He who controlling the organs of sense and action by the power of his will, and remaining unattached, undertakes the Yoga of Action through these organs, Arjuna, he excels.'

'Fear is the biggest cause of illness. Transfer your faith from pill to Providence; put your trust in Madhava (God), not in medicine; resort to prayer, *sadhna dhyana* and not to injection. They are the vitamins you need' (Sai Baba).

'The body has a wonderful capacity of adaptation and endurance. It is able to do so many more things than one usually images. When ruled by the central truth of the being, one would be amazed at what it is capable of doing. Calm and quiet, strong and poised it will be able to put forth the effort that is demanded of it, for it will have learnt to find rest in action and to recuperate through contact with the universal forces, the energies it expends consciously and usefully' (Aurobindo). Being an instrument for realization, the body must be kept clean, strong, healthy.

Body Health:

One of the health magazines has summed it up beautifully: 'Do you leap out of bed in the mornings with a song on your lips, a sparkle in your eyes and a spring in your steps?

Or is your rise to face the day and all its challenges a more cautious, slower process — a matter of checking gingerly on your current mental and physical condition (like seeing if the car will start without trouble)?

If you don't feel as fit as you should, take comfort — you are not alone. Only one in four feels really fit. More and more people are finding that they are permanently 'under the weather', and that orthodox medicine does not have the answers. Doctors are overworked and busy...the waiting lists for treatments are too long...and while prescription drugs may rid us of the symptoms, they don't always get to the root of the problem — and they may have even side-effects that are worse than the ailment they are meant to be treating.'

Small wonder, then, that so many of us are beginning to ask what are the alternatives. There is a growing awareness that other more natural approaches to fitness and well-being actually have sound basis...and that, in many cases, the gentler alternatives actually work.

There is a great revival of interest in herbal preparations that will liven our mood and help chase away everyday complaints.

Naturopathy:

It is the hub of healing art. The name may sound

strange, but the methods of naturopathy are as old as the hills—and probably just as familiar. Nature cure methods have been used for centuries. These include correct feeding, fresh air, sun baths etc. Naturopathy is a constructive method of treatment which aims to remove the basic cause of disease. It is now being increasingly realized that health is normal condition of the body brought about by living in accordance with the laws of nature. There is a move among intelligent people to move away from chemical drugs. In the USA fifty million Americans are estimated to patronise Drugless physicians, Nature-cure physicians with Osteopathy and Chiropractors.

Spas and saunas, massage and diet — are valuable aids to health. Everyone needs fruit and vegetables every single day. But most people don't know how to go about getting the amount of antioxidants that are found in recommended diets. Or even what antioxidants are. The fact is, for years scientists have known about highly reactive molecules called free radicals that can do serious damage to our cells and wreak havoc on body tissues. While we can't see this damage, it can be compared to the rapid browning of a cut apple or the rusting of metal. And there is increasing scientific evidence that links this free radical damage to chronic diseases such as cancer and heart disease. That's where antioxidants come in. Scientists are now paying more and more attention to them, since studies have shown that antioxidant nutrients such as Beta Carotene and Vitamins C and E, help protect against harmful cell damage. Among the studies currently being conducted throughout the world are a number relating to the possible roles of antioxidants in reducing the risks of chronic diseases. Early positive findings are leading to further research. In the meantime let us follow the advice of America's Surgeon General: 'Eat a balanced diet including plenty of antioxidant-rich fruits and vegetables, reduce fat, don't smoke and have regular medical checkups. And for those of you who simply don't eat a good balanced diet, consider a vitamin-mineral supplement or fortified foods such as breakfast cereals and juice drinks.' Natural habits, regular physical activity and healthy diet are most important factors for good health.

One need not be a hypochondriac to be interested in one's own body — to want to keep it in a peak condition and to be concerned about the treatment it gets when things go wrong. It is a mistake to neglect the body and let it waste away. True there should not be excessive attachment to it, but not contempt or neglect either.

While on the subject of body health, let us briefly go into the question of aging. According to studies made on aging, especially in the USA (where centenarians are expected to number 1,00,000 by the century), living to 100 is no big deal. As to what makes centenarians tick, here are a few observations:

With most of them, it is a matter of keeping busy.

Some spend hours daily strengthening body and mind. They read scriptures and newspapers.

Most have a discernible pattern of orderliness in their lives, much of it is the result of having been associated with farm life.

Slightly more than half of the centenarians were associated with religious life.

The ability to laugh was a factor; alertness with a sense of humour.

According to Swami Purna who is a great living Yogi and has mastered aging:

'Many do not realize that the physical body is designed and intended to live normally 150 years. That is without being a high Yogi, who may extend that time enormously. Living in this sense means remaining healthy, sound and fit until age 150. It seems that one thing humankind has mastered is the ability to shorten its own lifespan. Most people do not live in health beyond 50, and extension of life is often an extension of suffering rather than health. In some of the lesser developed nations the average lifespan is 35 years.

The question is how to keep this body in good working order for its full lifespan and also how to get it to carry on into realms of increased creativity and fulfilment. Boredom evaporates once one knows how to live, create and proceed to the goal of life. Firstly, to live 150 years one must de-program oneself out of negativity. However one is programmed, the mind, senses and body function accordingly. The brain, that incredibly complex computer, does its work by following the data it has been fed. If one plants a tree of thorns one cannot expect it to bear sweet fruit. The brain is made up of billions of cells or circuits, tiny entities working unitedly and independently to serve one's every whim and desire. They respond to each thought one creates, both fear and fancy. Whatever is programmed will be unfolded.'

During my visit to the USA (1993) I was surprised to know that the average American is 30 years older functionally than he/she is chronologically. The fact is, an active 60-year-old and an inactive 30-year-old have equal physical work capacity. Inactive people give aging a bad name, because many people think it's quite normal to look and perform as older. When these individuals see a normal, fit individual, they remark how young he or she looks, when in reality all they are saying is evidence that regular physical activity, along with a healthful diet, will help you look and feel younger. Apparent aging can be blamed largely on inactivity. Also we may recall what an old Lama said about aging:

'Age is not in the years heaped upon our body but in the weariness of spirit laid in your heart and mind at any time.'

Adding years to life is not that important, it is said, as adding life to years. Life divine is life worthy of living — in the quest of the Self and in service of humanity, better still, all living beings.

Weight-loss:

Today the weight-loss industry generates a lot of money, which shows how desperate people are to lose weight. Even with the best intention the success rates for weight-loss are very discouraging. Of all the people who start on a weight-loss programme only a small percentage lose weight. About 95 per cent of them eventually regain some or all of their weight-loss. This is because of lack of proper exercise and due control on diet.

Blood Pressure:

It is estimated that upto 20% of world's population have high blood pressure. Only 50% know about it. Only 25% are being treated. Only 12% are being treated effectively.

The apparent epidemic of high blood pressure these days is mainly blamed on the fearful increase in the amount of stress most of us have to cope with. Not the age-old human worrying about food or shelter or safety, but the stress of meeting the deadlines in work, paying bills, keeping our jobs, coping with inflation, even the tension of daily commuting. Relaxation of mind and body, either through a sport, hobby, meditation or otherwise, is very important. We must organize our life in such a way that we give ourself sufficient time for every significant activity. Especially for appointments and travel it is a sound practice to keep a little extra margin of time. Here I am talking more on the basis of personal experience.

Tension:

The sense of strain. The feeling of inadequacy, the pessimism. Certainly there is too much tension, too much uptightness in our lives. To get rid of excess tension — for some stress is inevitable and according to some eminent medical doctors even desirable — three things are recommended:

Practise relaxation of the physical body, relaxing every muscle, stretching various parts of the body and then let them go limp.

Relax the mind, through concentrated imagination of some beautiful scene of forest, sea, mountain; imagining which enables one to touch tranquillity in the midst of stress.

Refresh the soul by recalling and meditating upon great passages and great promises from scriptures or any other good books you have read.

Modern medical science is moving towards recognition that in illness of any kind, from common cold to cancer, emotional stress, and also fear play a part. Many doctors would concede that prayer is a good way to control anxiety and promote healing. Hope, faith, truth — these seem to be 'basic keys to healing'.

Age-old techniques of meditation, aimed at heightening awareness and fighting the ill-effects of stress, may have scientific basis, doctors now believe. Meditation can help gently and effectively to cope with the stresses of modern life. Aches and pains, bad backs, pulls and strains, frozen shoulders, sciatica...everybody and every *body* — suffers wear and tear. Is the best treatment — what we generally follow — to take a pain-killer and go to bed until it is better? Or could we get back on our feet with Yoga practice?

There are many techniques and exercises to combat stress which we can practise easily and pleasantly at home.

Breathing techniques to enhance feeling of well-being; herbal remedies culled from the wisdom of the ages; relaxation routines to fight fatigues.

Importance of diet and exercise:

It is good to know advantages and disadvantages of alternative diet. Vegetarianism is rightly attracting attention the world over, as a healthy habit. Masters on the path of spirituality always insist on complete abstinence from all meats, fish, fowl and eggs. Also from all alcoholic beverages or intoxicants and other opiates and stimulants, one dulls the thinking faculty. Animal passions flare up within and render one insensate to higher impulses in life. There is an appropriate aphorism: 'As is the food, so is the mind.' We should eat that which is clean and conducive to body-health and purity of mind. Vegetarianism and honest earning are two very important principles.

A natural diet, comprising vegetables, fruits, nuts, butter, bread and cheese in moderate quantities, is highly nutritious for the health and strength necessary for carrying on obligations of life, either earthly or spiritual. We must remember what an eminent physician has said: "We dig our graves in the kitchen and more deeply with our teeth."

If one acquires a simple knowledge of nutrients — minerals, vitamins, proteins and carbohydrates — he or she will see that vegetarian diet leads to good health, both physically and mentally. Approaches to dieting and fasting, methods of cooking to preserve vital vitamins and minerals and discovering which foods are really healthy, and which are simply fads — are very important.

Exercise is a highly crucial factor in promoting health. Tied, as most of us are, to office desk, kitchen stove, or work-bench...we would benefit enormously from sensible tips on exercise, from Indian Yoga and the less known Chinese ritual based on T'aichi Ch'wan; techniques that will soon have us feeling and looking our best.

Sleep and relaxation:

These two are most important instruments in maintaining good health. Sleep is a natural restorative process. How funny that man is losing the simple way to sleep. American people use more than 12 million sleeping pills every night. 'If you do not get sleep, start doing *'simran'* (remembrance of the Lord) and you will fall asleep, it is a better pill', says Maharaj Charan Singh (of Radha Swami Satsang, Beas, Punjab).

If one is very tired, then one must stretch out on the bed, relax, loosen all the nerves one after the other until one becomes like a rumpled cloth in one's bed, as though one had neither bones nor muscles. When one has done that, the same thing must be done in the mind. Relax, do not concentrate on any idea or try to solve a problem or ruminate on impressions, sensations or emotions you had during the day. All that may be allowed to drop off quickly; one gives oneself up, indeed like a rag. My friends are surprised how quick and sound I can sleep, after working hard for long hours. A little bit of prayer before sleeping helps improve its quality and that of dreams.

People in the cities have forgotten the art of relaxing. Sitting in a secluded place, lying down under a tree, sitting by the side of a lake or a river, watching birds or listening to their musical sounds, walking alone for long distances, have all become unfashionable. Everyone wants to pack up more in 24 hours.

Hurry, hurry hurry. You cannot go on hurrying for long without spoiling your health. Mental tension, high blood pressure, heart disease, stomach ulcers are the consequences. Wear and tear of the body is more when you run it at high speed than at low; the engine of the car and the human body suffer in the same way.

Yoga:

In real sense Yoga is union with God; it means joining of individual soul with the Universal Divine Being. This union is effected through offering oneself to the Divine. At their highest level, all religions are so many different paths to the same goal, the ineffable and the indescribable union between the human and the divine.

According to Swami Purna: 'Yoga implies unity, integrity, balance and attunement to nature. It is a method of growth based on physical fitness, mental profoundness and Self-realization. If the individual grows, all of life grows. Yoga is not a religion, a political movement or a dogma; it is a way of bringing harmony within diversity. It respects all cultures, creeds and nations, and it nurtures the higher instincts of humanity — compassion, cooperation and peace.'

As it is, physical culture has been overemphasized especially in the West to the detriment of other aspects of life. I would like to quote a line of deep significance, from Gurudev on Yoga: 'Yoga is evenness of mind — a peace that is ever the same.' We shall revert to this aspect of Yoga a little later.

Presently we are discussing body and what keeps it healthy. Of course the body is closely related to mind. A weak sickly body means a weak mind also. Yoga arouses indomitable power of the human mind. Interest in Yoga is now at an all time high. During the past thirty years people all over the world have come to recognize the great benefits which accrue from Yoga. Not only do they surpass the benefits provided by other systems of self improvement for the physical body (aerobics, calisthenics, jogging, isometrics, sports etc.) but they also expand one's mental and emotional aspects. Yoga is concerned with the whole psycho-physical being.

Complete control of mind is necessary for success in

Yoga. For this reason Patanjali has declared in his most important verse:

Yogaschitta-vritti-nirodha

i.e. Yoga is the cessation of mental waves; rising above thoughts. He prescribes eight scientific steps (*ashtang*) of Yoga:

1) *Yama* — physical disciplines : Truthfulness
Non-violence
Non-stealing
Celibacy (chastity)
Non-covetousness

2) *Niyama* — moral observances : Purity
Contentment
Austerity
Self Study
Reliance upon God

(Together these form ten commandments of Yoga — important in life.)

3) *Asana*: Discussed in brief, separately.

4) *Pranayama*: A separate sub-section on Pranayama is given in subsequent pages.

5) *Pratyahar*: Bringing the sense organs under the control of will, not to allow the mind to exploit the senses without control.

6) *Dharna*: Concentration. Fixing the mind. It requires practice, patience and perseverance. Purity of mind with intensity of longing is needed for this.

7) *Dhyana*: Meditation. It helps one to elevate oneself to bliss and peace. (There is a separate section on it, in Chapter 6.)

8) *Samadhi*: Spiritual union between the individual soul and the supreme Self. It is a state of oneness and sameness that cannot really be explained by the written word. We shall talk about it briefly in a later part of this chapter. (More about it again, in Chapter 6.)

To keep the body and mind healthy one must practise *Yoga asanas* (postures) and *pranayama* (breathing exercises). There are a number of Yoga practices. Many books describe them with illustrations. One can select some suitable ones and practise regularly. One would do well in learning the technique of right postures preferably under the personal guidance of an adept in the beginning. The practice should be regular, continuous with faith and devotion. Practice for a month or two will render all rigid tendons, muscles and bones very elastic.

The difference between Yoga and ordinary exercises is that while the latter develop the superficial muscles of the body only, asanas are intended for the thorough exercise of the internal organs viz. liver, spleen, pancreas, intestines, heart, lungs, brain and the important ductless glands of the body, which are called endocrine glands viz. thyroid and parathyroid at the root of the neck, adrenals in the spleen, pituitary and pineal glands in the brain which play a very important part in the economy of nature, in maintaining health, in metabolism and in structure, growth and nutrition of different kinds of cells and tissues of the body. Asanas make the glands to secrete more of their reactive fluid in the body. Certain asanas also stimulate voluntary and involuntary nervous system and its plexuses (*chakras*).

Yoga asanas are good for any age. Even old people can practise most of them. In case of those medically not fit, consultation with doctors so as to which type of asanas are not good for them is necessary.

Pranayama is the yogic practice of breath control. It is very useful in tranquillizing the mind. Actually *prana*, life-force, often interpreted as breath is consciousness, the most subtle life essence that pervades all manifestations. Prana is the sum-total of all existing energy in the universe. All functions of the body have prana as their life-force.

Pranayama involves control by a triple process: inhalation, suspension and exhalation. It causes proper elimination of carbon dioxide.

Today we all live in an age where stresses and strains are necessary evils as observed earlier. The practice of *pranayama* supplies more oxygen to the blood. The life-force which permeates all the cells of the body can work only if it receives oxygen from the atmosphere around it.

The oxygenated life-force is the strength and the maintainer as well as the master of the human body. According to the author of Hatha Yoga Pradipika: 'Life is what exists as long as air (which serves· as the vehicle of life-force) remains in the body...such air should be controlled.' Ancient Indian medical science enumerates as many as eighty diseases caused by the unhealthy movement of the air in the body.

Disbalance in our *pranas* produces tension and disbalance in different parts of our body. According to the Indian medicine text the three humours — *vayu* (wind), *pitta* (bile) and *kaph* (phlegm) become disturbed. If these three humours are not in harmony, many diseases develop in the body.

Practice of pranayama increases the alpha waves in the brain. The brain functions well only if all our brain centres receive a sufficient amount of oxygenated blood. The different techniques of pranayama, it is claimed, can remove many diseases including nervous disorders. The respiratory system improves which also improves the state of mind and brings about refinement of sense perceptions. Also a sense of peace and harmony is experienced.

Pranayama exercises provide a complete and comprehensive exercise for the lungs — their proper and full contraction and expansion. These strengthen the heart, too. The beginner must get hold of a good book on pranayama. Much better, however, and a certainly preferable course is to learn pranayama techniques from an experienced teacher. Wrong type of breathing exercises can be harmful.

Kundalini:

In recent years a lot of interest has developed in this aspect of Yoga. The yogis describe it as a coiled spring at the base of the spinal cord, called muladhara chakra, sacral plexus. When activated, aroused and channelised upwards, it works and stimulates the other plexuses of the nervous system. Joyous effects are experienced, as a result.

The *Kundalini,* however, remains a mysterious concept signifying 'Grand Potential'. It has not been possible to explain it completely in terms of known anatomical structures or physiological processes, although many theories and conjectures abound in literature.

Certain yogic postures and breathing exercises are, however, credited with awakening of *Kundalini sakti* (serpent power) causing motivation of many unsuspected and unexpected faculties leading, in the language of Yoga, to the realization of the Self.

In view of the growing interest in Kundalini Yoga, a fairly detailed note is added on it as Annexure IV. At its end, a brief reference is made to 'Sex' as very often, especially in the West, Kundalini is mistakenly linked with it.

We may now briefly talk of the deeper spiritual aspect of Yoga. Yoga does not want a turning away from life. It demands spiritualization of life. Yoga is not forsaking of action but it is efficient performance in the right spirit.

Yoga, as a way or practice towards union with Divine, is not opposed to any religion or any sacred belief. It is purely scientific, spiritual and universal. It does not contradict any one's sincere faith. It is an aid to the practice of the basic spiritual truths in all religions. Yoga implies abiding continuously in God and to live at peace with man and all. Yoga is Union with God. God dwells in all. Yoga is thus union with all.

We must feel at every step that we belong to the Divine; we must have the constant experience that, in whatever we think or do, it is always the Divine consciousness that is acting through us...then even the smallest thing to which we do not usually pay much attention or care, ceases to be trivial and insignificant; it becomes full of meaning and it opens up a vast horizon beyond.

Yoga, says the Gita, will empower the mind with wisdom — Yoga not merely of the contemplative type but virile action promoting the good of humanity. Success or failure — never mind — we must practise evenness of mind in the performance of our duties. Evenness of mind is enforced as the keynote of all Yoga.

Hara — secret of the belly:

I had several occasions to talk to a friend of mine, Mr. Vinod Dhawan, who is a scholar of spiritual studies and an ardent devotee of the Lord. We have been sharing many ideas on the spiritual path.

Happily, one day he introduced me to 'Hara — the vital centre of Man'. It is the name of a book written by Karlfried Graf Von Durckheim, a well-known German philosopher and psychotherapist, who discovered, learnt and later practised the tradition of Hara in Japan.

The Japanese term Hara means the physical embodiment of the original Life Centre in man and this is considered to be in the region of the navel or, to be precise, a little below it.

Right posture and correct breathing are two characteristics of the Hara practice.

The man practising Hara — concentrating on the life centre — is composed. Unnecessary movements and all restless jerking and twitching of the limbs cease.

By Hara the Japanese understand an all-inclusive general attitude which enables man to 'open himself' to the power and wholeness of original life force. The mundane power which Hara bestows is merely a bye-product of the unlimited power derived from contact with the Greater Life. Supernatural power is released, so it is claimed, through man's liberation from the limitation of his ego.

Hara is thus regarded as a connecting link between Being beyond space and time and our existence between space and time.

While discussing with Mr. Dhawan the growing popularity of Hara not only in Japan but also in the West, I quoted from Granth Samata Prakash a couple of verses regarding the importance of the navel region, according to Mahatma Mangat Ram Ji. These are:

> नाभ कंवल है अचरज थाना, जां में बसया श्री भगवाना।
>
> The navel 'Lotus' is a wondrous locale one can experience as seat of the Lord.
>
> नाभ कंवल में पवन नित गरजे, मुकन्द सरूप परगट सरजे।
>
> In the navel 'Lotus' the breath resounds powerfully and the splendorous Almighty is experienced as Supreme bliss.

Our mysterious mind:

It is said 'Man is what his mind is'. Mind has no form. It is an emanation. It is an expression or characteristic of consciousness. Mind is the highest of all sensory powers, precursor of all perceptions. All objectified consciousness has its origin in the mind. As we cultivate and train the mind so shall we become. In short, in the make-up of an individual, we can say that as the thought, so the mind; and, as the mind, so the man. We must also remember that thoughts have weight and subtle forms. It is necessary to understand the mind's incredible abilities, powers and creativity. Everything starts in the mind. It can be turned towards that which is unwholesome or towards that which is wholesome. Mind is a great trickster too. By giving rise to hopes and expectations, it remains attached to them.

Mahatma Mangat Ram advises us to have a clean, calm and unconditioned mind.

> मन के औगन तब ही जायें। झूठ का जब मोह मिटायें।।
>
> Mind is cleaned of its defilements when too much attachment to the ephemeral body is eradicated.
>
> मन सत कर्मों से निश्चल होता है और मलीन कर्मों से चंचल होता है।।
>
> Noble deeds lead to calmness of mind; evil ones make it restive.
>
> विरत रहत मन निर्मल भयो। साची शोभा प्रभ की लख लेयो।।
>
> An unconditioned mind is a pure mind which can perceive the real glory of God.

The functions of mind are multiple. It records events and remembers things. It produces ideas, thoughts and works as an inventive and creative instrument. 'It controls, guides, governs and activates the entire bodily system.' It is the greatest gift of life and a veritable *Kalpatru* (wish-fulfilling tree). If we want *bhakti* (devotion) it will develop *bhakti* (devotion) and give us bliss. If we want *asakti* (passion) it will plunge us headlong into it. Mind can be a foe as well as a helpful friend.

When the mind is almost wholly dominated by the body and its demands, as is the case with most persons, it is best to begin gradually, in little things, to dissociate the mind from the body.

Troubles always strike at the body, for this is a law of life; in spite of difficulties, we should keep such mental neutrality that the mind is not affected by outer conditions. 'Let us always think of our mind as a garden; and keep it beautiful and fragrant with divine thoughts', as Swami Chinmayananda puts it.

The mind is miniature universe. The universe is expansion of mind. It is impossible to even broadly assess all states the mind can assume. Broadly, these are three in nature, called *gunas* (moods):

Satvic (pure)	stands for stability, humility, innocence, truthfulness, faith, silence, peace, desire for liberation and other virtues.
Rajasic (action, passion)	represents movement in the nature of tremendous activity, ambition, greed, ego, aggression and mental unrest.
Tamasic (inertia, ignorance)	tends to indolence, turpitude, negligence, negativity, dullness, stupidity, depression and darkness.

The three *gunas* (moods) are interdependent and interpenetrative; they do not exist independently of each other in their purity. They generally occur in combinations. 'Reality', however, as discussed earlier in Chapter 2, is beyond them and is untouched by them.

Mind follows the trails of impulses and instincts. This is its nature. It also manufactures any amount of delusion. A good mind must have compassion, great sense of beauty and be capable of right action. Its relationship must be right. As J. Krishnamurti observes: 'Blessedness of order is when the mind has not a single desire and the senses are operating fully and totally...The mind must learn to be silent, remain calm, attentive, without making noise.'

'Our mind consists of dual, invisible gigantic powers; the conscious and subconscious. One is a giant that never sleeps. The other is a giant which when asleep is powerless. It is called the subconscious mind. When awakened its potential power is unlimited. When the two work in harmony, they can affect, use, control or harmonize with all known and unknown powers. When properly controlled by sane intellect, there is no limit to what the mind can reach.' In fact the mind knows no limit except that we ourselves place on it. Dr. Wayne Dyer, in 'Sky's the Limit', says:

> 'You are whole human being. Body and mind are involved in every single human action. Your mind need to be challenged and exercised as regularly as your body.'

Exercise for the mind is cleansing it of unnecessary thoughts, a sort of emptying out of trash, and keeping it young, fresh and sensitive. Not to curse it, but to caress it with loving thoughts, wise counselling and brightening it with the Divine presence in us. Victory over mind is won not by compulsion nor by artificially induced methods that suspend the mind temporarily, but by knowledge and understanding alone.

Some say the mind should not be maligned or castigated; mind is a good boy. I, too, personally think that way. The natural tendency of the mind is to become fine unless we force it to go downwards. Constant vigilance, however, is the necessary price of liberty. When the mind becomes pure, a little free from the dead weight of sense experience and the consequences of sense life, it soars up, lightened.

Mind has the right to ask questions. But as J. Krishnamurti says: 'The state of mind that questions is much more important than the mind itself. Any question may be asked by a slavish mind, and the answer it receives will still be within the limitations of its own slavery.' Mind must be both pure and free. A self-disciplined mind is a great asset.

Somebody asked Gurudev: 'Please advise on how to control the mind? He answered:

> 'Surrender to God and remembrance of His Name are the methods to control the mind. Having learnt the

right way from any spiritual adept, and with faith you will be able to control the mind. One who can control the mind for a minute is perfect practitioner, is truthful and can experience God. One who can control for five minutes is a fully realized soul.'

In reply to another question Gurudev tells how the mind gets peace when it has faith, not doubt: 'it does not find stability in anything created by it, on the contrary it becomes stable in the source of its creation. Meditation promotes health of mind.'

Austerity of mind is described in Gita as 'cheerfulness of mind, placidity, habit of contemplation on God, control of the mind and purity of inner feelings — all this is called austerity of the mind.'

Tranquillity of mind is possible by consciously withdrawing the senses from the excessive charms and temptations of the world.

Intellect (*Budhi*):

Very often mind and brain are equated or bracketed. The brain is part of the body but brain and mind are not identical. 'The brain breathes mind like the lungs breathe air.' For our study we shall take brain as the instrument of thought. It is the seat of mind. It examines arguments for and against and gives decision. It is the intellect, a quality of the brain, which ponders over thoughts of the mind and reasons out. To use intelligence over mind is like using a steel tool to sharpen an iron instrument. Both are similar substances, or the same material, but one is superior in quality to the other.

Mind and intellect both, in fact, function in the realm of thoughts. It is only due to their functional differences that they are called by two names. When distinction is made between the mind and intellect, the mind is defined as the seat of emotion and the intellect as the seat of reason and discrimination.

Mind, intellect, memory and ego are, in fact, parts of consciousness itself; the mind thinks, the intellect decides, the memory records, the ego develops the sense of doership.

The relationship between sense organs, mind and intellect is lucidly described by Mahatma Mangat Ram:

> 'Mind is the power which wishes to use the organs of perception and action for gratification of desires. Intellect is the faculty which decides on the right or wrong aspects of mind's inclinations or desires.
>
> The organs act the way the mind runs. And movement of the mind depends on the discretion of the intellect. Thus the correctness or otherwise of the actions of the organs of perception and action ultimately depends on the state of the intellect. The purer the intellect, the more peace-yielding would be the action. And, the reverse will also be true. With impure intellect one's actions would be peace-disturbing correspondingly. In the final analysis the purity of life depends upon the purity of the intellect.'
>
> (Samata Vilas)

सब कल्यान और बन्धन का भाव बुद्धि पर ही है। बुद्धि की शुद्धि सत् विचार करके और सत् निद्धियास करके है।

Emancipation of bondage depends on the state of intellect. Right concepts and right contemplation make intellect pure.

बुद्धि की लीन अवस्था सत् सरूप आत्मा है।

Intellect in its immersed state is the true self—the Atman.

जब बुद्धि आत्मा का अन्तर में साक्षात्कार कर लेती है, तब शारीरिक क्रिया में निरमान निर्मोह होकर विचरती है।

On realizing Atman — the Inner Being — the intellect

remains humble and unattached while guiding body-actions.

'The human brain', observes J. Krishnamurti, has been living in disorder which means conditioned for millions of years. It lives on that conditioning and considers it as security. There has to be breakthrough in the conditioning, to create order which is harmony.' He adds: 'Order comes only when there is understanding, learning about the disorder.'

Can the brain realize the truth? How can we realize that which is above thought, through the process of thought? Perhaps we can, provided we see without prejudice, without anything surrounding the fact. Again, as Krishnamurti puts it: 'It is necessary for a brain to become very young, fresh, innocent, alive, youthful. This is only possible when there is no psychological registration.'

Mahatma Mangat Ram has described the perfect and imperfect states of *budhi* (intellect). The entire activity of the world, he observes, is based on the state of our *budhi*. When it merges into Self, it turns into Reality itself.

Four are the dark states of the *budhi* and three of its brightness, as briefly summarised from Gurudev's observations:

The first dark state is when it becomes too egoistic of the body and remains absorbed in sheer selfishness and directs all sorts of ugly actions. No belief in God.

The second dark state is to be drowned in all types of foolish superstitions, to be attracted to sinful actions.

The third state of darkness is to undertake worship of different forms of gods and goddesses, even undertaking sacrificial acts such as killing of animals as offering to them, for one's selfish ends.

The fourth dark state of *budhi* is to worship gurus, pirs, prophets etc. for one's selfish gains and for personal popularity. And for this purpose also to do some sort of prayers, a little bit of charity, visiting places of pilgrimage and so on.

The three bright states of *budhi* are described as:

- One : to distinguish between truth and untruth and to love good acts.
- Two : to know God as truth and to distinguish between truth and delusion, to worship one God and to remain away from undesirable worldly objects. (To have an attitude of detached attachment towards the world generally.)
- Three : to rise above all bodily desires and defilements, to remain in a state of contentment and equanimity and knowing one's real self, to be absorbed in its bliss.

Our individual soul:

The soul is the essence of the Lord, a drop of the Divine Ocean.

We live mostly in our surface mind, life and body, but there is an inner being within us of which we are generally unaware. We must be awake to it and open the ranges of this inner being. This inner light and force — our soul — when we live with it and its vast possibilities, can shine in our outward lives too. It is called psyche or *nafs*. If we equate mind with the stream of consciousness, the soul is the source of this stream.

Body has two forces, one which instigates, the other which enlightens. The former is avarice, the latter is Divine refulgence. The embodied soul comprehends cravings of mind. On realizing the Divine enlightenment within, it will overcome the instigating force.

The soul is the divine spark that dwells in the centre of each being: it is the divine in man. The soul is the eternal essence at the centre of psychic being. 'The soul of man is immortal and its future is the future of a thing, whose growth and splendour has no limit.'

Antonio Machado in 'Is My Soul Asleep' says:

'No my soul is not asleep
It is awake, wide awake.
It neither sleeps nor dreams but watches,
its clear eyes open
far off things, and listens,
at the shores of great silence!'

Khalil Gibran refers to another aspect of the soul:

'If soul is the element in man that relates to God, Spirit is the element that is identical with Him.'

'The man who realizes "It is the Supreme Life that shines in and through all life" does not waste words. His pleasures and his love are then all in the soul. He becomes more enlightened among the philosophers. Knowledge and discipline are mutually complementary' (Mandukya Upanishad).

Spirit (*Atman*):

We have to go deep, deep within and find the eternal essence of our being to know the creative reality in us. This reality — as stated in Chapter 2 — is also known as *atman* or Self, 'unruffled by the fluctuations of the mind', as Ramana Maharishi calls it.

According to Rigveda it is 'desireless, firm, immortal, self-existent, contented with the essence, lacking nothing. One does not fear death who knows HIM, the Atman — serene, ageless and youthful.'

We must also accept that while Spirit is Infinite man is finite with his specifically overlay of body, mind and soul veiling the Spirit within him. As the veil is lifted, so does the Spirit in us shine. In other words when the film that separates the knower from the known is removed the self sinks into the Spirit, that is Infinite.

Mahatma Mangat Ram has, time and again, drawn our attention to our true, sublime self — the Atman. Here are a few of his pertinent observations:

अपना निरमल रूप विचार। पावें परम शान्त सुख सार।।

Think of your pure, sublime self;
you will find tranquillity and real peace.

देह ममता को त्याग के, आतम पूजे जोए।
"मंगत" मिटे चित कामना, तब पूरन ज्ञानी होये।।

Anyone abandoning attachment to the body and meditating on the Absolute Self (Atman), gets rid of mind's desires and can achieve perfect enlightenment, says "Mangat".

Some more of his sayings, translated in English, are:

- Faith in Atman destroys *unatmic* emotions — superstitions, over-attachment to worldly things, bodily and worldly shackles.
- Atman contemplation destroys *unatmic* contemplation — desires and designs for body alone conceived as the world.
- Experience of Atman destroys unreal aspect of the world and its illusion.
- Knowledge of Atman is not limited to any country, any time or any other physical feature of nature. That formless consciousness is all-pervading.

Our true 'self' is that reality — the Spirit — that unlimited power which supports all life. It is recognized only when we transcend the mind and intellect. To become ourselves is the one thing to be done; the true ourselves is that which is within us — the divine being, the spring of perennial joy. To become self-revealed by going within, to discover the spirit and to express that in all our being and living — this is spirituality.

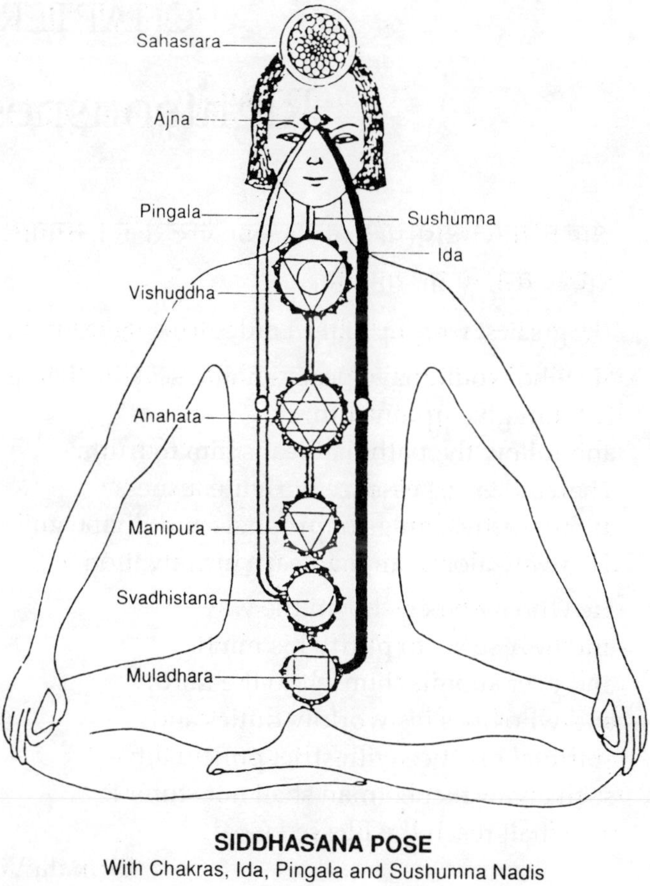

SIDDHASANA POSE
With Chakras, Ida, Pingala and Sushumna Nadis

CHAPTER 4

Righteousness

'सबसे पहले सदाचारी होना बड़ा जरूरी है। भगवान की सबसे बड़ी पूजा यही है।'

The greatest worship of the Lord is to be righteous in life.

He who would have peace should seek his Being
Let him give up untruth,
and follow the path that leads him to truth:
Therein lies his essence of righteousness
and of the teachings of prophets and divine guides.
That way alone can man earn his salvation

He who has been shown the way
and ever seeks to purify his mind
and ever submits himself to the Lord,
and who does his worldly duties and
spiritual practice with strict punctuality—
such an awakened man shall not stumble
and shall reach the Blessed Goal.

(Samata Vilas)

'If a man is right his world will be right.'

According to an old saying of Jainism (Tattva and Artha Sutra) 'Right belief, right knowledge, right conduct, these together constitute the path of liberation.'

Whenever I think or talk of righteousness, Rotary International's 'Four-way Test of the things we think, say or do' comes prominently to mind:

1. Is it the TRUTH?
2. Is it FAIR to all concerned?
3. Will it build GOODWILL and BETTER FRIENDSHIPS?
4. Will it be BENEFICIAL to all concerned?

Man in his most natural innocence of life seeks to be just, to be loving, to be kind, pure, merciful, compassionate, courageous and moral in every aspect of life. But as we know it is both difficult and important to be moral in a world which is constantly changing and offering fresh series of choices. Pearl Buck (first American woman to win the Nobel Prize for Literature) puts it plainly: 'People are what they want most to be. They may not have all they want to have — that is less important anyway — but they are in themselves, what they want to be.' Let us choose to be right!

Men can excel one another only in piety, according to the Holy Quran. 'The noblest of you in Allah's sight is the most righteous of you.' It further says: 'Righteousness does not consist in whether you face towards the east or the west. The righteous man is one who believes in Allah (God)...who for the love of Allah gives his wealth to his kinsfolk, to the orphans, the beggars...Be charitable. Allah loves the charitable.'

Mahatma Mangat Ram's observations on 'righteousness' serve as a lighthouse in the unchartered sea of practical life:

- That is righteous living in which the tendencies of the senses are brought in a proper equilibrium.
- Let man ever remain steadfast on the path of righteousness.
- Righteous sentiments purify the mind and enable the intellect to realize the real nature of Being.

- Let us think of true righteousness, meditating on one Supreme Being. He is the giver of everything, have faith in His support.
- Firmness in righteous conduct is achieved only through consistency in dedication to the Truth.
- To spend life in noble deeds is the most important duty (and responsibility) of man.
- Deepen your love for the person who falls from a principle (stumbles from the path of truth). Lift him/her up through your intense love.

The five-fold path shown by the great spiritual master comprises:

1) *Sadagi* : Simplicity
2) *Seva* : Selfless service
3) *Satya* : Truth orientation
4) *Satsang* : Sublime association with the True minded
5) *Satsimran* : Meditation on the Name — the Word, the Absolute

What a coincidence! Another great saint, Shirdi Sai Baba, also prescribed five steps to reach the Lord: simplicity, truth, service, *satsang* and remembrance of the Name.

Following these simple principles, not taking them as authoritarian 'Do's', but deeply understanding their significance and following them out of conviction, not compulsion — that is what the Master himself suggests.

In Satguru's words:

"The highest degree of purity may be through what one eats, through personal conduct and through fellowship. Purity in and of food may be maintained by avoiding intoxicants and not eating meat. Purity of personal life means to lead a life of contentment with what one earns honestly. Purity of conduct denotes to speak and act in accordance with what is true. That may be said to be holy fellowship which is characterised by persons of true righteousness. When purity with such (spiritual) praxis becomes constant, the intellect awakens and thereby firmly treads on the path of Truth. The heart of life's advancement lies in it alone."

Simplicity:

सादगी यानी अपनी कामनाओं को शुद्ध करना, अपने आहार व्यवहार में शुद्धि अखितयार करना और अपनी जरूरतों को कम करके दूसरों की जरूरत पूरी करना।

Simplicity implies sublimation of personal desires, partaking simple diet, having honest dealings.
And, fulfilling others' needs by curtailing one's own.

सादा खावन सादा लावन, सादा वचन विलास।
"मंगत" रहनी देव की, जो पाये तो पाप विनास।।

(Samata Prakash)

Simple food, simple dress, simple thought and speech — these make life god-like, devoid of any sins, says Mangat.

Mahatma Mangat Ram who was one of the greatest living saints of the 20th century, was also one of the simplest and humblest. On simplicity he has placed special stress.

'The first among noble principles', he observes, 'is the principle of simplicity. It enables one to restrain unnecessary desires and purifies the intellect. Thus, self-restrained and purified one comes to seek happiness that is true and genuine.'

Simplicity, as he explains, implies simplicity in dress, simplicity in food and simplicity in thought.

Simple dress promotes humility and love, develops modesty and respectfulness in behaviour. And one can afford living on a modest income.

Simple (vegetarian) food promotes health, purifies the intellect and helps the mind acquire strength for restraining desires.

Food and dress have a direct impact on the mind. It is, therefore, imperative that they be plain and simple, if one wishes to attain real happiness.

Simplicity of thought means innocence, freedom from malice and simple conversation — impartial, truthful and thoughtful. Simplicity of thought makes one peaceful and others happy; one also escapes many a sorrow. 'Simplicity is the very foundation of true and righteous life. One who would get rid of one's sins and attain salvation should adopt the principle of simplicity with firm determination because luxurious living is the root of all sins.'

'God the Truthful and Ever-Pure Lord is pleased only with him who is simple hearted, guileless, true and innocent. The more truthful, simple-hearted and straightforward is a man, the deeper is his realization of self and the cleaner his perception of God, the Blissful Father.'

Desire:

'Desire is a malady', says Mahatma Mangat Ram. 'Through right effort, one can be free of it', he adds. There is no end to our desires and cravings. Keeping desires under control is verily the greatest worship and allowing them free vent to control us is the greatest of follies. We must restrain our desires and be active in the service of others. This way, the wise tell us, we will be able to reach the bliss of desirelessness.

Fettered by desire one is not at peace even for a moment. 'Desire is the badge of subjection with its attendant discord and suffering.' It mostly governs our superficial life, the life of satisfaction of senses, of the play of passions. If we allow the subjective being in us to be at the mercy of the objects of sense, that life is life of desire. In order to get rid of desire, we must put an end to the cause of desire, the rushing out of the senses to seize and enjoy their objects. We are not talking of the physical renunciation of the objects of senses but of an inner withdrawal, a renunciation of desire. We should not forget that it is the feeling of 'doership' which creates web of desires. It is also true that 'to conquer a desire brings more joy than to satisfy it'. Here is an appropriate Urdu couplet:

ترکِ لذّت نہیں لذّت سے کم
کچھ مزا اس کا بھی لینا چاہیئے '

Tark-e-lazzat nahin lazzat se kum,
Kuchh maza is ka bhi lena chahiye

Abstinence from relish is itself a relish;
Must enjoy the pleasure of negating things too.

As normal human beings we must adopt proper balance between our minimum physical needs and tremendous source of bliss inside us, the liberator within us. If we do that we can, in the words of Gita, move among sense objects without attraction or repulsion for them. 'It would amount to turning the vital being from a troublesomely dominant power into the obedient instrument of a free and unattached mind', as Sri Aurobindo puts it.

Consumerism: the dreadful monster:

The rat race for material possession, the craze for a quick buck, corrupt ways of amassing wealth, unabating desire for material success by the urban and industrial societies is blindly pushing the growing youth groups towards dismal ditches of consumerism. The corrupt politician and the capitalist bureaucrat all have become cogs of a big consumer machine. It has turned them into work alcoholics with insatiable thirst for economic exploitation and money power.

To save the youth from the engulfing trends of consumerism, we must seek a dialogue with them, in our own household establishments, on the contemplative ways of life leading to the personal and universal happiness of mankind beyond national boundaries. They have to re-fashion their own lives, knowing the human worth of each ideology they confront during their lifetimes. Once they understand what spirituality is, what it stands for, where it leads to and where to turn when in conflict, in doubt, they will not succumb to self-eroding materialism. They will make their own evaluation and take their own decisions. High enlightened quality of life with a sense of fulfilment of life's goal has always withstood the outrages of time. They have to realize this truth on their own.

Happily, consumerism in some sections of capitalistic or even socialistic societies is fast collapsing to a level where people are driven to alarming frustrations. They find hollowness in their lives and are in search of practical alternatives to the monstrous consumerist way of life that devastates the natural resources in each country and kills the global ecology for total annihilation: Spirituality stands for equilibrium and balanced growth and rejects mad consumerism.

One wonders if a psychology of "scorn of excess" is built up across the globe, would it not be good for the individual, and good for the planet. If we have during the centuries turned into the subconscious of mankind that affluence is the penance for human ills, it should be equally possible to indoctrinate ourselves with the truth that fewer material needs hold the key to human happiness. If renunciation comes to be socially more respectable than the possession of riches, mankind will then have attained maturity on this earth.

Renunciation (*Vairagya*):

It is an art, a mastery one achieves by careful study of the chemistry of yearnings. Renunciation indeed is a state of detachment from that which is false and transitory. It is not running away from the necessary or unavoidable things and situations in life. It is an intelligent attitude to life. It is a secret of living in peace with the world.

> 'Renunciation is experienced when the intellect is free from all impurities. Renunciation arises when the intellect understands the becoming-nature of the world, when it knows that all gross forms, including the body, are subject to change and comprehends well that no material object has the power to bestow true peace... Renunciation is the only way to get rid of the primal ignorance that makes the living being confound himself with the body, the abode of delusions, desires, sense-enjoyment and perpetual fear and sorrow. The easiest way to eradicate this ignorance is that of service, of offering all that one may desire for himself to others. That way one gradually gets rid of desires and comes to be established in one's own blissful being.'
>
> (Samata Vilas)

Swami Chinmayananda says:

> 'Rude shocks in life such as loss of property, sudden bereavements, disappointments in love and such other causes may temporarily make us realize the falsity of the values lived by us in our day-to-day life of competition and selfishness. Man, under these stresses in life, has a feeling of renouncement, for the time being. But this is only a passing mood. In many of us this mood does come at some time or other, but soon it passes off as an impotent impulse.'

There is difference between outer abstention and inner renunciation. One may denounce the object of sense but desire for it cannot easily be rejected. If the Supreme is met, the desire is lost.

A true renunciate is one who is ever ready to give up his personal comforts for the sake of others with an attitude of utter humility. The path of renunciation consists in viewing every form of service in the light of Divine Will.

Detached attachment is another aspect of renunciation. Sheer attachments do bind us. Here is a wise piece of advice from Shirdi Sai Baba, who says:

> 'To attain our goal in life we have to cast off the four chains of attachment. These are attachment for money, property, relatives and name/fame. Freedom from these four attachments earns liberation.'

Attachment to a bigger cause for helping humanity loses its stink, as Swami Chinmayananda observes:

> 'Attachment becomes a clog or a painful chain on us only when it is extremely ego-centric. To the extent we work for larger schemes to bless a larger section of humanity, to that extent the attachment loses its poison and comes to bless the ego.'

J. Krishnamurti has a beautiful observation on non-attachment:

> 'Living lightly as a guest in one's own house, or in one's body. To be a guest is to have no sense of attachment; to step lightly on the earth.'

Isavasya Upanishad says: 'Enjoy through renunciation.' That is the only way through which our actions do not create bondage. 'All the actions that we perform can be used to deepen the delights of spirituality', as Swami Rama says in his commentary on the Upanishad. We shall revert to the question of renunciation of action vis-a-vis its performance in the next chapter.

Contentment:

Spirituality does not exclude working for progress or towards perfection. However, it suggests that we cultivate the virtue of contentment, in the sense of being satisfied with whatever has been the achievement at a particular point of time or stage. Contentment does not mean passivity; or inactivity, it implies acceptance of results — as coming from Him — after having done our best, at any stage of a project or operation.

Contentment is a personal quality. To be contented with what we get for ourselves is a real virtue. The contented man even though poor is happy. The discontented man even though rich is sad. It is greed that makes man poor in life, for the abundance of things does not make rich. 'Give up your growing greed; adopt moderation and contentment in life', advises Mahatma Mangat Ram.

Here is an interesting Chinese quote:

The practice of Tao consists in subtracting
day by day
Subtracting, yet again subtracting,
Till one reaches nothing.
And through this very nothingness
Everything gets activated.

(Tao Te Ching)

Nothingness is supreme intelligence—nothing contains the whole universe — as J. Krishnamurti puts it. Nothing contains all (as zero contains all the numbers) — but we are afraid to be nothing.

While discussing contentment, it is not suggested that one should not try to have minimum necessary physical and emotional comforts. To be content with one's right self-interest is just right. For one's pure good interest, however, one should have full faith in one's real Self and adopt moderation in enjoyments / passions related to sense organs.

Ego:

Ego-sense in the individual is considered as the source of all troubles; it acts as barrier between the soul and God. Even though a non-virtue, ego need not be condemned outright. It is surely the instrument for individualization; it makes each one a separate being, in all possible ways. While ego is what helps us to individualize ourselves — very necessary to an extent while living and working in the world — it also prevents us from becoming divine. Again it is a question of a balance, a golden mean, a middle path. Let us first become conscious individuals. And then see that our ego does not remain limited to the "I", "I am", "I want". It must lead us to looking into ourselves and ask 'Who am I'. It is only then we can move from lower *aham* (ego) to higher *aham* (the Self), the ego will then vanish into vastness. 'Annihilation of ego-sense in us is the becoming of God. When we totally detach ourselves from our misunderstandings and false values of a delusory life with the knowledge of the True and the Eternal, the ego evaporates away, leaving behind only the Absolute Truth in all its purity and grandness.'

We must keep our soul clear of the clamour of ego, and cleanse it of all self-deceipt, hypocrisy and vain self flattery. 'By the subordination and disappearance of the ego, the Divine life Power, a force of self-affirmation, the affirmation of the Divine within us, the central being, the secret Imperishable Person — the Atman — can emerge.'

> देह अभिमान जाए भ्रम काल । घट में परसे पुरख दयाल ।।
>
> As the illusion of self-pride (ego) is cast away, the perception of the Absolute benevolence dawns within.
>
> (Mangat)

'When we put ourselves at the centre of universe and all things exist only in relation to us, that is egoism — a celebrated stupidity.' Everybody is a little egoistic and at least a certain proportion of egoism is acceptable, as stated earlier. When we condemn 'ego' we should not confuse it with 'self-esteem', which is just desirable. Self-pity, self-condemnation does not generate self-respect. Besides caring for our self-respect — in which confidence and belief are most dramatic factors, that affect mental health — we should build up self-esteem in everyone we come in contact with, through understanding, courtesy and compliments.

Many people forget the difference between ego and determination. That is a trap. Let us understand very clearly that self-confidence is different from ego. It is of supreme importance in the material as well as spiritual progress. Here I would like to quote very aptly two well-known Urdu verses of Dr. Iqbal (the great poet philosopher), one about ego, the other about self-esteem:

مٹا دے اپنی ہستی کو اگر کچھ مرتبہ چاہے
کہ دانہ خاک میں مل کر گل و گلزار ہوتا ہے

Mita de apni hasti ko,
Agar kuchh martaba chahiye
Ki dana khak main mil kar,
Gul-o-gulzar hota hai

Shed aside the ego, O man,
If thee seeketh elevation
For when a seed mingles with soil,
Only then it sprouts into a blooming flower.

خودی کو کر بلند اتنا کہ ہر تقدیر سے پہلے
خدا بندے سے خود پوچھے بتا تیری رضا کیا ہے

Khudi ko kar buland itna,
Ki har taqdeer say pahley
Khuda Bandey say Khud puchhay,
Bata teri raza kya hai.

Exalt thy being, O man,
To heights so high,
That obliged feels the God,
To seek thy choice,
The choice of thy destiny.

To quote Mahatma Mangat Ram on the subject of ego:

- The body ego is exceedingly subtle and deceptive force.
- As long as the intellect is in the grip of ego, it is a prisoner of innumerable desires and due to frightful play of mind and senses it is ever restless.
- The real cause of human being's restlessness is the feeling 'I am the doer'. The knowledge of imperishable and uninvolved Reality within gives freedom from the feeling of doership.
- Every effort should be made to get rid of the impurity of ego, that is, doership. Liberation from ego is great blessing and major goal of life.

Ego is like a rope made of many strands — pride, self importance, greed, desires, cravings. The sacred texts mention nine types of pride: birth and social status, physique and strength, beauty and handsomeness, intellect, morals and virtues, psychic powers, spirituality, wealth and possessions, knowledge and talents.

We cannot destroy ego completely, but can certainly reduce it progressively. All bitterness and complications in life come from the ego refusing to abdicate. We can begin by surrendering the will of the ego to the Divine Will at every opportunity and finally in a constant way. One has, however, to be sincere and spontaneous. Sai Baba suggests: 'To eliminate ego, strengthen the belief that all objects belong to God and that you are holding them in trust. This will prevent pride; it is also the truth. Egoism will be destroyed if we constantly tell ourselves, it is He not I. He is the force, I am an instrument.'

Ramana Maharishi has another and highly interesting way of dealing with 'I' which is generally equated with ego. In the very asking of the question 'who am I', he says, one comes to know the real 'I', the Self. To quote him:

> 'When the mind turns inward questioning 'Who am I' and draws near the heart, the fellow who called himself

'I' sinks crest-fallen and the One Awareness rises of its own accord as 'I'. And though it appears as I, it is not the ego, it is the whole, it is the real Self.'

The Maharishi thus speaks on the same theme:

'If the first person exists the second and the third persons will also exist. If the reality of the first person is enquired into and the first person ceases to exist, the second and third persons will also cease to exist and all will shine as ONE. This is one's true nature.'

Humility:

Humility is, indeed, a great virtue. It is a virtue of the cultured. 'It is the richest jewel one can wear.' As Gurudev Mangat Ram says:

> 'There is lack of humility on account of the absence of spirituality... Lead the life of humility and humility will kill the ego within you. With the disappearance of ego everything will fall in its proper place.'

'In reality true happiness comes from submersion of ego and the attainment of true bliss in the state of humility and equanimity (Samata).' Mahatma Mangat Ram prays for being blessed with it. Prophet of Islam proclaimed: 'Poverty (humility) is my glory.' Christ said: 'Happy are those who are humble, they will receive what God has promised.' St. Augustine laid great emphasis on the virtue of humility. 'Humility first, Humility last and Humility throughout' was the supreme theme that he had to give to his students when he rose to deliver his convocation address to them.

Goodness:

In all parts of the world one religion or the other is followed. There are certain cardinal principles which are same in all religions. We may call them fundamental principles of life. To follow them is 'goodness'. This way 'goodness' is an individual as well as a social need. And, goodness is a strength and not weakness.

Gurudev says: 'Goodness looks not at the defects of others. It only does what is good for others...Nobility of character means to be available to the redress of others. Be humble and helpful.'

For one who sees God in everyone, 'goodness' becomes spontaneous, coming effortlessly as the breath of one's nostrils. It gives mental state of happiness.

How to face today's world—where evil doers seemingly flourish more—while remaining steadfast on the righteous path? A friend of mine, an honest civil servant, told me that he found the answer in the following quote from Paul Brunton's 'The Inner Reality':

'Be ye harmless like a dove but wise as a serpent.'

In today's world while it is necessary not to harm others it is also necessary not to get harmed as a result of our goodness. If our goodness gives an impression of weakness, the fault lies with us and we have to remove this fault by proper introspection.

Non-violence:

'Goodwill towards all beings is the true religion', says Buddha. 'Cherish in your hearts boundless goodwill to all that lives.' Respect for all forms of life and non-violence towards animals are some of the foundations of spirituality.

Who hurts and harms living creatures, destitute of sympathy for any living being, let him be known as outcast, declared Buddha. He also said: Blessed are they who earn their living without hurting others.

Today, we are faced with the menace of terrorism, which has become a world problem. Killing human beings has become a mad sport. This must end!

The need is to radiate the grand principle of the Family of Man on the divine ground of loving and compassionate desire for the well-being of all. It costs very little but counts very much.

We must treat all living beings with loving thoughts, with thoughts generous and deep, purged of all anger and hate. That is real and positive non-violence. Then we shall not harm anyone through word and deed. Mahatma Mangat Ram says: 'It is the highest duty of every man to cultivate nature of non-violence (*ahimsa*). A life that is characterised by *ahimsa* is holy and beneficent.'

Anger:

Simplicity of thought demands, among other qualities, absence of anger. Gita has described where anger can lead us to:

> *Krodhad bhavati sammohah sammohat smrtivibhramah*
> *smrti bhramsad buddhinaso buddhinasat pranasyati*
>
> From anger springs distraction;
> From distraction, discomposure;
> From discomposure, irrationality;
> And from irrationality, ruin.

We are usually angry when someone differs from us. We forget that 'as long as you cannot forgive the next man from being different, you are still far from the path of wisdom'. The more we understand others, the more we are tolerant. And tolerance is not action, it is an attitude. 'Tolerance, patience and understanding are the highest virtues every man should develop', says Buddha.

Anger is the real enemy of man. Intolerance results in anger. By anger one only creates veritable hell around oneself, making others and himself suffer. According to an old Chinese saying (Meng-Tse): 'Never give way to anger, otherwise in one day you could burn up the wood you collected in many bitter weeks.' There is another old pithy saying: 'Man who gets angry quickly becomes old quickly.'

If we try to question the work and basis of anger everytime, we shall find that it is some hurt felt to our ego. Very often it is non-fulfilment of certain desires or things and happening against expectation that flares us into anger. As Sai Baba observes: "Wrath springs from thwarted desires. I do not expect anything from others, so their actions cannot be in opposition to my wishes." What a peaceful state of mind! It is Confucius who said: 'Demand much of yourself and little of others. Thus you will be spared much vexation.'

Dealing with others:

The most important single ingredient in the formula of success is knowing how to get along with others.

We have all the time to deal with others. How do we speak and behave? Do we realize presence of God in others, when we deal with them?

मीठा सब से बोलिए, रखिए सब से हीत।
नारायण सर्वज्ञ है, रमया सब के नीत।।

'Speak sweetly to everyone, love all,
for God is all prevalent, present in each one.'

(Mangat)

"Sweet tongue imbued with humility
O' Nanak! is the essence of all virtues."

Kabir says: 'Always speak in a way as calms others as also oneself.'

As Bible says: 'Pleasant words are a honey-comb, sweet to the soul and healing to the bone.' 'A cheerful look brings joy to heart.' The Quran says: 'If a man greets you, let your greeting be better than his — or at least return the greetings. Allah keeps count of all things.'

Behaviour, indeed, is the mirror in which everyone shows his image. W. Clement Steve says in 'Success Unlimited': 'The Universe is like a great echo chamber. Sooner or later what you send out comes back. If you love people that love will be reflected back to you. If you sow anger and hatred, anger and hatred are what you will get. If you think mainly of yourself and your own interests, people will never be drawn to you. If you put others first and yourself last, everyone will be your friend.'

Besides language of words, there is the body language. The science of body movement tells us that 50 per cent of information on character, impact and creditability of a person is conveyed by body language. It is a major means of communication. We must be careful in movements like wrinkling the nose, wagging a finger, making a fist, raising the eyebrow etc. Our eyes can transmit signals about our innermost feelings towards other people. A look can be soft, penetrating, sharp, stern, tender, vacant, shy. We must harmonize our inner and outer attitude, so that we feel more relaxed in ourselves and in our relations with other people. Speaking gently both with words and body must be backed by our feeling kindly towards others.

Let us note here that particularly good behaviour, special regard and consideration for the old in all respects is a moral duty and social desirability of the younger ones.

The younger generation should preserve age-old tradition of LOVE & CARE FOR THE ELDERLY both in the family and the community. The number of old is on the rise, all over the world, on account of increase in life span. Let them not be neglected. Do not push them to old-age homes. Give them affection and care at your own places if you can. Gurudev advises that some time spent in the company of the old is very useful; one learns from their experience.

Generally we have a tendency to too harsh a judgment of others, a readiness to see and stress their faults and not to see enough of their good sides. If we are patient then the other party will think of our patience with respect and honour, and possibly review his or her mistake. And, thus the way for correction becomes easy and smooth. Everything done by the person who is disliked, appears to be gravely wrong, and gives rise to disputation. There is an old Chinese saying:

> 'Be kind and you will realize that your judgement of others was too severe!'

Gurudev says: 'Self improvement leads to improvement of others too.'

We must be severe with ourselves, indulgent to the imperfections of others, just and beneficent to all mankind. We must develop the habit of never complaining about the behaviour of anyone, unless we have the power to bring about change in his or her nature.

As Christ has advised: 'Go easy on others, then they will do the same to you. And why quibble about the speck in someone else's eye — his little fault — when a board is in your own?' And, Kabir says the same thing in his simple words:

> Men laugh, and make fun,
> Of others' shortcomings,
> and never look to their own
> which are countless, not few.

Swami Bhoomananda Tirtha in his book 'Dear Souls Become Human First' has three very good pieces of advice on behaviour:

1) Everyone should have the discernment to put up with the slips and errors of the others, more so of those around him. Simply because of one mistake or another, one's friend or relative does not become otherwise. To accept an all-correct person, one does not need any great virtue or wisdom. To accept, on the other hand, one, in whom there are mistakes side by side with virtues, is the real goodness. Human behaviour should be tuned to this end.

2) "*Na abhinindati na dwesti*" means do not either praise too much or hate too much. "*Veeta-raagabhaya-krodha*"— always transcending this will mean trying to transcend the mind's natural forces of attraction, repulsion and fear. These

are the oft-repeated statements of the Gita. Sri Krishna describes these as the sure traits of the wise and the illumined. Are not these the ways of handling and sublimating our mind and its propensities? If these are the qualities to be developed, is not every bit of thinking and action, done throughout the day, whether it is within the household in the manner of talking to and reacting to the relatives, assistants, servants or bosses to be regarded as piece of Sadhana, the spiritual refinement process?

3) People generally develop a flair for religion and religious routines, and so too for spiritual or yogic pursuits. And they are indifferent to the day-to-day behaviour and behavioural expressions. You will find several people flaring up during *Pooja* they perform or the worship they offer. Often the quarrels will be with their own wives, family members, etc.

Yajurveda invokes friendship with all living beings:

'May all beings look on me with friendly eyes,
May I look on all people with friendly eyes,
May we look on each other with friendly eyes.'

The way to keep mind happy, in relation to others is to move about in Brahman (the Absolute). It includes the fourfold practice:

Maitri : friendship
Karuna : compassion
Mudita : joyfulness
Upeksha : detached attachment

The Bhagavad Gita says: 'When a person responds to the joys and sorrows of others as if they were his own, he has attained the highest state of spiritual union.'

Sai Baba advises:

'Firstly, you must forget whatever help you have done to others. Secondly, you must forget whatever harm others have done to you.'

Extremely difficult, yet highly ennobling and chivalrous attitude to develop!

Selfless service:

सेवा करे मन होए निरमाना। साचा ठाकुर तिस कियो पहचाना।।

'Selfless service imparts humility
It enables one to perceive the Almighty.'

(Gurudev Mangat)

'Man in his ceaseless pursuit of wealth employs all kinds of corrupt methods to gather it.
One who earns with the sweat of his brow, and gives a part of his earnings to others, is the one who knows the way to God realization.'

(Guru Nanak)

All religions deprecate wealth which is neither earned through pious means, nor is employed in the service of God.

'We make a living by what we get but we make life by what we give.' And the miracle is this — the more we share, the more we have. I would like to quote here from Bible:

'Do not be hard-hearted or tight-fisted towards your poor brother.'
'If a man shuts his ears to the cry of the poor, he too will cry out and not be answered.'

"By love serve one another" is the exhortation of St. Paul. A Persian text says, "Service exalteth the server."

Selflessness is true religion. 'You want to search for God, why don't you see him in the poor, the distressed and the weak/infirm', declares Vivekananda. He adds:

'In the world take always the position of the giver. Give everything and look for no return. Give love, give help, give service, give any little thing you can, but keep out barter. Make no conditions and none will be imposed. Let us give out of our own bounty, just as God gives to us.'

His master Ramakrishna goes a step further when he says:

> 'If you find someone who is unselfish, all-loving, and deeply concerned for the well-being of all, there you will find the true realization of God.'

Kabir said, "By giving away money it will not be lessened. If you are not satisfied, you may try for your own self." So says Mahatma Mangat Ram, too. He further advises:

> 'If you make some donation in a gathering or a society, and have your name noted or announced prominently, it is not good. You must first understand what is real service (including donation) then serve (silently). You will see what spiritual joy you will get then.'

A Punjabi saying: Donation or selfless help of any kind should be done *kujjke* (in privacy), *rujjke* (to heart's content), *pujjke* (as quickly as possible).

The offerings in all cases should be free and voluntary and should not be inspired by any thought of reward or be the outcome of impositions from without, for, then instead of being a source of liberation they become the source of bondage.

All sufis and saints have laid much emphasis on service to humanity, next only to worship of Allah. Constructive work for the amelioration of mankind and betterment and development of society comes under service to humanity on which much stress has been laid by Syed Ashraf, a well known Sufi. He says that an idle man is worthless of all and those who are engaged in some constructive work, are in service to humanity and thus in reality they are in service of God.

Mahatma Mangat Ram has much to tell us about selfless service. Following are his selected sayings on this highly important aspect of righteousness:

- Service is the principle that sustains the world. Service is the way to self-purification from impediments, the way to supreme bliss and absorption therein.
- Devotion to God and selfless service are the only means for eradicating the impure impressions from the screen of psyche.
- Service is the supreme path that leads man to salvation.
- All sacred scriptures proclaim that selfless service is the highest virtue. On rendering selfless service the mind becomes humble and then one perceives the Almighty Lord.
- Man should serve others as the air, water, earth, the sun and the moon serve various creatures continuously in a natural way. (Nature constantly reminds us that we should live to serve the society, not to plunder it.)
- He who is bereft of the spirit of service is bereft of humanity; a victim of demonic passions of greed, infatuation, pride and jealousy, he ever remains in a state of unrest—this is like living in hell.
- Peace comes increasingly to one who progressively and selflessly serves others with his body, mind and possessions.
- Through self-sacrifice, comfort ye those who are weary and heavy laden.
- One who would serve others to escape from some calamity or adverse circumstances, or resort to it for popularity or some other gains, shall never come to know what real service is nor shall that one ever truly come to practise it.
- Glorious indeed is the path of service, the path that purifies those who follow it and delivers them from sins and brings them everlasting bliss.
- Sin does not stick to a man who gives himself up to

the service of others. Let every person resort to it with utmost earnestness.

- One given to selfless service develops many traits: consideration for others, detachment, harmony, humility, renunciation, calmness, contentment etc.

Gurudev further says: 'The real benefit of life is to serve others. This will eliminate your desires and bestow bliss on you. There is no religion as service, no sacred knowledge as service...It is the sacred rendering of service to others which explodes the poisonous mind of confusion...If you do nothing else but serve others conscientiously you will certainly succeed in life, overcoming countless confusions and infirmities.' He distinguishes between self-interest and selflessness as looking after one's own comforts and caring for others' comforts. 'Those who merely work for their own well being, depart from the world unhappy, while those who make others happy leave the world merrily.'

Gita teaches us not only of selfless service but also that each action of ours should be based on selflessness. It considers imparting of knowledge as the best type of selfless service. It says:

> 'The welfare of society is based on sacrifice. The best among the sacrifices is the giving of knowledge (education).'

Sublime Association of the True (*Satsang*):

Company of the good does a lot of good. If we associate with righteous people we develop righteousness ourselves.

> जीव की बन्ध और मुक्त हालत का विचार करना और बंधन स्वरूप कर्मों का त्याग करना और निर्बन्ध अवस्था की प्राप्ती का सत् यतन करना — इन भावों का विचार सम्मिलित होकर करना अस़ली सत्संग है।

'Real *satsang* (truth-oriented association) is that where people get together and deliberate upon what binds their embodied soul and what frees it; to give up actions that cause bondage and to adopt means which bring emancipation.'

(Mangat)

'The first principle of *Satsang* is that of togetherness; second, to reflect prudently on self improvement; third, to listen and reflect what is righteousness (real *dharma*), to learn from the lives and teachings of all realized personages; fourth, to ponder over the real purpose of life; fifth, to recognize means for overcoming obstructions in following the right religious law; sixth, to obtain freedom from blind faith and to adopt/develop belief in God; seventh, to find the cause of one's spiritual debility and achieve liberation from sorrow. There are numerous other benefits.'

(Samata Vilas)

It is through *Satsang* that one is able to discriminate between that which *IS* (truth) from that which is *NOT* (Untruth) and to cognise what is good and what is evil.

One acquires the disposition of right thought, right belief and right endeavour by participating in a serious *Satsang* — the sublime association of the true and the good. It is through such association that one achieves real peace, too.

Righteous Living:

'Let not man be careless about what he eats, how he earns his living and the kind of people he associates with. Let him abstain from food that gives rise to sloth and passion, and refrain from ways of livelihood that are dishonest and deceitful, and also from the company of the wicked, the foolish or the frivolous. It should be remembered that good conduct is the first prerequisite for earnest spiritual endeavour that leads man to final beatitude. The fetters that tie creatures down to worldly life are indeed very hard to break.

The great did not earn their salvation cheaply — high indeed was the price they were called upon to pay. But in the long run, they did succeed in earning it during their life-time itself and lived truly blessed and liberated even before their death and became paradigms of righteous living for future aspirants for salvation to emulate and live up to.

The glory of human life lies in attaining autonomy from all such strictures as belong to non-being. A person who sees his actions in the light of divine will, who sees everyone as his own self, and who believes that his comfort is identical with the comfort of others — such a person is truly righteous.'

(Gurudev Mangat Ram)

At the end of this chapter I would like to recall some specific suggestions of Gurudev given in reply to questions asked from time to time, regarding nature of righteousness, right conduct and purity of life.

The Nature of Righteous Life:

Discarding unnecessary comforts of the body — following principles of simplicity, truthfulness, selfless service, righteous fellowship and contemplation.

How to overcome the five enemies within: lust, anger, greed, attachment and ego-sense?

— Anger is overcome by loving everyone.
— Pride and greed are overcome by serving everyone.
— Attachment and lust are overcome by knowing and remembering God as Truth.

Right conduct:

Good conduct implies pure performance (of duty) prompted by pure intention and backed by Atman-orientation.

Life shall be righteous if attention is paid to the following points:

Be simple in life, and natural in habits. Cheat none. Keep away from intoxicants and undesirable show-places. Both of them corrupt the intellect and increase restlessness.

Dissociate from those who are unrighteous. Do not talk of evil actions. Their very thought affects the mind.

Cultivate the fellowship of the noble ones. Their company has sublime influence.

Purity and discipline of life:

Purity and discipline of life consist in:

- Pure food — to stay away from all intoxicants, meat etc. and to eat according to appetite whatever pure food is available at the proper time.
- Pure livelihood — to remain content with one's rightful honest income and to work honestly and within certain time limits.
- Pure conduct — to remain true in word and deed; one is what one utters, does or lives.
- Pure company — to associate with noble and truthful persons and to adopt good thoughts.

CHAPTER 5

Attitude to Work

'This world is the plane of action, and act we must, whether we like or not.'

(Gita)

Krishna thus speaks to Arjuna:

'When you perform an action, do not think of the results or reward. But then, do not delude yourself that inaction will help you. No, you have no right to inaction, either. Do not attach yourself to anything. Do your work with earnestness of mind. You must be unaffected by success or failure. It is this evenness of temper which is meant by *Yoga*.'

Mahatma Mangat Ram calls this evenness of mind as an attribute of Samata — sameness in all circumstances. He says:

When action is performed freely, passionlessly, neither grief, nor joy is felt; there is no sense of 'doership'.

निर्वास करम चित लेप न करे। करम करे नहीं खेद चित धरे।।

Action, free from sheer self-interest, does not smear the mind. Acting thus one does not afflict the mind.

Gurudev thus defines action:

'Every living being is doing one thing or the other all the time. Thinking is also an action. Speaking too is an action. Physically doing a thing is action all right. Everyone acts according to one's nature.'

(Samata Vilas)

Some selected verses of Gurudev on *Nishkam Karma* (selfless action) may be aptly quoted here, even though we came across his views on non-doership and selfless service briefly in the previous chapter too.

इच्छया ममता मोह चुकाई। निष्काम करम घर सोझी पाई।।

One truly understands the meaning of selfless action, when one is above desire, attachment and infatuation.

करम का करता भाव त्याग । निष्काम करम में उठ के जाग।।

Give up the feeling of 'doership'. Wake up in selfless action (as per Lord's will).

पाप पुन्न दोहे लीन समाई। निष्काम गती सो सत कहलाई।।

Sin and virtue cease to be in the state of true non-doership (one then acts merely as an instrument of God).

निष्काम करम मैल को धोए। साचा सिमरन तब परगट होए।।

Selfless action cleans the dirt (of the mind).
One can then truly engage in God-remembrance.

In answer to a question what is *Nishkam Karma* (selfless action) Gurudev's answer, as always, was simple and straight:

रज़ा में फना।
होना न होना प्रभु की इच्छा में देखना।।

To completely surrender to God's will.
To see His will in whatever happens or does not happen.

Work as worship:

"Perform actions as worship of God", says the Gita. "Therefore, renounce the selfish desire for personal gain! Act, but not for personal gain or honours. Act impersonally. Act non-egoistically. Act sacramentally. Let your every action be an offering to God!"

Here is a very beautiful story; a little story full of wisdom. A story of an artist. His paintings were much admired, but he never noted down his name on any of his paintings.

One day, a dear friend comes to him and says to him: "Your paintings are marvellous! They have the power to attract. Why don't you give out your name?"

The artist is silent. The good friend asks again: "Why don't you give out your name?"

And when the painter is hard pressed, he takes his friend to a corner where a painting is kept. He lifts up the painting and says to his friend: "This painting will answer your question." Beneath the picture are written the following words: "Master! may the painting draw many unto Thee! But may my name be forgotten!"

The very heart of the teaching of the Gita is in these words of the artist!

> 'Fill the span of life given to you with work and worship.'
>
> (Isavasya Upanishad)

A good and spiritually realized friend of mine, late Gumnam Sahib, used to speak spontaneously soul-inspired verses in Urdu. One of the many which impressed me deeply is:

نظر آئے جسکو بخود تو ہے سب میں
عبادت میں اپنا وہ ہر کام جانے

Nazar aye jis ko Khuda khud hai sub main
Ibadat main apna woh har kam jane.

'One who sees God Himself present in all, for him each act is an act of worship.' He often flattered me by saying that I lived the saying literally.

'Work done in the true spirit is meditation.'

'Work, indeed, is body's best prayer to the Divine.'

'Even the tiniest work is a flower placed at the feet of God.'

(Sai Baba)

What is the true or the right spirit which makes work a worship? When we work as an offering to the Divine. But the work has to be done to the best of our capacities, leaving the results to the Divine. Let nothing short of perfection be our ideal in work and we are sure to become a fine instrument of the Divine. 'Accept thyself humbly, yet proudly, devotedly, submissively and joyfully as a divine instrument', advises Sri Aurobindo.

Perfection as ideal:

'There is no greater pride and glory than to be a perfect instrument of the Master' (Sri Aurobindo).

The nature of the work done, as above, is of little importance and we can do any right work without losing contact with the inner presence. Any work done well and carefully, for the sake of the Divine, without desire or egoism, with calm tranquillity, in the spirit of *samata* (oneness, equality) is a means of dedication.

It is the spirit or consciousness in which the work is done that matters most; the outer forms vary greatly for different natures. It matters little if the job is called 'high' or 'low'.

I am particularly inspired by the following saying of Sri Aurobindo:

'All work done for the Divine, from poetry and music to carpentry or baking or sweeping a room, should be made perfect even in its smallest external detail as well as in the spirit in which it is done, for only then is it an altogether offering.'

The work has to be perfect, this must be our consistent aim. The Divine works through our nature. If it is imperfect, the work will be imperfect, mixed, inadequate. In that case the work will be done according to our weakness, not according to the purity and power of the source. Like ego we have to remove the veil of nature. We must develop quietude in action itself. 'Action without desire is possible, action without attachment is possible, action without ego is possible.' Let us strive for that liberated state in action.

If we want perfection in any work, we need:

— quietude of mind, not to be disturbed by anything,
— strong will and right effort; one cannot succeed in anything without a strong determination,
— not entertaining negative thoughts or self-defeating thinking,
— absolute faith, faith that which is for the best will happen,
— opening to Divine Force and allowing it to work through us, and
— avoiding depression and boredom which result in lack of initiative in everything.

We must also remember that challenges are the stuff of life. Coping, getting along, become a well adjusted person, that is not good enough. Striving, devoting serious effort or energy to something — it involves having some direction and energy. That is something. But for achieving perfection, excellence in every way is the way.

Some people think that in countries like India it is religion that has made people lazy and indifferent towards work. That is partly true. Wrong application or interpretation of religion cripples work culture. Scriptures do not suggest inaction. The Gita, for instance, is all about the importance of work. It says: *'Yoga karmasu kausalam'*, Yoga is excellence in action. It is not a text for the old and retired. It is for the young and working people, as well. We ignore its message, and instead conveniently interpret religion to mean only prayers (necessary and important though prayer is), temples and God. Working hard and honestly is very much a part of being truly religious.

Gurudev says:

> 'Whether it is personal work or service to others, one must have strong urge to complete it well and in time. One would certainly succeed thus in whatever one has taken in hand.'

Whatever we do must be done wholeheartedly. In this connection, I would like to quote Abraham Maslow who describes 'Muga' — the term used in Zen-based Japanese culture — a state in which you are doing whatever you are doing with a total wholeheartedness, without thinking of anything else, without any hesitation, without any criticism or doubt or inhibition of any kind whatsoever. It is a pure and perfect and total spontaneous acting without any blocks of any kind. This is possible only when self is transcended or forgotten.

> 'Let our work speak for itself. No covering it with an excuse. Excuses are just the expressions of our weakness in the field of action. Revelling in our tiredness; joyous in our exhaustion; blissful with our fatigue; we shall still work on inspiredly in our endless love for Him who is thrilling us into performance from within. He tickles and our giggles percolate in suffocating laughter through our daily action.'
>
> 'Let our work stand by itself. Let the world estimate our

success, criticise our failures, laugh at our hopes, smile at our visions — we shall work on for Him, in Him, with Him, as He commands us. We will always do lovingly our best.'

'While thus working we must cultivate in ourselves a special brand of independence — spirit which shall sustain us, both in the busy market place and in the meditation-seat. In the midst of the contending crowd or in the peaceful solitude, this daring spirit of freedom and fearlessness alone should spring forth from our consciousness that we are upright and pure, diligent and clean both in our thoughts and actions.'

('We Must' — Swami Chinmayananda)

Gospel of work:

The Swami describes it as under:

'And let us work. With our physical passions and emotional impulses dedicated unto the Lord, with a wakeful intellect policing our lust, greed, pride, arrogance and such other lower urges, let us work in love and in charity with deep sympathy and all tenderness. Work, when undertaken in this attitude, becomes a rewarding fulfilment in itself: whatever be the final result. Inspired by the Lord-at-the-altar-of-our-heart, when we work thus in love and joy, the achievement comes to exhibit a glow, at once divine and unique, bringing forth untold happiness to the world around us. Even if our plans break down, our schemes fail, our purpose gets shattered, our efforts become wasted, we shall find some miraculous Power secretly pouring unending success into our fields and accomplishing things which we never planned, showering blessings all around which we never conceived. This then is the Gospel of work.'

Mahatma Mangat Ram says that an action done with a selfish motive chains one. That done as duty frees one. He repudiates the statement made by some that spirituality makes people lazy. He affirms that *Vedanta* does not make people inert or indolent. On the other hand it teaches valour, bravery and helping others. On the nature of actions, good or bad, he has a highly pragmatic view: 'Pious actions are those which give you genuine joy, inspire your heart and provide you with a sense of peace. Such actions as create worry and turbulence are of the nature of sin.' Purity of actions is pure wisdom, he says:

> जब कर्म ही पवित्र नहीं तो योग और तप क्या ?
>
> When actions themselves are not pure, what use is Yoga and penance?

He recommends purity of action coupled with dedication to God: a great combination indeed! Says he:

> 'The one who, first of all, has purified the path of action, has given up unbecoming actions and taken to sublime ones, then has surrendered the fruit of even good actions to God, has achieved the state of selfless service. Simultaneously, who is steadfast in right remembrance of God, such one alone can reside in inner Absolute reality.'

As a highly pragmatic piece of advice he says: 'There must be judicious allocation of time for service to self and selfless service to others.'

We must always remember that the only work that spiritually purifies is that which is done without personal motives, without desire for fame or public recognition or worldly greatness. Let appreciation of our work follow, but not be sought for. Our job should be only to do any good work in close union and deep communion with the Divine in us.

Karmayoga:

Yoga of action is 'the worship of the Supreme Being in the form of action; every act that we do volitionally or intellectually, can be converted into a contact with the Eternal.'

Dr. Radhakrishnan commenting on Gita says that Krishna does not consider the world as an illusion and action as a snare. He recommends the full active life anchored in the Eternal Spirit. He advocates detachment from desires and not cessation from work:

> 'The state of spiritual freedom consists in transformation of our whole nature into the immortal law and power of the Divine. The freed soul is inspired by Divine knowledge and moved by the Divine will. His body, mind and spirit work flawlessly together and attain rhythm expressed in the ecstasy of joy, the illumination of knowledge and the intensity of energy. Liberation is the transfiguration of the whole man. He does the duty expected of him without travail and with freedom and spontaneity. He knows he is only the instrument for the work of God; then God works through him.'
>
> It is this state that one can say in the words of Gurudev:
>
> तू कर्ता तू धर्ता, सर्व तेरी आज्ञा।।
>
> 'O Lord! You are the doer and the supreme controller. Everything happens under your command.'

The wise advise: 'Let the Source work through you, Identify only with the Ultimate and do not become deluded by the trickery of one's own ego.' That is also the state which is described as 'inaction in action', since then the Lord works through us; we become only faithful medium.

करम करे ते रहे निहकरमा। निष्काम कर्म यह निरमल धरमा।।

'Inaction in action — this is selfless work and pure religion.'

(Mangat)

Work, according to Gita, again can be our means of inner spiritual birth when personal desires and personal emotions no longer govern it, where the dualities fall away; where the action is no longer our own, where the universal, the impersonal, the divine works out through us its purpose in the world. This is what is really meant by being the instrument of the Divine. And, this is Karmayoga.

Krishna, however, superimposes a higher law also that work must be done without desire, without attachment to any fruit or reward, without any egoistic attitude or motive, as an offering or sacrifice to the Divine. Desireless action may be defined as a life of action, or work, on the one hand and a life of non-attachment and devotion to the Supreme Being on the other — this is achieved through renunciation of fruit of action which should be done for the good of community, and in the spirit of YAJNA, that is to say sacrifice or offering to God, in gratitude for what has been received from HIM.

Mahatma Mangat Ram says: 'One who engages himself in the tasks of the world with a vigorous discipline as well as follows the path of the spirit is blessed with the awareness of fearlessness.' He has also a very practical piece of advice for worldly people: 'One must not depend on others for one's living; honest work and honest earning is necessary.'

The first necessity obviously is an entire spirit of self-consecration in our works. All our actions must be performed as consecrated acts, devoted to the Eternal. 'Skilled hands, precise care, a sustained attention — and one completes the Matter to obey the Spirit' (The Mother).

Having worked with craftsmen for over fifty years, I know how dedicated master craftsmen consecrate their work. They worship Viswakarma (the Lord of crafts), worship their tools and in some cases, for instance the Shilpis, carvers of stone in South India, keep fast before starting on sculpturing of great stone figures. Here is a story of a Chinese master craftsman whose work was considered by people as 'the work of God':

> Woodworker Ch'ing carved a piece of wood and made a bell stand, and when it was finished, everyone who saw it marvelled, for it seemed to be the work of gods or spirits. When the Marquis of Lu saw it, he asked, "What art is it you have?" Ch'ing replied: "I am only a craftsman — how would I have any art? There is one thing, however. When I am going to make a bell stand, I never let it wear out my energy. I always fast in order to still my mind. When I have fasted for three days, I no longer have any thought of congratulations or rewards, of titles or stipends. When I have fasted for five days, I no longer have any thought of praise or blame, of skill or clumsiness. And when I have fasted seven days, I am so still that I forget I have four limbs and a form and body. By that time, the ruler and his court no longer exist for me. My skill is concentrated and all outside distractions fade away. After that I go into the mountain forest and examine the heavenly nature of the trees. If I find one of superlative form, and I can see a bell stand there, I put my hand to the job of carving; if not, I let it go. This way I am simply matching up 'Heaven' with 'Heaven'. That's probably the reason that people wonder if the results were not made by spirits."

The Divine Shakti (power) must be known and felt within us as the true and sole worker. There must be no egoism of any kind in the attitude of the instrument. Never say: 'Behold God's power in me.' That power works in all.

Bible says: 'Commit to the Lord whatever you do and your plans will be successful.'

Attaining a state where action ceases to be a bondage, where action ceases to decay life, where action is permeated by great eternal peace — that is the right attitude to work. Dynamic activity supported and supplemented by eternal peace — two great apparently contradictory things — this teaching is the greatest blessing of Vedas. They teach us how to act yet remain non-acting.

Maharishi Ramana's 'Updes Sạra' a small book setting out in a nutshell the profound philosophy of self-enquiry of this great saint, says, in the opening verse itself, that God is the dispenser of the fruits of action — *Karma-phala-dhata.* "The effect of karma is two-fold: one the immediate seen effect in the physical sense, the other is the effect left by the action on the mind of the person, a subtle latency called 'sanskara' which will come to fruition at a later date as a '*prarabdha karma*'. Therefore, what then is the technique to get over the trick played by the double-edged weapon of karma? If 'Karma' is performed without an eye on personal benefits, but entirely as an offering to God, as a service to the people concerned, not only the old '*sanskaras*' or the latencies find a way out, but also no further latencies or '*sanskaras*' are impressed on the mind. Thus the mind gets cleaned which in turn prepares the ground for *moksha*, or liberation."

We may next consider two more aspects of action: Renunciation and 'holy indifference'.

Renunciation in action:

'True renunciation', according to the words of Krishna in the Bhagavad Gita, 'is a matter of letting go of all actions which are prompted by personal desires and whims. To rise above self-serving actions and, instead, perform God-directed actions is the way of soul freedom in this world. It is possible for us to live out of divine consciousness even while we fulfil our daily duties and harmonize with the guidelines which are designed for fair relationships among people in society' (Roy Eugene Davis).

Action rightly renounced brings freedom;
Action rightly performed brings freedom;
Both are better
Than mere shunning of action.

....

The wise see knowledge and action as one;
They see truly,
Take either path and tread it to the end;
The end is the same,
There the followers of action
Meet the seekers after knowledge
In equal freedom.

(Gita — Translation by Christopher Isherwood)

Below are also Mr. Isherwood's highly pertinent remarks:

"In general, mankind always acts with attachment; that is to say with fear and desire. Desire for a certain result and the fear that this result will not be obtained. But there is another way of performing action; and this is without fear and without desire. The Christians call it 'holy indifference', and the Hindus 'non-attachment'. Both names are slightly misleading. They suggest coldness, lack of enthusiasm. That is why people confuse non-attachment with fatalism; when actually they are opposites. The fatalist simply does not care. He will get what is coming to him. Why make an effort?...The doer of non-attached action, on the other hand, is the most conscientious of men. He does not run away from life; he accepts it, much more completely than those whose pleasures are tinged with anxiety and whose defeats are embittered by regret. No matter whether he is sweeping a room or calculating the position of a star, or taking the chair of a meeting, he does it to the utmost limit of his powers — so carefully, so devotedly, so wholeheartedly, that the dividing line between the chosen activity and the necessary chore disappears. All work becomes equally and vitally important. It is only towards the results of the works that he remains indifferent."

Aldous Huxley in his foreword to the Gita (by Christopher Isherwood) says that St. Francois de Sales (of France) was never tired of insisting on 'holy indifference'. "He who refers every action to God", writes Camus, summarising his master's teachings, "and has no aim save His Glory, will find rest everywhere, even amidst the most violent commotions." So long as we practise this 'holy indifference' to the fruits of action, "no lawful action will separate us from God, on the contrary, it can be made a means of closer union". Here the word 'lawful' supplies a necessary qualification to a teaching which, without it, is incomplete and even potentially dangerous. Some actions are intrinsically evil or inexpedient; and no good intentions, no conscious offering of them to God, no renunciation of the fruit can alter their essential character.

Inertia is not freedom. Again, the binding quality of an action does not lie in its mere performance, but in the motive or desire that prompts it.

Renunciation refers not to the act itself but to the frame of mind behind the act. Renunciation means absence of desire. If we have to give up anything or any action let us give up what God does not like.

As Ramana Maharishi advises even the *jnani* (a real soul) need not withdraw from action but may work in the world though with complete detachment. For him *karma* (action) has become *akarma* (inaction) because he has no sense of doership. *Akarma,* he further describes as unnecessary activity.

Mahatma Mangat Ram, too, as we have seen, tells us merely to give up 'doership' which is responsible for bondage. The aim is not to discourage right action but to weaken the sense of individual doership and the selfish desire which drive one to unenlightened action. He adds:

'Doership is the primordial darkness the origin of all pollutions...

'In its ego of 'doership' the intellect undertakes various types of activities, through organs (of senses and action) promoted by three types of desires — sublime, moderate and stupid — and remains totally absorbed in the game of desire-satisfaction. Simultaneously binding itself with the duality in the fruit of action, it remains miserable in the fire of likes and dislikes. Not for a moment thus can it attain real peace. To understand this tragedy of life is true wisdom.'

(Samata Vilas)

'Wise people know that true renunciation is a matter of giving up all actions which are prompted by (personal) desire; relinquishment of the results of all works (including personal) is the highway of freedom.'

(Bhagavad Gita)

Creativity:

Creative work has its own significance. The *Ananda* (true happiness) of creativity is not the pleasure of the ego in having personally done well and being somebody. Says Aurobindo:

'That is something extraneous which attaches itself to the joy of work and creation. The Ananda comes from the insurge of a greater Power, the thrill being possessed and used by it...the exaltation of the uplifting of the consciousness, the illumination and its greatened and heightened action and also the joy of beauty, joy of power of perfection that is being created.'

Calm, positive mental activity is revivifying. Yet many people wrongly associate creative activity with strain and go about it with a tense, nervous attitude.

There is another dimension of creative work — the art

of uniting what one loves with what one works at. They say that when you are creatively involved in your life, you have no time even for illness or tiredness.

Great artists, painters, musicians, scientists, craftspersons and distinguished people in many other creative avocations have proved, by their dedication and intense interest in what they did, that they expressed, through their work, the divinity in them.

Living and acting now:

"Today is the day to attempt. Today is the day we can achieve. Today is that golden day, given unto one and all — to Give...to Share...to Serve."

Another healthy attitude towards work is the art of living now. Now is the only time we really have. We must give up continuous regret, remorse, self persecution for the past. No doubt one has to learn from past mistakes, decide firmly to avoid repeating them and get on with living now, packing our bags of past mistakes and miserable memories. We must carry with us and cherish all the wisdom, truth and beauty, all the sources of inspiration that our own life history has bequeathed us.

'Seize the day, trust the tomorrow as little as possible.' Futurising can become the most destructive of habits. Even planning, which is necessary for meaningful future actions, can become present moment pleasure.

> 'The present alone is the time when we can work and achieve, grind and gather, give and serve. In the "past" we can now do nothing; in the "future" again, we can now accomplish nothing. In the "dead" moments of the past, and in the "unborn" moments of the future, we can never act. These living "present" moments are the only fields to be hammered at and wherein are all the glories of life, all the gains in existence.'
>
> (Swami Chinmayananda)

Marketing and Management:

Some readers may wonder what has this subject to do with 'Attitude to Work', the heading of this chapter. Apart from the fact that the subject is of special interest to me I imagine each one of us has to be a marketing person especially, salesman, in one way or the other, in any work or avocation. I have always believed, also tried practically, the efficacy of spirituality in marketing (against so much of marketing in 'spiritualism', for which the West provides a particularly 'flourishing market'). Recently I read a very interesting book by D.G. Mandino: 'The Greatest Salesman in the World'. It says:

> 'Everyone of us is a salesman no matter what his or her occupation or profession. Most of all, first he must sell himself to himself in order to find personal happiness and peace of mind.'

Regarding failure, Mr. Mandino says: 'He who has never failed is he who has never tried.' Further, 'Failure will never overtake you if your determination to succeed is strong enough.' He and many prominent authors have, inter alia, referred to self-awareness, the faith in God and the power of prayer in successful salesmanship, marketing and management.

Success as a word and as a concept has different meanings for different people in different contexts. Success, as a variable, by nature is elusive. It is certainly contingent on contextual, situational, organisational, societal and cultural factors.

I would like to talk of managerial success. Among the various factors, the competence of managers appears to be the primary factor that determines managerial success. Researches in the field of human resource management are striving towards identification of these competences that contribute to managerial success:

verbal communication (with humour as an aid),
managing time and stress,
decision making,
creative problem solving,
motivating people,
delegating,
articulating a vision,
self-awareness,
team building, and
conflict management.

These ten are considered the most vital management competences in several mid-level and upper-middle level managers (Whetten & Cameron 1991).

In Chapter 10, we shall briefly revert to the role of spirituality in modern management. The happy combination of the two should and does work very well. My modest experience confirms it.

A few years ago I met late Swami Chinmayananda (whom I have quoted at a number of places in this book) in the train, while travelling from Delhi to Pathankot. We were in the same compartment. I was rather surprised to see that the Swami was reading a book on Management (an American publication). Being curious I asked the Swami how come he was reading a book on Management while one expected a person like him reading or discussing about spirituality alone. He replied by saying that each one of us had to know the art of management while planning, directing or executing any activities even in the spiritual field. One has to know the principles of good management including management of time, for success in any line. Incidentally while we met in the train, the Swami was going to Dharamsala, a hill station, where his Mission has set up a beautiful Ashram (a retreat) Sidhbari, in picturesque surroundings.

During discussion the Swami was happy to know that

marketing and management were the subjects of my interest and that I could very well go on with that interest with my interest in spirituality. He was pleased to observe that a really spiritual person can spiritualize life and all its good activities.

May I again draw on a great Upanishadic wisdom? The Isavasya Upanishad says: 'You may live longest life doing work in a detached spirit and dedicating everything to God. Thus alone can we escape the contamination of work and sterilize life.'

A question of ethics:

I would like to mention another aspect of work, the growing modern business. Business ethics are constantly being called into question. There is growing number of ardent believers in their importance. The Bishop of Oxford, the Right Reverend Richard Harries, is one of them. In his book 'Is There a Gospel for the Rich (Mowbray) he says:

> 'For too long there has been a tendency to assume morality only applies to private domestic life, not business. People have been rather schizophrenic about their attitude towards morality, believing it applies solely to their personal lives and does not affect them at their work. But those with strong moral sense surely will want to apply it in both private and business lives. If they don't, it is total contradiction of what it is to be a human being.
>
> Religions generally have been at fault for not underlining the importance of business, industry and commerce. We all depend upon business in one way or the other and we have to increase society's resources before society can share in those same resources. The process is integrally linked but care must be taken that wealth is not created at any price.'

The intangible wealth:

In modern economics and business education, under 'Marketing and Management', the terms such as 'productive resources' and 'wealth creation' have, of course, been used in the material sense. There is another wealth — priceless and limitless: the awareness of divinity within us — cognition of which also requires deep search and intensive effort. There is no comparison between the two types of wealth! (However, their correlation, matter and spirit, can work wonders in the world of action.)

Problem solving:

Every problem can be taken as a challenge. It may be reiterated here that the real men of achievement are those who have the heroism to feel more enthusiasm in their work when they face more and more difficulties. As Swami Chinmayananda puts it: 'You are successful and creative, when you see an opportunity in every difficulty.' We go further with him in the following para:

'When we have a problem to solve or a challenge to overcome it often becomes the centre of our attention. We can become very absorbed in the problem as we think or worry about how we are going to find a solution. We may even become tired or grouchy when we are trying hard to work things out. There is a better way than "wrestling" with our problems, a way shall we call it a spiritual way, that not only provides us with creative solutions to our problems but allows us to relax while finding these solutions. This way is the way of spiritual awareness, realizing that with God there is a solution to every problem, and that as spiritual beings who are of God we can find these solutions in God. How do we do that? The first step is: we take our attention off the problem and put our attention on God. To help us do this we can remember that God is present everywhere — there isn't anywhere we could go and be apart from God. When we are bright, awake, happy and fulfilled — God is there. When we are unaware, unhappy and faced with problems, God is there, too. So a problem can even be an opportunity for us to remember that God is near, God is in charge, and that with God we will find a way. When we turn our attention to God and trust that a solution will come, the mind which has been thinking so hard and trying to find the solution is able to rest and become quiet. When the mind is quiet, we are able to hear the inner voice of intuition, the voice of God within us. We find the right answer to any problem.'

There also is a nice little story:

One night a man had a dream. He dreamed he was walking along the beach with the Lord. Across the sky flashed scenes from his life. For each scene, he noticed two sets of footprints in the sand: one belonging to him, and the other to the Lord.

When the last scene of his life flashed before him, he looked back at the footprints in the sand. He noticed that many times along the path of his life there was only one set of footprints. He also noticed that it happened at the very lowest and saddest times in his life.

This really bothered him and he questioned the Lord about it. "Lord, you said that once I decided to follow you, you'd walk with me all the way. But I have noticed that during the most troublesome times of my life, there is only one set of footprints. I don't understand why, when I needed you most, you would leave me."

The Lord replied, "My precious, precious child, I love you and I would never leave you. During your times of trial and suffering, when you saw only one set of footprints, it was then that I carried you."

(Margaret Fishback Powers)

Attitude to Suffering:

Who does not have to pass through a difficult time now

and then? We must remember that suffering is simply a natural consequence of past errors, not a punishment, just as a burn is the natural consequence of playing with fire.

Indeed adversity and suffering may sometimes turn out to be the greatest help and purifier of the soul; surprisingly they turn out to be opportunities in disguise. Dadu, a famous sixteenth century saint, has recalled a homely example of the goldsmith beating the gold to purify it:

> 'What grudge does the goldsmith bear the gold
> when he beats it with his hammer?
> He frees it from all blemishes,
> that it may be worn about the neck.'

Our attitude to suffering should be positive, to take it in the stride of life. Troubles are often the tools by which God fashions us for better things. Remaining still with trust in God's will is the best thing to do. 'The prayer of the righteous man is powerful.'

> संकट हरण मंगल का दाता, प्रभ का नाम चितार।
> "मंगत" जतन यह सार है, नित ही नित जप सार।।

> Name of the Lord is the trouble-shooter.
> Remember and try this right remedy always, says Mangat.

Another saying of Gurudev:

> अधिक संकट जो आन व्यापे, निश्चल रहे सतनाम को जापे।।

> If even a great calamity overtakes us, we should remain still and remember God.

There are two kinds of stillness — the helpless stillness of inertia which heralds dissolution, and the stillness of assured sovereignty which commands the harmony of life.

Suffering entitles us more to the Grace of God. He will never let the righteous fall. He is our Father, He is our Friend and He is the Dispenser of our destiny — so whatever comes from Him is for our good. So I heard from Maharishi Rabindra Nath Tagore in 1937 when I was a student at Lahore (now in Pakistan). And, I continue to have fairly firm belief in this pearl of wisdom.

Now what about any blockage of or hindrance in our way. The obstacles which the physical presents to the spiritual is no argument for the rejection of the physical, for in the unseen providence of things our greatest difficulties can turn out to be our greatest opportunities. I have seen this happen in practical life if one is not egoistic. 'There is also a special thrill in riding over a storm. Anyone can hold the helm when the sea is calm', as Publius Syrus has so graphically said.

There is an Urdu couplet which fits in very well here:

تندیِ بادِ مخالف سے نہ گھبرا اے عقاب
یہ تو آتی ہے تجھے اونچا اڑانے کے لیے

Tundiye bad-i-mukhalif se na ghabra ay uqab,
Yeh to ati hai tujhe ooncha udane ke liye.

Do not worry about or fear facing the opposing wind,
O' Uqab (a high flying bird)
It comes only to make you fly higher.
(Like a kite flying higher with strong opposite wind.)

In facing troubles we must keep up hope and not allow ourselves to despair. Here is a Sufi saying:

> 'In the hour of adversity do not be without hope. For crystal rain falls from black clouds.'
>
> (Nizami Ganjawi, 12th century
> Persian poet of Azerbaijan)

Depression:

All depression is bad, it lowers the consciousness, wastes the energy and opens to adverse forces. To yield to depression when things go wrong is the worst way of meeting the difficulty.

The cause of depression is generally some desire or demand within us, conscious or subconscious, which could not be satisfied. 'The best way is to be conscious of it, face it calmly and steadily throw it out' as Aurobindo suggests. He also has a witty remark: 'the vital (in us) can never remain constantly in joy and peace, for it needs their opposites in order to have a sense of the drama of life. If it were not for the rocks in its bed, the stream would have no song.'

'It is the opposite which is good for us', said Heraclitus, a Greek philosopher about 500 B.C. His argument was that it is not good for people to get all they wish to get. 'It is sickness that makes health pleasant; evil, good; hunger, satiety; weariness, rest.'

Now what is the remedy to eradicate depression when it does come in. Let us watch or witness it from a distance, from the stand of our real self: *Sat, Chit, Anand.* It would vanish. This is the unfailing spiritual remedy.

Here is a small story:

Who has not heard of Martin Luther, the German priest who initiated the Reformation and started Protestantism as opposed to the Roman Catholic Church. Once he got into a mood of great depression. For days he would not smile and would hardly talk. One day his wife fed up with his "blues", dressed herself in total black as if for mourning and appeared before him. Luther was surprised and asked why she had worn such clothes. She exclaimed: "God is dead!" Luther angrily retorted: "God can never die!" Then his wife quietly said: "If that is so, what is there in the world to depress anyone?" Luther immediately came to his senses and from that day never wore a gloomy look.

In a sense, depression is the sign of acute egoism. It is not the soul but the ego and its pride that feels defeat, dejection or humiliation. Self-pity, self-complacency or vanity, all these are signs of ego.

Fear and Worry:

Perhaps the greatest obstacle in the way of man's progress is fear, a fear that is illogical, unreasoning and often unreasonable.

Fear destroys and perverts all seeing. It is destructive energy. It breeds illusion. It dulls the mind. It destroys dignity. We should not allow fear to paralyse our will and nerves.

Mahatma Mangat Ram tells us of the fearless state in the following words:

> 'Fearless, indeed, are men of faith, and such men are not afraid of death. The fearless state is attained when the intellect, by abandoning the swing of doubt or uncertainty, attains firmness, and orients itself towards God. Otherwise fear, in one form or the other, crops up. By abiding in the continuous recognition of God as the only cause and creative principle, we no longer have any fear; the truth becomes our fortress. How can lack or limitation (causing fear) affect us if we have inner, actual acknowledgement of this fact?'

He need have no fears who has found refuge or asylum in the Supreme Being. He needs no fear who wishes others well and is occupied in Godly service. 'Fear enters when God is shut out of life', says Paramahansa Yogananda.

Prophet Muhammad says:

> 'Beware, verily the friends of God will have no fear, nor they grieve.'

David's Psalms in the Bible have the following soul-lifting message:

> 'The Lord is my light and my salvation
> whom shall I fear?
> The Lord is the stronghold of my life
> of whom shall I be afraid?'

The teachings of all Faiths lead us to fearlessness and strength. The delight of awareness of the ultimate Existence and the value of cheerfulness in one's daily responsibilities are important in Upanishadic teachings.

Fear and anxiety are perverse forms of will. With faith in God — and in ourselves — there is no fear. Living the way we generally do, fear is our shadow. It creates imaginary terrors. Even if there is real danger, fear does not help; it clouds intelligence, takes away presence of mind and prevents one from seeing the right thing to do.

One fears what one does not know. When fear comes if one succeeds in putting upon it consciousness, knowledge, force, light, one can cure it altogether. One must keep a perfect equanimity in the presence of all beings, all things and happenings.

Closely related to fear is worry and depression. Every one is beset with anxiety — or shall we say worry — of one kind or another. The student is anxious how he fares in the examination; parents are worried (at least in India) over the choice of a match for their grown-up daughter. A money-lender is uneasy thinking whether he will be able to recover the money or not. The poor man is deeply concerned about his livelihood while he who earns is concerned about how he should invest his wealth so that his corrupt and concealed earnings do not get revealed and confiscated. Politicians are anxiously finding ways and means of seizing power, whereas those in power worry about not losing their grip on the seats of power. In short anxiety and worry, in one form or the other, is present everywhere. So the question is: how can one be released of the fetters of worry?

If we think deeply, we will find that frustration, despair or some doubts are lurking in man's mind about his future. These are the root cause of his worry or anxiety. But a clear analysis would show that anxiety, worry or doubt do not help. On the contrary they are harmful. Thinking of evil or failure, or being afraid of them, brings them on one's head. To be worried or feeling helpless is denial of one's self-confidence. One may think, have dreams of future, but one should not be visualising horror or harm. One must think but not as a pessimist does. Here is a nice little poem which is greatly helpful for the fearing, worrying type:

HAVE FAITH

The worry does no good at all;
But does a lot of harm
It puts across lines on your face;
and dissipates your charm;
Whatever is to be, will be;
That worry cannot change;
It only serves to dim your joy;
And all your friends estrange;
This lack of confidence in Self;
That causes worry's fright;
A lack of faith in God's Design;
Your happiness will blight;
Then cast aside the gloomy thoughts;
And bid your dark fears flee;
Live in the light of faith and love;
Joyful and worry free.

(Author Unknown)

Kabir says:

चिन्ता चिता समान।

Worry is like burning fire.

कबीरा चिन्ता क्यों करे, तुम चिन्ते क्या होए।
मोरी चिन्ता हरि करे मोहे चिन्ता रहे न कोए।।

Why do you worry O' Kabir? Your worry would not help!
God is taking care of you; you need not worry at all!

Gurudev says:

कारण करता जान के, मन की चिन्ता त्याग।
"मंगत" देह पिण्ड जिस दिया, रहो चरण तिस लाग।।

Trust the Lord as the Causative force and abandon your worry. Hold fast to the sacred feet of One who has bestowed you with body and life.

Fear, worry and anxiety of any kind would vanish if we have a calm certitude and a complete trust in the power of the Grace to shelter us from everything. Cessation of fear comes with the contact of God. With the help of meditation we are able to rise above all fears and worries, able to shed them all.

Death and its dignity:

Death is the greatest fear — most subtle and the most tenacious. (Please see Annexure V for author's experience.)

How can one overcome this fear? Here are some formulae worth trying:

1) The knowledge that life is one and immortal. Only forms are countless, fleeting and mortal. Life does not die.
2) It is absurd to fear something one cannot avoid.
3) Give up, by and by, attachment of people, places and things; knowing we have to leave them all one day.
4) Learn to die while living. This is difficult but most desirable. Desirelessness drives the fear of death; then one lives with it all the time. We can begin by learning to die to small things first.

"Death can take away everything that is outside us, and if we have grown our inner being, if we have found peace, blissfulness, silence — which are not dependent on anything outside — the question of fearing death does not arise at all" (Rajneesh).

Saints maintain that the final goal is reached by dying while still alive. The human birth of one who has attained this state is fruitful.

> 'O Nanak, one who has died to live,
> His coming here is fruitful.'

And Paltu says:

> All die without exception
> dies the whole world,
> But few there be who know how to die.
> One who dies while living, O Paltu,
> Crosses the ocean of the world with ease.

Bulleh Shah states that "if thou diest before thy death, such a death will bear fruit." But Kabir says it is a rare one who obtains the fruit, by dying while living:

> Tall is that tree,
> Its fruit is in the skies within;
> Rare is the bird
> Who tastes it. He alone.
> Will eat that fruit, O Kabir,
> Who dies while living.

In the Quran it is written, "Die thou before thy death." Maulana Rumi says, "So long as man does not come out of his body, he will remain ignorant of the inner vision."

Some saints have likened daily meditation to a brief death, in the sense that one dies temporarily to the world, while totally attending on the Supreme Being within. It is perhaps in this sense that St. Paul said: 'I die daily.' Maharaj Charan Singh has developed this idea deeply and widely in his book: 'Die to Live'. The Mystics refer to the process of vacating the body and withdrawing the consciousness to the third eye — the central place between the two eyes, in the forehead — as 'dying while living'.

Mahatma Mangat Ram says:

मारग तत्त ज्ञान का, मर जीवत हो पाई।
"मंगत" दुबधा त्याग के, सतरूप समाई।।

To die while living leads the way to the essence of knowledge,
"Mangat" thus did away with doubt and realized his true-self.

Death is not separate from life. When death is accepted we become balanced, as we accept the day and the night, the summer and the winter—both the light and darkness. There is time when the fall comes and the leaves have to leave the tree.

Here is a beautiful quotation about birth and death and immortality of soul:

'Birth is not a beginning.
Death is not an end.
There is existence without limitation;
There is continuity without a starting point.
Existence without limitation is Space.
Continuity without a starting point is Time.
There is birth, there is Death.
There is issuing forth, there is entering in.
That through which one passes
in and out, without seeing its form
that is 'Portal of God'.'

Life has its blessings, death has its blessings. All that God gives us has to be taken in deep gratitude, even death.

There is a way of even becoming immortal after death as Kena Upanishad says:

'Since He is the Ear of the ear, the Mind of the mind, the Word of the word, the Breath of the breath, the Eye of the eye, therefore, the wise having given up (self identification with these) depart from the world to become immortal.'

The dilemma of death has been an astonishing well-spring of speculation, inspiration and creativity through the ages — one of the central issues addressed by virtually every religion and belief system. Schopenhauer called death 'the truly inspiring genius of philosophy!' Thomas Mann wrote: 'Without death there would scarcely have been poets on the earth!' Michelangelo said: 'No thought exists in me which death has not carved with his chisel.'

'It is the denial of death that is partially responsible for people living empty, purposeless lives', writes psychiatrist and author Elisabeth Kubler Ross.

A great Indian saint saw death as a source of self-realization. Here is his story:

Maharishi Ramana, Venkataramana, as was his name in childhood, was born on 30th December, 1879, at Tiruchuli, a village 30 miles south of Madurai, Tamilnadu (India). As is the case with such spiritual giants he took little or no interest in his studies. His only joy was reading the biography of 63 saints called Periyapurana. In the middle of 1896, he prepared himself to experience death. Lying alone he felt that he was unlinked from the physical body, he was different from the body. This, of course, was the flash point in his life, which was also the rediscovery of himself. This theme of self-discovery, he developed into a precise science. 'Who am I' is the most important question, he says. 'For the ignorant the 'I' is limited to the body, whereas for the *jnani* (knower) the 'I' shines as boundless awareness.'

Let us also remember that while our body is mortal, our soul is immortal. Krishna says in Gita: 'The soul is never born nor dies...It is unborn, eternal, everlasting, ancient.'

'It is not the end of the physical body in any case that should worry us. Rather our concern must be to live while we are alive.'

Kabir says so sweetly about life and death: 'When you came into this world you cried, but everyone else rejoiced.

During your life-time, work and serve in such a way that when it is time to leave the world, you will smile at parting while the world cries for you.' If we hold this thought, we will always remember to consider others before ourself and serve the world selflessly, while we live.

Kabir again says: 'The world is afraid of death, but I am happy about it. I am waiting for my death to merge into bliss supreme.'

Socrates believed that 'the best preparation for death is in the best possible discharge of the duties of life.'

David Cohen talks of another dimension of death:

> 'It is through acceptance of the finiteness of our individual existence that we are enabled...to devote each day of our lives — however long they may be — to growing as fully as we are able.'

जीवन में कुछ कर लयो, होएं मुसाफर अन्त।
दुर्लभ सेवा जगत की, और याद भगवन्त।।

Do something in your lifetime, you know it will end one day. Two great things to do are: service of the world and God-remembrance.

(Mangat)

Gurudev further observes: 'Childhood is eaten up by youth, old age eats up the youthfulness, ultimately death devours the years. This is the tragedy of an embodied soul.' He adds: 'When man sees himself as Eternity and his body as Death, seeing the immortal in the mortal body, he sings, with supreme love, the glory of the Lord, his Self, and himself lives in self-forgetful humility.'

Gurudev also advises:

जीवन में हरी रूप ध्यायो। अन्त काल हरी रूप समायो।।

One who meditates on Almighty sustainer of all, during life-time, merges into That ultimately.

He also advises: 'It is essential that before passing away from the world, all mental conflict and defects be overcome so that the highest and fearless state of Being is realized.'

Further,

भूल कर न कीजिए, कूड़ी देह का मान।
"मंगत" एक ही पलक में, उड़ जाए धूल समान।।

Be not ever proud of your untenable body, even unwittingly,
It can puff off any moment like dust!

मुर्शद कामिल जगत में, एको मौत पहचान।
जिस मरना मन मानिया, करे न दूजे हान।।

Treat 'death' as the perfect teacher, in the world
One who accepts 'death' as inevitable shall harm none.

It is a known fact that man comes to the world empty handed, empty handed he departs; whatever his possessions, nothing will go with him. But we forget this fact.

Gurudev also says:

सम्पत बहु संचत करी, पर चली राई नहीं साथ।
"मंगत" भरम गुबार में, ले चलया खाली हाथ।।

One may collect lots of wealth but nothing will go with him, not even a mustard seed (the tiniest thing), when he leaves the world.
He departs empty handed, but loaded with lot of confusion and affliction.

Fate vs. Effort:

While talking of work and action in the physical sense and heightening its significance from the spiritual angle, one comes across the constant controversy between issues of fate and effort, destiny and freedom of action. Some would say:

'We make our destiny.' Many others would hold fate as the main force.

Let us clear our ideas on this perennially controversial but fairly pertinent issue.

Much depends on our attitude. We have the capacity to think whatever way we choose, it can be self-defeating attitude or self-fulfilling attitude.

God as we believe is not a sole willed, arbitrary dictator. In His Kingdom there is free will exercised for the solutions of various problems facing humanity.

Swami Ishwarananda, an eminent contemporary saint, whom I had the privilege of meeting, personally, says: 'Man alone has been invested with the freedom of choice. Both angels and animals have been deprived of this gift.'

Vedanta does not suggest developing a thick-skin, an insensitivity to whatever happens. Referring to those whose reaction to things usually is:

> "It is all *prarabdha* (fate)" or "Nobody can overcome *maya* (worldly illusion)" or much worse, "Everything is His *lila* (play). What can we do?"

Swami Ishwarananda Giri remarks:

> 'This is perverted form of misquoting Vedanta. It throws a bucketful of cold water on the spirit of true living...True living demands an exercise of one's power, an eagerness to progress and achieve, a capacity to respond to each thrill of life and rise upon the increased understanding of life's deeper and deeper levels. The root of all this, of course, is the fundamental faith that one can do it.'

'Whatsoever a man soweth, that shall he also reap' is a well-known Biblical saying. Mahatma Mangat Ram says the same thing in very simple words: '*Jo bije so katna*' (as you sow, so shall you reap). Kabir says it with a simile:

If you plant a cactus
How will you reap mangoes?

Gurudev's brief view on destiny is:

'Noble shall be the destiny of the one who channelises properly his dispositions through self-exertion, meditation, proper reflection and conduct, who patterns his life-style in accordance with the lives of great men. It is also necessary to see every event and deed in the light of Divine Will. Believe in God while doing good, and avoid that which is evil.'

Regarding destiny, Swami Vivekananda has highly invigorating views:

"We reap what we sow. We are the makers of our own fate. None else has the blame, none else has the praise. The wind is blowing. Those vessels whose sails are unfurled, catch it, and go forward on their way. But those that have their sails furled do not catch the wind, is that the fault of the wind? Is it the fault of the merciful Father, whose wind of mercy is blowing without ceasing, day and night, whose mercy knows no decay? Is it His fault that some of us are happy and some unhappy? We make our own destiny. His wind blows for saint and sinner alike. He is the Lord of all, the Father of all."

'Destiny is not a matter of chance, it is a matter of choice. It is not something to wait for, rather something to work for.'

'Each man is his own absolute law-giver, the dispenser of glory or gloom to himself; the decreer of his life, his reward, his punishment.'

('Light on the Path')

There are yet other views:

Destiny — yes it is there. But God's grace can do or undo anything. Grace is abundantly bestowed on a few who have wholly surrendered themselves to and merged themselves in God.

Love of God and total surrender to Him ensures removal of obstacles by Him.

وہی ہوتا ہے جو منظور خدا ہوتا ہے
بات بگڑی ہی بن جاتی ہے جب فضل خدا ہوتا ہے

Hota hai wuhi jo manzure khuda hota hai
Bat bigdi ban jati hai jab fazale-khuda hota hai

It is God's will that prevails
Even a spoilt situation gets straight with His grace.

Sai Baba says: 'If you win the Grace of the Lord, even the destiny can be overcome.' He adds: 'Act, act with all your might and with all your mind, make full use of the skill, capacity, courage and confidence that you are endowed with. Then God will bless you.'

'Placing your burden on destiny and keeping quiet means diminution of effort...without effort and prayer destiny and grace are not gained.'

Destiny and determination to work supplement each other. The liberal take to the dynamic life of purposeful activity whereas the weak and the timid ones depend on fate.

Henry David Thoreau has spoken highly of the man's will and man's determined effort in the following words:

'If one advances confidently in the direction of one's own dreams and endeavours to lead the life which he has imagined, he will meet with success unexpected in common hours.'

बगैर सत यत्न के कुछ प्राप्त नहीं हो सकता।

'One cannot achieve anything without right effort.'
(Mangat)

'Since one's own past effort it is that has ripened into fate, one can with greater present effort change one's fate.'
(Ramana Maharishi)

Destiny is what we meet with in life; the attitude we meet it with and the action we take is our free will.

Personally I like to think that destiny is nothing but carry-forward resultant of our previous actions. Life is like a bank account in which our good and bad actions act as deposits and drawals or credits and debits — the balance at any time being the destiny. By current good actions — in which we are comparatively free—we can change our destiny.

According to a long prevalent and rather rigid view: 'In the plane of matter and on the level of ordinary consciousness, you are bound hand and foot. A slave to the mechanism of Nature, you are tied to the chain of Karma (action and reaction).'

'But it need not be so', says Aurobindo. He adds, 'You can shift your place if you will...Once you draw yourself up out of the whirlpool and stand high enough, you see you are free...You are not then bound by the consequences of your actions...You belong no longer to what is moved but that which moves.' True freedom comes when one knows one's own self and is not influenced by self-created fear and misery.

In the above state we activize the presence of God in us. In that state no sin or virtue touches us.

Man, indeed, is the architect of his life. It is given to him to make or mar himself. The ebb and flow of human fortunes are something attributed to past *karma.* Yet destiny can be overcome by man's reason and will. 'This is possible only for those who gaining control over the disintegrating forces inside their self and outside in the world negate their influences, affirm the forces of integration in their thought and will, establish themselves in a state of equipoise and are set on the path of realizing the Divine.'

Here is an Urdu couplet on fate:

شکایت کی جو قسمت کی تو دل کہنے لگا چپ رہ
مقدر آپ اپنا ہم مٹاتے ہیں بناتے ہیں

Shikayat ki jo kismat ki to dil kehne laga chup reh,
Muqaddar ap apna hum metate hain banate hain

When I complained about my fate, the heart advised 'Be silent! We ourselves make and unmake our destiny!'

There is an interesting statement by Aristotle on fortune/effort. "It is better to be happy as a result of one's own exertions than by the gift of the fortune."

There is another angle of bad luck. In adversity nobility shines through, when a man endures repeated and severe misfortune with patience, not owing to insensibility but from generosity and greatness of soul. A truly good and wise man will bear all kinds of misfortune in a seemly way, and will always act in the best manner that the circumstances allow, even as a good General makes the most effective use of the forces at his disposal, and a good shoemaker the finest shoe possible out of the leather supplied to him, and so on with all the crafts and professions.

I would rather close this quite controversial subject by saying that fate and free will are only two facets of one indivisible energy. The best attitude — along with our doing the very best under any given circumstances — is to have faith in God and take everything coming from him, as Mahatma Mangat Ram observes:

प्रभ की आज्ञा मन माहीं विचार।
जो वरतावे सो सुख कर धार।।

O' mind! Remember ever God's will;
And, treat all that comes from Him — as for your good only.

Christ, too, said:

"And we know that all that happens to us is working for our good, if we love God and are fitting into His plans."

CHAPTER 6

Relation of Man with God

'The Supreme is that from which all beings are born, that by which they live and that into which when departing, they enter.'

(Taittiriya Upanishad)

'That which is the creator of all and in which everything dissolves. He is the remover of all troubles, all pervasive, without beginning and end, permeating all living beings as 'sameness'. He knows what goes on within each one. Knowing Him means knowing all, and experiencing Whom the intellect becomes He. That is what is known as God — a state of perfect contentment and perfect bliss.'

(Mahatma Mangat Ram)

Regarding the relationship of man and God, there are three different philosophies advocated by India's three great religious philosophers of their times. These are:

- Madhva: Man and God are permanently separate.
- Ramanuja: You are a part. He is whole. You are the drop. He is the ocean.
- Shankaracharya: You are God: 'Tat Twam Asi'.

The three are not mutually opposed, but are different points of view. God is seen through three different angles:

— Body consciousness
— Intellect consciousness
— Pure consciousness

Mahatma Mangat Ram was definite in his views about God's existence in man's body-temple. He also says how it could be discovered therein:

पांच तत्त देही का कोट। तिस में पेख अत निर्मल जोत।।
नाम जपत अगम कला प्रगासी। देह मन्दर में मिले अवनासी।।

See within this five-element body a supremely pure light. The repeated remembrance of the Lord is an incomprehensible but enlightening art that enables one to find the Immortal Supreme Being in the body-temple itself.

Oneness of man and God:

'The Divine dwells in the inmost being of Man. It is the inner light, the concealed witness. It is the life principle. God is one though He is called by different names. Various are the paths that lead to Him. God dwells in all body-temples as the Atman.'

It is said God without Man is as impossible as Man without God. They are incomplete without each other. Man is instrument of God. Somebody has wittingly remarked: 'God is man's treasury. Man is God's treasure.'

God without the creatures is no longer God because he is precisely the God of the creatures. That shows the intimate relationship between God and Man. It is an oft-repeated remark that God created man in his own image. Its meaning is that he endowed man with his divinity. Many cults gave God human form, while God is formless. As Voltaire says in his witticism: 'God created man and man returned the compliment by creating Him in his own image.' Someone else has stated: 'One reason why man created God was that his love sought a subject of perfect excellence in his imagination and gave Him objective existence.' 'As a matter of fact when one attains true knowledge, God ceases to exist separately.' Everything then becomes One, so says Gurudev, on the basis of his experience.

Before going further with exploring or defining the relationship between God and man, we would do well in clearing our concept of God in the light of what Mahatma Mangat Ram has observed:

साहब लावजूद है, लामजहब जलाल।
"मंगत" कहे सुन काज़िया साहब दा सही अहवाल।।

God is without body; He is Splendour, with no religion,
that is the truth about the Lord, listen O' pious person!
says 'Mangat'.

'God is that ultimate conscious state or reality by the power of which every phenomenal category of the phenomena exists. A spiritual state free of and from desires and actions, when the intellect attains the state of 'sameness'...

God is another name for that state of 'sameness' of your intellect in which you rise above dualities — distress and comfort, loss and gain, birth and death, honour and dishonour, acquisitiveness and renunciation — and thus move in the world in perfect equanimity, unaffected by pleasure and pain.'

Reproduced below are two questions asked by a devotee about God and Light, with answers of Gurudev:

Devotee: What is the meaning of the term *Ishvara*?

Gurudev: *Ishvara* (the Supreme Being) is a state of being, and the realization of this state results in the perfection of intelligence.

Devotee: What is the meaning of Light?

Gurudev: The term "light" connotes the state of Ishvara — perfection of intelligence — and

> the realization of this state means the removal of the veil of ignorance. It is the power of Light which removes the veil of ignorance. Negation of ignorance means the state of rest and peace. Light, indeed, may be said to be that divine energy which destroys ignorance.

Here are two rather delicate questions asked of Gurudev about Rama and Krishna considered by Hindus as incarnations of God:

> **Q:** Do you believe (in the divinity of) Rama?
>
> **Ans:** *This* believes in the Supreme Lord in whom Rama believed and about whom Krishna spoke in Gita.
>
> **Q:** Is it possible to attain the state of Krishna?
>
> **Ans:** Yes indeed! Krishna had reached the ultimate state whereby he was able to know his essential nature. You, too, shall be like unto Krishna when you will come to know your essential nature.

How bold and deep are these answers! Only one merged with totality—in complete state of realization—could speak in such unequivocal terms.

Mahatma Mangat Ram believed in the Life-force which permeates all beings from ant to elephant. That is his conception of God, and not the One seated in the Heaven above. He has described the state of 'samata', perfect equanimity, when the mind is completely silent, as the state of Godhood. And that is our true-self.

Here are a few lines giving briefly the thinking of some philosophers on the issue of God:

- For philosopher Kant, God is a moral certainty and not a product of reason.
- For Voltaire, the theist is a man firmly persuaded of the existence of a Supreme Being as good as He is powerful...he knows that God acts and that He is just.

- For Locke, the order and the wisdom observed in the universe provide sufficient evidence for the existence of a Creator.
- For Spinoza, the very existence of the Universe is proof of the existence of God.
- For Kierkegaard, God is the Universe.

Let us now turn to some more saints and seers what they have to say. Sant Tukaram, a great saint of Maharashtra (India), refers to relationship between the Creator and creatures in the following words:

'If water in hail is removed, where would hail be? Creator when separated from the Creation, where would the Creation be?'

Baba Farid, the renowned Muslim saint (quoted copiously in Guru Granth Sahib, the sacred book of Sikhs), speaks in the same strain:

'Farid, the Creator is manifest in His creation;
the Creation is in Him;
Cavil not at any one, He pervades all.'

Guru Nanak thus speaks of all-pervasiveness of God, in the heart of each one of us:

'In every heart thou are hidden
In every heart burns the light
God created the entire universe and
then hid Himself in every atom of it
Unknowable, without end
Unfathomable, beyond description.'

Kabir quotes God thus:

Where dost thou seek Me?
Lo, I am beside thee!
I am not in outer rites and ceremonies
I am by thee, with thee, within thee.

Shams Tabriz, a celebrated Sufi poet, has dramatically described oneness of man and God in the following words:

'O, pilgrims for the shrine', where go ye, where?
Come back! Come back! The Beloved is here!
Ye, who are seeking God! Yourself are He!
You need not search! He is verily ye!
Why will ye seek what was never lost?
There is Naught-Else than ye!
Be not in doubt lost!'

Ramana Maharishi rightly remarks that the fact of immanence of God — that God is everything and everything is God — is not to be merely intellectually comprehended but realized and experienced through continuous practice. He makes it abundantly clear that 'our *sahaja* or natural state is the fullness of consciousness which is bliss'.

Sheikh Sa'di, the celebrated Sufi poet of Persia (Iran), too, sees the divine reality permeating everything. He considers everything other than God non-existent. He does not see anything except God:

> 'Man reaches a state where he sees nothing other than God. Look how unlimited is the status of man! I am joyous in the world because the world takes joy in Him. I love all the world because the world comes from Him.'

Realization of God:

There exists no gap between God and the world. This is the truth about man and God too. The feeling that one is away from God is the cause of the struggle to unite oneself with Him. Such a feeling is based on ignorance, a wrong attitude. And, it is our own attitude which determines our distance from God. Even if we assume that God is away from us, we cannot deny: "We are from God and to Him shall we return."

Buddha says: 'You have not to seek Reality (God). You find *IT* in you.' And yet 'no material eyes can see Him though He sees all eyes' as the Quran says.

'He who knows his own self knows God' (Muhammed).

'God resides in the hearts of all; only the minds of some are not with Him. When one realizes the Almighty, compassion fills him internally and overflows outwards and he sees Him as the Omnipresent. The *bhakta* (devotee) who is blessed with the vision of God sees Him at all places, in all things and at all times and all in Him.' These are the words of Swami Panarimalai of South India (Reference his book 'The Holy Panchakshara).

He further says: "There is difference between the presence of God and consciousness of His being present in us. We are religious only when we are able to have that consciousness of God."

God is the best object of study. He who seeks God intellectually is certainly better than the one who is completely ignorant of His existence. Feeling of God is better than intellectual study and experiencing God is the highest goal of life. Still it is better to become God than to experience Him.

Swami Chinmayananda describes God-man relationship by giving a simple simile:

> 'What is the relation between the bedroom space and the atmospheric space? Just so is the relationship between the soul and God.'

Worship:

Many of us adopt various forms of worship to be close to God, treating Him as distant from us. We go to various places of worship. However, it is not where we worship that counts, but how we worship. Is our worship spiritual and real? 'He (the Lord) is always with us all and we can all be in constant contact with Him if we do the needful which is simply to love HIM', says The Mother. 'The god within needs no other God to be worshipped. All that is needed is the awakening, the awareness or the consciousness of the inner being.' The transmitting of emotional forces into spiritual energy is accomplished through the process of worship. The worship of the Supreme Being seems to have lost its place in modern life, though, as Swami Sivananda Radha says, 'still we worship football heroes, boxers, movie stars'.

The Mother adds: "Yet there is in every man and woman, coming to the foreground in precious moments, the value, the greatness and the rightness to worship that which is a great inspiration. Somewhere within everyone there is the knowing of a greater Power, and it is in this inner knowing that generates within us the urge to worship. When we recognize that we are a bridge between two worlds, the mental-physical material on the one hand and the spiritual on the other, and when we walk over this bridge, there is suddenly a profound humility as we realize the great and awesome power." She makes yet another pertinent point: 'Worship is not done for the benefit of God or Guru.' It is, indeed, for our own benefit. It helps to discover and confirm, time and again, the divinity in us — the search of God within. In passing we may touch the subject of idol worship. Gurudev says: 'Real idol worship is to serve living beings through body, mind and wealth. Not to hurt anyone by thought, word or deed. Feed the hungry, clothe the naked and help the needy and helpless, in any way you can.'

As regards worshipping idols or pictures of 'God-incarnates', prophets, saints and sages, he would advise worship of their 'ideals' — in the sense of appreciating and adopting them. Once a devotee asked him about the Reality — the nature of Supreme Being. His question and Gurudev's reply are:

Devotee: What, sir, do we mean when we say that Reality is both qualified and non-qualified?

Gurudev: Reality in itself is qualityless. When we impose attributes on Reality, it is called the process of superimposition, a process in which qualities of one object are superimposed upon another object which does not have those qualities. Imposing of qualities on qualityless Reality received its initial impetus from a kind of worship or devotion which desires that the object of worship should have a concrete form — and form implies qualities. When Reality is conceived of as non-qualified, it means the pitfalls of superimposition are avoided.

That explains how the idea of idol-worship was born. Difference between idol worship and worship of the Absolute has been explained as:

a) To serve humanity, knowing that God is present in all beings — as much as one can, keeping in view the needs of others — is real 'idol worship'. In this worship one believes in God as the doer, the omnipresent and the supreme inspiring force, whose glory is manifested in each particle, and one offers to Him one's invocation accordingly.
b) To believe in God as non-doer, uninvolved and unattached, and to contemplate of such attributes, in inner meditation — is the worship of the Absolute.

Gurudev ardently advocates worship of one God — the Supreme Being. Let us note some of his observations:

ईश्वर को छोड़ कर देवी देवताओं की पूजा करनी जहालत (मूर्खता) और नास्तकपन है।

To worship gods, goddesses (and stars), leaving aside the Supreme Being, is nothing but stupidity and atheism.

उसतत कीजे प्रभ एक की, जो जल थल पूर समाई।
"मंगत" दूजा भ्रम काल है, जो छिन छिन रूप वटाई।।

Sing the glory of one God alone who permeates everywhere on land and sea. All else is illusory and mortal that changes moment to moment, says 'Mangat'.

सरब परकाशी शकत जो, मन में सदा आराध।
"मंगत" दीनदयाल प्रभ, सब दूर करें अपराध।।

Worship within yourself the Power that illuminates all, God, the Merciful, will pardon all your guilt, says 'Mangat'.

अपने आप का कीजे जाप। जल थल देखे अपना प्रताप।।

Recollect repeatedly your own real Self
Observe your own glory (everywhere) on the land and water.

बिन सिमरन और नाम ध्यान। दूजा करम पाखंड पहचान।।

Without remembrance and contemplation of one Lord's name all other acts (of worship) are mere show.

मिथ्या भरमन त्याग के, सत्‌रूप जो ध्याए।
"मंगत" साचे हरजन सो, दुर्लभ जग में आए।।

One who meditates on (worships) his Real Self, not running after falsehood, such true persons are rarely born in this world, says 'Mangat'.

The following verse of Yunus Emre's — the best known Turkish popular mystic poet of thirteenth century, constitutes a pregnant expression of the God-man relationship in terms of the conception of a "unity of being" (*wahadat-al-wujud*):

'God permeates the whole wide world
Yet His truth is revealed to none
You better seek Him in yourself
You and He aren't apart, you are one.'

Self-analysis:

According to this conception of "unity of being", man is a microcosm in which are encompassed all the attributes of the macrocosm. Therefore, a human being cannot arrive at a knowledge, a comprehension of the Absolute without a knowledge of self. That is why also Yunus Emre considers self-knowledge to be the basis of all cognition, cardinal knowledge:

'Knowledge should mean a full grasp of knowledge:
Knowledge means to know yourself, heart and soul.
If you have failed to understand yourself,
Then all of your reading has missed its call.'

The conception of unity of being was amplified into a pantheistic model precisely by Jalau'ddin Rumi — famous thirteenth century philosopher and greatest mystical poet of Islam — who left a significant mark on the works of an entire generation of Sufis of Asia Minor. In a lyric, Rumi describes his search for God after having realized the nature of his own ego. He moves from creed to creed and dogma to dogma. Not finding Him in temples, institutions and symbols, he returns unto himself and discovers Him there in the sanctuary of his own heart.

'We are all divine, but we hardly know it. And in us, it is precisely that which does not know itself as divine, which we call ourselves.' Swami Ashokananda, in his book 'The Soul's Journey to its Destination', says: 'God made us in his own image. Why we now feel separate from God, separate from Creator and more and more identified with this physical form, and forgotten we are souls?'

Our miserable state — experiencing ourselves as limited, mortal, finite beings — is only apparent. In reality, we are still divine!

The aim of self-analysis is not merely self-knowledge but simultaneously also self-perfection, purification of one's "spiritual heart". Uniquely he who has succeeded in removing evil, hate, envy, pride from his heart is able to become conscious of his unity with God — figuratively speaking, to achieve a lovers' union, to find eternal life within himself.

Glimpse of God:

> As a fish cannot live out of water
>
> As the thirst of the chatrak (rain bird) can be quenched only by the rain drop;
>
> with a like intensity the saints yearn for the Lord
> Only the sight of Him can satiate their thirst for Him.
>
> (Kabir)

Each one of us must have experienced at some time or the other the feeling of something immense, incredibly immense inside oneself. That is a glimpse of God, if I may say so.

Sri Ramakrishna was asked if one can find God in a very short time. He replied:

> 'Verily, verily, I say unto you that he who wants Him finds Him. Go and verify it in your own life; try for three days and you are sure to succeed.'

A devotee asked the Master, "Sir, how can we attain God?" The Master took him to the sea and immersed him under water. After a short time he released him and asked him, "How did you feel?" The devotee replied, "I felt as though my last moment were come — the condition was desperate." Upon this the Guru said, "You shall see God when your yearning for Him will be as intense as your yearning for a breath of air just now."

"I must attain perfection in this life; yes, in three days I must find God; nay, with a single utterance of His name, I will draw Him to me!" — by such violent love the Lord is quickly attracted. The lukewarm lover takes ages to reach Him, if indeed he does so at all.

There is also a famous oft-repeated parable of Rama-krishna about how to have a vision of God:

> 'Through intense love one attains vision of God. The attraction of a husband for a chaste wife, the attraction of the child for the mother, the attraction of worldly possessions for a worldly man — when a man can blend these three into one and direct it all to God, then he gets the vision of God.'

Are we serious? It is said, God has been trying to get attention of each one of us, but some of these: problems, business, fun, friends, sports, hobbies — have prevented it. 'The Most Beneficent One never keeps the door shut. He is ever waiting, only it is we out of some strange illusion wander the outskirts, sometimes careless to enter, sometimes afraid to enter' (Sri Aurobindo).

There is another illusion or misconception we sometimes suffer from: When we think, say or do anything not good or decent, hiding it from others, we assume 'nobody is seeing us'. We forget God in us is all the time as constant witness. If we remember this relationship we would be saved from many wrongs. He knows every aspect of ours — good or bad. As the Quran says: 'Whether you hide what is in your heart or reveal, it is known to Allah.'

Intellectually, we say He is everywhere, but only a few really feel convinced. We say God is watching us and He's always with us. Why are we imperfect then? Aren't we frightened of Him, awed by Him, that He's watching us? We do bad things only when we think that nobody's watching us, and that we don't have to account to anyone.

Merging with Self:

Sheikh Nooruddin of Kashmir known as Nund Rishi, a Muslim saint who was highly inspired by Lalla, a great Hindu lady ascetic, says: 'The greatest curtain between man and God is the ego of man.' He further says: 'One who wants to be with God, should adopt no other path than that of self-annihilation (*fana*). That is the last stage when man completely merges with his real Divine self.'

Khwaja Kaki of Chisti Sufis describes three signs of the friends of Allah: first to be as generous as the ocean, secondly to be as affectionate as the sun, and thirdly to be as humble as the earth.

Bhakti (Devotion):

This is a word often used in India and is also becoming popular in other countries. It means devotion, surrender, love of God, personal relationship with God, mysticism of love. The love of God comes to be only when one firmly believes in and thereby orients the will towards God. Inwardness increases this love. We may also remember that 'love of God is not an easy path; one has to die while living'.

In Hindu scriptures there is mention of nine types of *bhakti*. Most of them have assumed outward forms and external demonstration. But, as Mahatma Mangat Ram has described, the real nine-fold aspects of devotion/personal relationship with God are concerned with interior worship of *atman* (the Self) according to one's inclination. Brief excerpts from his observations in 'Samata Vilas' are:

1) *Shravana* (listening): To listen to the praise of one *atman* (inner essence—described briefly in the next chapter—of the universe and of Man) in the company of true-minded. Secondly to listen to the *Shabad* (Word) inwardly with full faith in the Immortal Being, at the same time fully understanding the mortality of the body and the world. 'When the mind resorts to the second kind of listening it gets cured of the malady of doership and becomes still and stable.'

2) *Kirtan* (glorification of the Lord): Not the type of singing and dancing, a sort of show or demonstration (which has become popular, of late). But speaking or singing genu-

inely in praise of the Almighty and His manifestation as natural outburst of feelings of love and joy which is possible only when one has listened to the Shabad (true Word) inside oneself, and experienced the presence of the Supreme Being. 'This vision fills the mind with wonder and ecstasy of love.' There have been sages who have glorified God in their songs and melodies, when the joy and wonder they felt refused to remain confined within the bounds of their human shell. The exercise in aping them can give only an ephemeral entertainment; it cannot be a genuine manifestation of God-vision.

3) *Simran* (repeated remembering): One becomes what one remembers, repeatedly. Remembering bears its true fruit when the rememberer and the remembered become one. Worshipping through repeated remembrance, on the inner plane, the One, undivided Being, with firm belief in the supremacy of the Divine force. This kind of remembering purges man of all sins.

4) *Pad sewa* (serving the feet of the Lord): It implies serving selflessly all living beings knowing that the Supreme Being resides in all. Service to and love for all living beings is real worship of the sacred feet of the Almighty. Knowing the all-pervasive nature of the Lord, one must with one's mind, body and wealth serve all creatures. Such a seer of sameness alone worships the feet of the All-pervading and becomes one with Him.

5) *Archana* (worship): To make happy the hearts of all living beings through the 'incense' of forgiveness and kindness, in utter humility. That man alone knows the glory of the Lord who worships Him in this form and this wise.

6) *Vandana* (adoration): Treating the entire world as transient and knowing the One Element *atman* as immortal and permeating all life, to bow to *IT* and respect all living beings, considering that the dust of their feet is precious. Such should be the depth of one's vision of the immanence, the all-pervasiveness of the Lord.

7) *Dasya bhava* (servant attitude): It means to worship, as a servant, the Supreme Being knowing HIM as the Almighty, the doer and the dispenser of destiny. Established in this spirit of utmost humility one reaches the Supreme. Those who cultivate this form of devotion experience the Lord as their Master.

8) *Sakha bhava* (treating as friend): To know the one *atman* as witness, everpresent, in the body and to treat Him as the best friend and protector. It is an attitude of intimacy, looking upon the Lord as one's nearest companion.

9) *Atma Nivedana* (Tribute to *Atman*) implies that one experiences *Atman* as inside and outside all forms, thus considering none as different from oneself. To view one *Atman* self-same Self in all beings; the cessation of the thought of 'me' and 'you'.

Those who follow the internal way shall pass through all these facets of devotion and eventually become one with the Self. External symbols or gestures do not lead one to the realization of the Lord, the Fearless. Only the inward oriented devotion can illumine the soul. One who, with a pure heart, goes inwards, knows the different modes of *bhakti*. 'They shall find the Lord who seek the Lord.'

Sri Aurobindo has also graphically described the Man-God relationship in the following paragraph:

> "Discipleship to God the Teacher, sonship to God the Father, tenderness of God the Mother, clasp of the hand of the Divine Friend, laughter and sport with our Comrade and boy-play-fellow, blissful servitude to God the Master, rapturous love of our Divine Paramour; these are the seven beatitudes of life in the human body. Can'st thou unite all these in a single supreme and rainbow-hued relation? Then hast thou no need to any heaven and thou exceedest the emancipation of the *Advaitiyam* (not having a second)."

So far we have been talking of Man-God relationship as

described by various saints and philosophers. But have not asked ourselves the purpose of our query.

Of course, we are not to seek relationship with God in order to acquire things. We are to seek a relationship with God, rather be aware of this relationship, because this alone will answer the yearning of the heart, the inner need of the soul. When we are centred in God-awareness we are resting at the very seat of creative power, the source of all that is. 'In the ego-less state of God-consciousness there cannot be the seer other than the seen.'

Faith:

सत विश्वास ही असली जीवन है।

'True faith is real life.'

(Mangat)

Faith can move mountains; it can work wonders. A man who has no faith in himself cannot have faith in God. Self-confidence and faith in God complement each other. Faith and steadfastness grow only on the soil of conviction. And, the only faith that is both complete and comprehensive is in life, its abundance and providence.

एक विश्वास सब गुन की खान।
"मंगत" दृढ़ विश्वासी को मिले भगवान।।

Faith is the mine of all virtues. Man with firm faith will reach God, says Mangat.

Gurudev adds: 'Trust in God alone shall bring peace and comfort upon you. When in midst of anguish, you shall be comforted if you firmly believe in God. That which seems to be difficult or impossible turns out to be natural only if one is established in God...One achieves total perfection only if one's heart is rooted in God.'

'True faith implies innocence; it is thoughtlessness...It

is to surrender our thoughts and let God or reality come to occupy us.'

Sai Baba has beautifully described what faith can lead to:

'Where there is faith, there is love,
Where there is love, there is peace,
Where there is peace, there is God,
and where there is God, there is Bliss.'

'Faith, faith, faith in ourselves,
faith, faith in God—
this is the secret of greatness.'

(Vivekananda)

He emphasizes self-confidence in the following words:

"The old religions said that he was an atheist who did not believe in God. The new religion says that he is the atheist who does not believe in himself."

Sri Ramakrishna, talking about faith, affirms:

"He who can resign himself to the will of the Almighty with simple faith and guileless love, realizes God very quickly."

Shirdi Sai Baba says in the same strain:

'With three virtues — simplicity, poverty and humility — you find God.'

Gurudev observes:

तेरी आस तेरा भरवस। तुद को सिमरूं गिन गिन स्वास।।

'O, Lord! You are my hope, you are my support!
I should be remembering you with each breath.'

(Mangat)

Faith, cheerfulness, confidence in the ultimate victory are the things that help, they make the progress in any field — much more so in the spiritual direction — easier and swifter. 'Without belief we cannot grow; self-limitation is the root of failure, for as we think we become', says Swami Purna.

Faith is not primarily an intellectual thing. Nor a kind of blind trust. It is rather a quality with which man is endowed. However, there is a yawning gulf between theoretical faith and its practical application in life.

'Vedic faith is previous to thinking and anterior to willing and deciding. It is precisely faith that makes thinking possible. When one acts with faith, one acts from such depth that hesitation is not possible' (Sri Raimundo Pánikkar).

The more complete one's faith, sincerity and surrender, the more will divine grace and protection be.

In answer to a question on Faith, Mahatma Mangat Ram explained as under:

> 'There are five states of faith. In the initial stage man has trust in the comfort of his own body, and directs all his energies towards one goal: to gather as many objects or instruments of physical comfort as possible. No consideration of right or wrong.
>
> The second stage is characterized by the orientation in which ethical values are given due place — a stage in which belief in right means for the acquirement of phenomenal delights is predominant.
>
> The third state of faith understands the perishable condition of all phenomenal experiences, and so is accordingly characterized by aversion of such experiences as are transient. Scarce are the people of this quality (of faith) in the world.
>
> The fourth state is characterized by firm faith in the Being of God. Men of this realm, indeed, are few in the world.
>
> The fifth state of faith is totally oriented towards God. Both success and failure are seen in terms of Divine Will and so both pleasure and pain are accepted with resignation. Men of such life may be counted on fingers.'

Superstition is not belief. Many people have different types of superstitions. These should not be given the status of 'belief', which, in spiritual terms, is a significant, positive force. Here are two interesting instances which make rather a light reading: A student would not change his pen with the most costly and prestigious pen because the ordinary pen used in the last examination secured him unexpectedly high marks. The student thinks there is some power in the pen which accounts for the high score. A girl student told her Professor that when she put on a blue saree during examination hours, it was her experience that she scored high marks.

'If this is our psychology in the enlightenment age we should be able to understand how the early man regarded relics of his ancestors, trees, animals, even pieces of broken jar, as sacred objects and experienced the emotion of awe, reverence and dependence in relation to them', says Prof. S.P. Kanal in his book 'What can take the place of God in Religion'.

Paradoxically, doubt can be healthy or destructive, depending on our attitude. There have been thinkers like J. Krishnamurti who believe that to be caught in (blind) faith or belief is the ending of doubt. According to them the religious enquiry in India was not based on faith, so it could move in any direction. Reasoning undoubtedly is the highest developed faculty of modern man. But, as Aurobindo holds, intellectual reason is not man's only means of knowledge. 'There is some greater godhood than the reason, some profounder or larger power of knowledge.'

Dr. Sir Muhammed Iqbal (quoted in earlier chapters too), known for his serious intellectual and genuinely perceptive mind, had denounced intellectualism and reason as hollow compared to Faith. He said:

> 'Faith gives the strength to sit in the fire like Abraham:
> Faith is God-intoxication, self-expanding:
> Listen, O dotard of modern civilization:

Worse than slavery is the lack of Faith.'

(Translated from Urdu)

Faith, however, does not take to the destination. Practice does. Without faith we cannot practise.

According to Mahatma Mangat Ram, again:

'The truth of the matter is that the intellect gains freedom from bondage by contemplating in faith and trust the Self.

Blessed, indeed, are they of true faith
and blessed, indeed, their faith
for "Mangat" did find rare the clay
that made men seek the truth.'

Let us remember that real faith does not live in words alone. It lives in action, the actions of everyday life. True faith is unwavering; it does not permit disillusionment.

Here is a small modern story about faith and effort:

A man named Smith was sitting on top of his room during a flood and the water was up to his feet. A fellow in a canoe paddled past and shouted: "Can I give you a lift to a higher ground?" "No thanks", said Smith, "I have faith in the Lord and He will save me."

Soon the water rose to Smith's waist. At this point a motor boat pulled up and somebody called out: "Can I give you a lift to a higher ground?" "No thanks, I have faith in the Lord and He will save me." Later a helicopter flew by and Smith was now standing on the roof with the water to his neck. "Grab the rope", yelled the pilot, "I'll pull you up." "No thanks", said Smith, "I have faith in the Lord and He will save me." But after hours of treading water, poor, exhausted Smith drowned and went to his heavenly reward.

As he arrived at the Pearly Gates, Smith met his Maker and complained: "Tell me, Lord, I had such faith in You to save me and You let me down. What happened?" To which the Lord replied: "What did you want from me! I sent you two boats and a helicopter."

Grace:

Speaking to Arjuna, Lord Krishna says (in Gita):

'Whatever is endowed with glory and grace and is full of vigour, that you may know is only a fragment of my own splendour.'

The Grace is a thing that surpasses all comprehension; it cannot be explained through words and feelings. The divine Grace is that which makes one march swiftly towards self-realization.

Faith is an important instrument in invoking the divine Grace and one can never understand its immensity, its exactitude, its organizational aspect. Everything falls rightly in the right place. However, one can perceive how intimate, wonderful and all-powerful Grace can be.

It is ultimately Divine Grace which leads a person to the supreme goal, that is union with the Divine. We must also remember that when our intentions are pure, presence of Grace appears rather readily.

'Then', as The Mother says, 'one lives in the Action and Presence of the Grace a life full of joy, of wonder, with the feeling of a marvellous strength and at the same time with a trust, so calm, so complete that nothing can shake it any longer.'

The Divine knows what is good for us. His Grace works for our good. Even when some untoward situation arises or some event, which we do not like, takes place, the same turns out to our amazement later exactly the right thing for us. That is the work of the Grace which is working all the time.

On seeking grace and blessing, Sai Baba says: 'You do not pray to Sun to make the rays fall on you, do you? Shining is His nature. He is doing it always. Remove the obstacles between you and the Sun and the rays are there.'

"So too, keeping the obstacles of Delusion, My-ness and I-ness between you and the rays of the Grace, what is the use of complaining that they do not fall on you. What can rays do?" he asks.

One of the attributes of the All-pervasive, Supreme Being, according to Mahatma Mangat Ram Ji, is Blessing Incarnate. We must remember it always. And deserve, not just desire, His Blessings. Speaking particularly of 'Grace', Gurudev says: 'Difficult it is to fathom the form and content of Divine Grace. Subtle and tender, like the mother's milk, is the Grace of God. Different are the ways in which Grace descends on the soul. As the reservoir of mother's love is inexhaustible, so God's love, in the form of Grace, is infinite and never-ending. The worldly people, bound to desires of the flesh, understand not the true intent of Grace. Grace they see in the form of fulfilment of desires...Few there are truly who understand the meaning of God's Grace. Grace is not a favour. Grace is the outpouring of God's love for the creature...It is not (just) the material success that characterises Grace, but the realization that the end of temporal life is painful. Blessed are they, with Divine Grace, who realize that life is suffering, and freedom from suffering is the goal to be achieved.'

'Man develops his mind in proportion to his love of God and God's grace descends on him in the same proportion — the greater the measure of his in-dwelling in God, the greater will be the grace of God.' According to an Upanishadic saying: 'The wind of grace is always blowing, what you need is to unfurl your sail.'

God remembrance, let us remember again, is an act of supreme merit, the highest blessing, unequalled wisdom, an ideal virtue, a divine endowment and the mother of all noble propensities.

Swami Purna says: 'The Grace of God is drawn magnetically into the vacuum created by trust, faith and egoless action. Profound truth is often paradoxical, not following the so-called laws of mental perception, which is limited by its very dependence upon duality.'

Gratitude:

We become aware of the Grace only when we are saved from some disaster, a serious illness or some other grave misfortune. When people are ill and get well quickly, they are full of gratitude but seldom do they think of being grateful while they are well, and yet that is a much greater miracle.

'Allah', says the Holy Quran, 'is bountiful to men and yet most of them do not give thanks.' Gratitude is the memory of the heart.

First of all we must be grateful to God — a humble recognition of all that the Divine has done and is doing for us. A loving recognition of the Grace received from the Divine.

To be grateful, never to forget wonderful Grace of the Supreme; the pure flame of gratefulness must always burn in our heart, warm, sweet and brightly to dissolve all egoism.

There is nothing which gives one joy equal to that of gratitude — for what one receives. Nature provides us so much for the joy of our soul: one hears a bird sing, looks at a little child, observes the charm of a flower, the grim grandeur of an overcast sky, the timorous twinkling of the stars in the midnight sky, the colourful magnificence of a sunrise or sunset, no matter what, suddenly one comes upon this type of emotion — deep and intense — that the world manifests the Divine.

If I may recall a rare personal triggering experience I had in Bhutan while posted there on a short U.N. assignment. It was during winter of 1978. One fine morning, during my meditative walk at Thimphu up in the forested hills beyond U.N. residential colony, I saw the rising sun, the way I had never seen it. A sort of divine radiance stretched straight from the Zenith all around me in a fiery blaze, enthralling the soul.

The distance between me and the sun, it appeared, had disappeared. I felt as if my being had lept the billion miles to be one with the sun. It seemed as if the sun was in me and I was in the sun.

I was never a worshipper of sun in a formal sense though I always greeted its first rays in the morning with reverence. But that morning, on seeing the sun in its benign glory, the following words spontaneously came out of my lips:

'Om Suryaya nama! Om Swasthya nama!'

(I salute to the sun, I salute to the giver of good health.)

My love of welcoming the first rays of the sun with these words has since become a regular habit.

What folly it was that all these years while I had been bathed in the solar glory but never felt the real touch of it. But now I felt the sun not just on the skin, but much deeper, entering the interstices of my being. The situation may be described as:

> 'The self in this person of mine and the being in the sun yonder — they are one.'
>
> (The Upanishad)

I am deeply beholden to God for this great experience!

'Thank you' — these two simple words are spoken from heart for any good done to us by anybody. For God, who has given us the very life and so many beautiful things around, our thanks have to be intense and indefinite. We must think of God intensely and thank Him, abundantly, for we owe our very existence in the world to his greatness and grace. We must always be grateful to HIM — as our Creator and the Creator of the Universe in which we live.

Prayer:

Prayer is a process through which we invoke the grace of the supreme spirit to inspire us with the spiritual strength needed to achieve the vision of Truth — God, and gain the perfection of life. It is not a formal ritual or a short-cut to *sadhna* (meditation) or a safety measure to ensure that God is not displeased. Prayer is a very positive and potent practice to invoke God's grace. Mrs. Beatrice Webb, known for having produced many works on social problems, with her husband Sidney Webb, writes: 'It is by prayer, by communion with an all pervading spiritual force, that the soul of man discovers the purpose or goal of human endeavour.'

Fight out ardent desire, egoism, greed, anger and other perversions, by true prayer. Further, it is through prayer that one can get over various psycho-physical deficiencies as Gurudev says:

حرص خودی، طمع، غصّہ اور بکار
حق نماز پڑھے کرے تن کا شکار

One of the greatest of British scientific thinkers, Francis Galton, is quoted in his biography as saying: 'Did I ever tell you that I have always made it a habit to pray before writing anything for publication, that there may be no self-seeking in it, perfect candour, together with respect for feelings of others?'

Prayer is neither words nor concepts. It is an appeal directly to the innermost reality. It is the stretching of the soul to the greater Power governing the world, for the fulfilment of one's need, for protection and aid in one's struggle. Whatever crudities there may be in the ordinary human approach to God by prayer — and there are many, as Sri Aurobindo mentions — especially the attitude which imagines the Divine as if capable of being propitiated, bribed, flattered with acquiescence by praise, entreaty and gifts — still this way of turning to the Divine has a significance. Praise of God, really speaking, is not a bargaining proposition. To praise God is to delight ourselves in Him. Too many prayers are made with a whining, self-effacing false humility. We must not fall into that pitfall.

شانِ دعا تو ہے یہی حرف سوال کچھ نہ ہو
ہاتھ اٹھا تھا کس لئے ہاتھ اٹھا کے بھول جا

Shan-e-dua to hai yahi
harf-e-swall kuchh na ho,
hath uthe thay kis liye
hath utha ke bhool ja.

'The dignity of prayer lies in not asking for anything. Why were the hands raised (in prayer)? Forget having raised them.'

In the words of Swami Chinmayananda:

'Prayer is not beggary. It is not merely an exaggerated glorification of some unknown entity called GOD, repeated mechanically by the mouth in a language which is unknown to the devotee. Prayer is invocation. With the mind contemplating upon the greater Reality of Life, the essential life that energises, actuates, thrills the inert world of matter into living creatures, expands itself and in this expansion it soars higher into kingdoms of joyous experiences and true unfoldments.'

Prayer is potent, but as supplement to, and not substitute for action. We must use all the talents awarded to us, in prayer and humble mood. Until then, we have no right to seek the help of the Lord, His intervention. Here is an interesting story illustrating the point:

A devotee of Hanuman (monkey-god of Indian lore) was once driving a cartload of grain to the market. On the way, the wheel got stuck and the cart could not be drawn forward by the bullocks. The cart slanted too far to one side and the bags fell on the ground. The devotee sat on the ground and started praying to Hanuman. He finished reciting the *stotras* (prayer verses) — the 108 names and even 1008 names. The cart did not regain balance. He began to blame Hanuman and started reviling Him for not coming to his rescue. Hanuman appeared and took him to task. "Foolish fellow, instead of applying all your strength on the job you have reviled Me, for not doing what is really your task. Come on, put your shoulder to the wheel; engage in *Karma* (action), contribute individual effort."

Prayer, no doubt, is the greatest power on earth. The power of prayer is to put the will and faith of man into touch with the Divine will as that of conscious Being with whom he can enter conscious and living relation. Prayer helps to prepare this relation. Its object should become higher and higher until we reach the highest motiveless devotion. Prayer for fulfilment of desires is a lower type of prayer, the highest prayer should be for desirelessness, even though God grants all our (genuine) requests, as Christ says:

> 'Everyone who asks receives; all who seek, find; and the door is opened to everyone who knocks.'

Addressing a Muslim gathering, Mahatma Mangat Ram once advised:

> Pray in the mosque of the body,
> using *prana* as the prayer rug
> Remember Allah with every breath,
> He hears you, opening the 'secret small window within'.

Do we know how to ask, what to seek and do we knock the door? Let us ask ourselves honestly. And, do we pray to God as if we are seeing HIM? If we do that our prayer will be in the nature of sincere and direct dialogue with HIM. 'Prayer is a joyous and free interplay between God and Man.'

Where to pray? Muhammad says: 'The whole of earth has been made a mosque for me.'

Prayer, belief, love and service go together. As Mother Teresa says:

> 'If you pray, you will believe,
> if you believe you will love
> and if you love you will serve.'

Kabir has a very practical advice for us:

'All remember God in adversity and none in prosperity.

> If you remember God in prosperity then there would not be any adversity.'

Everytime is prayer time: awake, walking, working and going to sleep. As Mahatma Mangat Ram observes:

> 'Spiritual contemplation is that process or praxis in which you constantly meditate inside and outside, on the disassociated, non-objective, light of consciousness, which will reveal the essential nature of the self, and by knowing which unity with the witnessing-self is realized.'

In answer to a question: How is it possible to continue the practice of remembrance and reflection while engaged in the activities of the world? Gurudev answered:

> 'The practice of meditative reflection of the Name, while engaged in worldly business, may be continued in this manner: Engaged in worldly activity one should go on performing one's duty. While performing the worldly (daily) acts, the inclination of the mind must be to revert back to the Name, as soon as they are finished...At the end of tasks the practice of the Name must begin with the same zeal which already exists in the mind.'

Before going to sleep we must concentrate for a few minutes, look into the day that has passed, remember when and where we have forgotten the Divine, and pray that such forgettings should not happen again.

Somebody has prescribed, very succinctly (good even for the busiest executives), 4 minutes prayer for a prosperous day:

- Think of your yesterday's mistakes.
- Assure yourself that you will improve from that.
- Seek the guidance of God for your fervent self-correction.
- Maintain inner silence.

In all pursuits, intellectual or active, our one motto should be 'Remember and offer; remember God and offer all our actions to HIM, leaving the result in HIS hands...' Generally very few people go to a temple, mosque or church with true religious feeling, that is, not to pray and beg for something from God, but to offer themselves, give thanks, aspire, give themselves. Self giving is true prayer. Let us approach God with no specific desire or preference, but in a wholesome attitude of surrender.

Then whatever turn of events assails us from time to time, whether fortunate or unfortunate, let us accept everything as a blessing of the Lord.

We may also remember what the Quran says: 'Surely God wrongs not men anything, but men wrong themselves.' Thus we shall not find fault with our fortune but pray earnestly for forgiveness.

Our prayer must also be reflected in our daily behaviour. We must heed the words of Jesus that God does not listen to the prayers of those who have wronged their fellow beings. We cannot be pious in the morning and ruthless in the afternoon.

Note: At the end of this book are given a few selected common prayers in Annexure VI. These are only by way of illustration. Truly speaking prayer being a personal communication between man and the Lord, one can use any words or no words at all. Here is a small story:

The Unseen Visitor: The story is told of a shabby old gentleman who everyday at twelve o'clock would enter the church, stay a few minutes, then leave. The caretaker was concerned for the valuable altar furnishings. Everyday he watched to be sure nothing was taken and everyday just at twelve the shabby figure would arrive.

One day the caretaker accosted him: "Look here, my friend, what are you up to, going into the church everyday?"

"I go to pray", replied the old man politely.

"Now come", the cautious caretaker said, "you don't stay long enough to pray."

"True enough. I cannot pray a long prayer, but everyday I just come and say, 'Jesus, it's Jim'. Then I wait a minute, then come away. I guess he hears me though it's but a little prayer."

Then, one day Jim was knocked down crossing the street and was laid up in the hospital with a broken leg. The ward where Jim quite happily lay was a sore spot to the nurses on duty. Some of the men were cross and miserable, others did nothing but grumble from morning till night. Slowly but surely the men stopped their grumbling and were cheerful and contented.

One day as the nurse was walking through the ward she heard the men laughing. "What has happened to all of you? You are such a cheerful lot of patients lately."

"It's old Jim", they replied, "He's always cheerful, never complains, although he is uncomfortable and in pain."

The nurse walked over to Jim's bed where the silvery haired Jim lay with an angelic look on his smiling face.

"Well, Jim, these men say you are the cause for the change in this ward. They say you are always happy."

"Aye, that I am, nurse, I can't help it. You see, nurse, it's my visitor. He makes me happy."

"Visitor?" The nurse was indeed puzzled for she had never noticed any visitor by Jim's bed. The chair was always empty during visiting hours. "When does your visitor come?"

"Everyday", replied Jim with the light in his eyes growing brighter. "Yup, everyday at twelve o'clock He comes and stands at the foot of my bed. I see Him there, and He smiles at me and says, 'Jim, it's Jesus'."

Surrender:

> 'And, who has a nobler religion than the man who submits himself to Allah.'
>
> (Muhammad)

सकल करम का कर्ता, जानो एक भगवान।
आप अकर्ता हो रहो, ये ही सार है ज्ञान।।

> Know Him, the Lord, as the doer of all actions. Take yourself (in all humility) as the non-doer (while devotedly acting as His instrument). This is the essence of the real spiritual knowledge.
>
> (Mangat)

> 'It is the sense of doership that causes suffering. The real cause of human unhappiness is nothing but ego. To be disassociated from the doership of ego, it is essential to meditate and remember the Name Absolute.
>
> Autonomy from the doership of ego is possible if one surrenders to the Divine Will. Dependence on God becomes possible if one, with a pure and loving heart, worships God...A loving heart alone will meditate truly and rightly.'
>
> (Samata Vilas)

There must be a total and sincere surrender. There must be an exclusive opening to the divine Power. 'We should not make behind our surrender a cover of our desires, egoistic demands and vital insistences. We must keep the temple clean if we wish to instal there the living Presence.'

'Self surrender, in utter humility, is the simplest, surest and nearest way to God.' It is not a matter of words, it is essentially an inner attitude.

'An inert passivity is often confused with the real surrender, but out of an inert passivity nothing true and powerful can come. We have to be efficient instruments in the hands of the Nature, the Divine. Doing things under HIS command, in perfect devotion — a devotion that keeps concentrated and silent in the depth of the heart but manifests in acts of service and obedience' (Aurobindo).

Self-effort and surrender are related. This may sound paradoxical but it is true.

The spirit of surrender to God does not imply that we stop our self-effort but rather a spirit of surrender to God is the fountain-source of energy, which allows us to perform our effort in a most dynamic manner.

We surrender to God in the true sense by exercising all that God has given to us, our mind, our intellect, our body, our sense of inner freedom. If we exercise all of these to the maximum and do our best, leaving the fruits or rewards of our action to rest in Divine hands, then we are performing the act of Divine surrender in the truest sense, so says a contemporary saint.

Shirdi Sai Baba says:

> 'Unless we surrender ourselves fully and unconditionally to the Supreme Divine Power, we are all the time feeling restless out of false sense of responsibility...Self surrender opens the flood-gates of the Divine grace for us.'

He who lives in the Divine Will from moment to moment, he opens more and more to the Inner Delights and Ecstasies.

Life has its ups and downs. Who has not some trouble or agony sometime or the other? Gurudev advises surrender to the Lord as the tried spiritual remedy.

> दीनदयाल की सरन में, सकल विनासे ताप।
> "मंगत" निरमल प्रीत से, नाम प्रभु चित जाप।।

> On surrendering to the Lord (of the lowly), entire agony is gone. Remember repeatedly from the core of your heart and with love the Name of the Lord, says 'Mangat'.

The Divine Grace and Power can do anything but with the full assent of one who has surrendered. "To learn to give that full assent is the whole meaning of *Sadhna* (meditation)" (Aurobindo).

Here is a small seven-worded prayer of surrender: 'Lord! Help me to will your will!'

Repentance:

Associated with surrender is the deep change of mind which repentance brings about. One rejects any undesirable activities, even so-called sins, feels sorry and takes a spiritual U-turn towards self-renewal.

When our sins bother us, remember God is actually trying to persuade us to repent and surrender ourselves to His guidance and perpetual concern for us. An unconcerned attitude can keep us from knowing God, but it does not keep Him from caring for us.

"Turn to Allah in true repentance. He is the Compassionate and the Merciful" (Muhammad).

We have not discussed so far what is sin. Nor do I propose to dilate on it. Different people have different connotations of sin. I would, however, like to quote Emil Ludwig, a great German/Swiss writer of early thirties, who described sin as under:

> "My view is that we sin in falling short of such efficiency as nature may expect, according to her gifts to us."

He describes the gifts as: health and vigour, spirit and intelligence. He worshipped creative power alone.

Ludwig was greatly inspired by Goethe who said:

> 'Before God the greatest is he who has brought his abilities to the highest point.'

Mahatma Mangat Ram defines 'sin' as any thought, word or act which disturbs peace of mind.

Silence:

Silence has been associated with the names of great saints. It is through silence that man can communicate with God. When man is silent, God speaks through him. The life of Gurudeva Mahatma Mangat Ram is an eloquent testimony to the truth of this statement. God manifested Himself in the holy words of the Vani — the revealed utterances.

Silence is golden. 'All profound things and emotions of things are preceded and attended by Silence', wrote Herman Melville, one of the loftiest and most eloquent of souls. He goes on to say: 'Silence is the general consecration of the universe. Silence is the invisible laying on of the Divine Pontiff's hands upon the world. Silence is the only voice of our God.' Silence, indeed, is the language of the realized.

Silence is not an absence, but a presence — presence of the godhood within us. Here our thoughts stop; we can hear someone else think. 'Silence is the condition of the being when it listens to the Divine.'

Ramana Maharishi, the sage of Arunachal, says: 'Silence is never-ending speech, the highest from the Grace, the most perfect 'updesa' (discourse).'

'A man who loves God necessarily loves silence', writes Thomas Morton. It is no coincidence that places of worship are places of silence. And it is only right that Quakers all but worship silence.

Swami Chinmayananda talks of another aspect of silence: '...The silent power of Truth, in irresistible efficiency, is constantly at work without strife, sound or confusion. As devotees of Truth when we work in the society, let us make use of this silent might of the ever-conquering Truth. We must learn to be cheerfully silent, gracefully silent, powerfully silent.'

'Make your life a Rose that speaks silently in the language of fragrance. For it is only in the depth of Silence that the voice of God can be heard' (Sai Baba).

'Once one has come to the stage of hearing the sound of silence, the external forms cease to enthral' (Swami Purna).

One must quieten one's mind; not to have restless, excited, agitated thoughts. At the same time one must never mistake inertia or a somnolent passivity for calm.

Quietude is a very positive state, a great strength. It is not in the outward circumstances that one must look for quietness; it comes from inside oneself. Deep inside the being there is peace which brings quietness in the whole being down to the body, if we allow it so.

The illumination of the soul is real silence. Without that merely keeping the mouth shut is not silence. Some adopt a vow of silence but communicate by writing on paper or slate, or they point out successively to the letters of alphabets or through finger signs. All this is pseudo silence. There is no need to attain silence. Silence is everytime with us. What we have to do is to remove all things that disturb it.

Still physical silence, not using the tongue, is good at times. It keeps out obstacles to meditation, and one can concentrate.

It is also good to be alone sometimes. We are always with people, with thoughts that crowd in, hopes that have not been fulfilled, or are going to be; in fact all sorts of recollections. 'To be alone is essential for man to be uninfluenced, for something uncontaminated to take place.'

According to Pascal, most of the evils of life arise from "Man's incapacity and inability to sit still in a room".

'To relax ourselves for an hour in a quiet corner and to compose ourselves to the serene silence within, is to open one's pores to the dynamic touch of creative life. This is meditation — this is the highest form of prayer too. At such peaceful moments, forget even to be curious to know the nature of silence. The condition and the behaviour of this inward poise, in its serene depths are divine beatitude itself.'

Silence is a blissful state, beyond the doctrine and divisions created by mind. We hold our words, we suspend our chattering selves, to feel the immensity of silence within us. 'In love we are speechless; in awe we say, words fail us', as Pico Iyer ends his remarkable essay: 'The Eloquent Sounds of Silence' (TIME, January 25, 1993).

J. Krishnamurti observes: 'In real silence there is no observer, no experience...Silence can only experience silence. Long periods of rest and silence can trigger the awakening of immense energy in us.'

Gurudev advises that we worldly people can and should observe silence — not only absence of physical speech but purging the mind of all thoughts — at least for some time in a day, one day in a week, or more whenever time and engagements permit. If we learn to be silent we will notice that we have talked much, too much. We should take refuge occasionally in the depths of our minds, in silence and in loneliness.

It is a habit of man — more accurately speaking, it is his nature — to speak without much purpose. Even while talking to others, we generally do monologing. Our talking thus turns into sadistic dominating, crude bullying. It is a kind of violence we inflict on others.

The restraint on speech means recognizing the existence of others. It means giving them the same status that we give ourselves.

When we are silent, we can also think better — can truly communicate with ourselves. And as for saying prayers only a silent man can do that.

Silence is not merely abstention from verbal activity — the use of tongue, as stated earlier. It has also an inner, profounder dimension. Abstention from verbal activity is comparatively easy. Inner silence is, however, hard to attain; it is possible only when the mind is purged of all thoughts — thoughts that are the creatures of memory. These thoughts are our scourge. They overcome us when we are awake. They haunt us when we are asleep. It is only when the mind is dead within us that we truly become silent. That is the moment when God speaks in us.

Silence transcends all actions and inactions. It is not to be confused with dullness. It comes into being with utter hard discipline. This is the aim of yoga — as the wise Patanjali told us long ago.

It is in this silence that the Word is heard:

'When the Word peals within
the mind gets lost in the Void;
it is in that inmost depth
— the abode of man's own being —
that bliss supreme resides,

says 'Mangat'. That is the glory of inner silence! In silence lies our beatitude, in speech our sin and suffering.

Guru Concept and Gurudom:

The literal meaning of the word Guru is 'One who removes darkness (ignorance)'. In reality God Himself, in the form of the Word is the One Guru present in everyone, as Mahatma Mangat Ram says in Granth Samata Vilas. He is the Light permeating all. Its realization by the intellect removes all darkness. To reproduce his words:

वास्तव में तो गुरु एक शब्द स्वरूप परमेश्वर ही है, तमाम अन्धकार को नाश करने वाला है, अखण्ड प्रकाश घट-घट व्याप रहा है...

Verily, the primordial Word-manifest of the Supreme Being — is the Guru. It dispels all darkness, and is present in all beings as ever-shining light.

Still in the world one needs (unless born as a highly evolved soul — as Gurudev himself was) a teacher. Men have to depend on guides and experts even in matters of the world — not to speak of matters that relate to the Spirit.

As Gurudev observes: "Even the saints and sages had to seek the way of knowledge from men of God. Krishna had to seek knowledge from Durvasa and Rama's guru was Vasisht. In the recent past Nanak gained his knowledge from Kabir...Even Kabir, a weaver's son, had to be initiated by Ramananda.

"The inner thirst is quenched at that time when the water of life is received from the loving stream of a true guru. Since the dawn of history man has always been in need of a teacher. Even for the purpose of empirical knowledge man is in need of a guru."

However, the real teacher can be one who is a realized soul; who sees Truth as it is in itself. It is the true seer alone who can point out the way. Of the many qualities of a true guru, narrated by Gurudev, a few are mentioned below:

जप तप संजम साधना, मोह माया से उदास।
पर उपकारी विरत जो, शबद आलख चित वास।।

He lives a disciplined and meditative life. Is away from attachment, kindness is his nature and he is conscious of the great Word residing in him.

बानी निरपख बोलदे, यह सतगुरु लच्छन चीन।
तन मन की शोभा तजे, रहे आतम में परबीन।।

His utterance is impartial. He is away from physical and mental glamour; remains absorbed in the *Atman.*

सब जीवों से एक दर्ष्ट, प्रेम समता ज्ञान।
वरन कुल नहीं मानदे, केवल सत ध्यान।।

He, the true Guru, sees all as equals, love of Samata — sameness — is his enlightenment. He does not believe in caste, creed or ancestory; truth alone is his contemplation.

इन्द्री भोग से रहे अतीत।
आतम भोगे सो गुर पुनीत।।

One who is away from enjoyment of sense pleasures, but rejoices in *Atman*, he is a clean guru.

मज़हब मज़ाहब सब से दूर।
साचा मज़हब राखे हजूर।।

A true guru is also away from religious tangles. Divine presence alone is his/her religion.

Even though himself a great Guru — a real one — Mahatma Mangat Ram was against Gurudom as such. He says: 'Gurus are not made. Gurudom is nothing but a process of making gurus.' He was against the pomp and show of gurudom. By misleading people, these gurus lead a life of comfort and luxury at the cost of others. He also held that it was better to remain without a teacher than to be a prey to a false teacher. He abhorred 'gurus' getting worshipped personally. Also he did not like their preaching to others what they did not practise themselves. Nor soliciting or even accepting gifts from their disciples or service in any form. A few of the generally observed characteristics of false gurus are:

कूड़ा दम्ब फैलाये कर, भोग विषे चित लाए।
औरों को उपदेश दे, नाम गुरु कहलाए।।

There are gurus in name with false outward show who would preach others, while themselves being engrossed in sense gratification.

अगम पंथ का साधन नहीं, नहीं साचो है अहसास।
तोते बांग पुकारते, संतन के इतिहास।।

Such gurus do not know the way to the Unknown, nor do they have true feeling. However, they repeat, ad nauseam, like parrot, sayings and stories of saints.

ना सत मारग सूझ कुछ, न मन में विश्वास।
पख वाद विखावते कलजुग के गुरनाथ।।

These gurus of *Kalyug* (present era) have no perception of the true path, nor do they have any faith; they speak false.

गुर कामी गुर क्रोधी, गुर माया चित धार।
ऐसे गुर की सेव से, कभूं न होए निस्तार।।

Any guru who is full of lust, anger and desires can never do any good to his devotees.

Asked specifically what should one look for in a genuine guru, Mahatma Mangat Ram pointed out the following nine criteria:

1. There is complete harmony in what he says and what he does; there is no dichotomy between theory and practice in his lifestyle.
2. His knowledge does not merely stem from books, but springs from the depths of life; he is learned not in books but in mind.
3. He is a paradigm of the peace of mind; a symbol of mental peace.
4. He is beyond the reach of temptations like those of wealth and honour, dignity and fame.
5. He remains for long time in *samadhi* i.e. absorbed in the bliss of the self.
6. He lives away from women; and does not allow any woman to meet him privately.
7. He is a man of utmost compassion; his heart is as soft and loving as that of a mother.
8. He remains constantly detached from the world; dispassion is his constant nature.
9. He is not affected by the nine-gates of the sense organs. Having killed his desire, he remains absorbed in the abode of the Imperishable Word.

Such a man transcends the sphere of *maya* (illusion) of three modes and remains established in the Self...Without constant spiritual practice one is a mere shell, like a pitcher without water.

Some people believe that man is uplifted spiritually when he is initiated by a Guru. Mahatma Mangat Ram was very clear on the question of initiation. He says:

> 'The task of Guru is to show the path. Necessary it is to follow the path and only then shall (spiritual) perfection be attained.'

Learning from any person necessarily involves a sense and feeling of respect, if not reverence, for whoever teaches. We perhaps cannot judge the institution of Guru in the light of the conduct of many modern gurus whose own lives and acts are very often shrouded in mystery, if not in dubiety. A real Guru need not awe or even impress the disciple by physical attributes — either of appearance or of atmosphere around.

It is Guru's own conduct, behaviour, way of living, attitude — and above all spiritual status — which really influence the disciple.

One need not discount, dilute or doubt the institution of Guru on account of aberrations, even when, unfortunately, these may abound. In fact a right guru also looks forward to and searches for the right disciple with as much intensity and eagerness as a disciple seeks the guru. Both the processes are difficult and are believed to be possible only with the grace of God.

Mahatma Mangat Ram further says that guru and disciple relationship runs over lives. He also qualifies Guru as synonymous with the word *Gyan* (gnosis), and disciple one who gains it. Without understanding the discipline of *Gyan*, there is neither any Guru nor disciple.

The fruit of meeting a true Guru is recognition of *atman*. Such a lucky one will speak always of God's glory, with veil of worldly illusion removed, says Gurudev. He adds: Guru is not body; guru is what guru says and lives. We, worldly people, are prone to worshipping guru's body or form forgetting his teachings, much less following them.

I am also reminded here of a relevant remark by Swami Purna — himself a grand charismatic personality, besides being a realized soul and a 'world-teacher'. He says: 'Attracted by the high radiation, pure love and compassion which the Guru emits, the form is taken for essence. This is very common mistake of the human being.'

Gurudev was so progressive as to envisage and declare: A stage comes when Guru-disciple relationship too recedes, the religious injunctions and prophets are forgotten. One has then risen above (the body fort) triumphantly, overcoming the mind.

Talking to some disciples towards the end of his life's journey Mahatma Mangat Ram remarked:

> 'If someone asks you about the form of God, read out to him Mahamantra. If Guru's form has to be described, explain the qualities you find in the saints (bodily states of every Guru, priest or prophet, have been different in all ages). But in all these shone the qualities: selflessness, humility, non-attachment, tranquillity and service of others.'

Regarding Samata Prakash and Samata Vilas, Gurudev said he had uttered what his Master (God) had made him speak 'The work is complete in itself. Coming generations will know through these Granths, what is Truth and what is untruth. These words have the force of uniting various religions and sects.'

CHAPTER 7

The Word and Meditation

Shabad:

In deep silence we hear within us *Shabad*. St. John calls it the 'Word'. Mahatma Mangat Ram calls it Shabad Braham (the resounding Reality within us). It is this mystical, the transcendent sound which is the Reality, the Master, the Creator, Life of all. By knowing it, he says, not only does one obtain release from all past afflictions, but also the fire of desires is extinguished.

As Bible says: 'In the beginning was the Word, and the Word was with God, and the Word was God.' This Creative Power is also referred to as the Logos, the Holy Ghost, the Spirit, the Audible Life Stream. In the Vedas it has been termed *Nad* or even sound. The Muslim mystics have called it *Kalma*, or Isam-i-Azam, the highest name, Sultan-ul-Akbar, the king of 'words', and Bang-i-Ilahi, the Voice of God.

The Word Imperishable, variously called — is the First born of Truth, the first offspring of the Absolute.

God has no name, in fact, because He himself is 'the WORD', though, as stated earlier, He has been called by various names as per countless attributes of godhood.

अनन्त नाम तिस पुरख के, सभी जान परमान।
"मंगत" जो चित में रमे, सो ही देवे कल्यान।।

Countless are the names of the Lord;
Consider them all authentic.
However, the one which becomes a part of one's consciousness, will be beneficial, says 'Mangat'.

But as Mahatma Mangat Ram says: 'Remembering of Name (of the Lord — any of the many) ultimately leads to unnamedness; absorption in the indivisible Word.' He further says: 'The Word is life. It is the Energy of life. When subjectively viewed, it is called the immanent Self, and when objectively thought of, it is referred to as the transcendent Absolute, or the Eternal Sound. The Self expresses itself in and through the Word. The Word in itself, however, is inexpressible.'

Saints and sages who have seen God describe HIM as inner resplendence and resonance. It is evident from the following verse of Guru Nanak:

'Within us is the light
and from within the light
emanates the sound;
We are attuned to the true Lord,
through the Word.'

He further says:

'Communion of the soul with the Word creates everlasting bliss.'

To hear or understand the Word is not a matter of the Will or the intellect alone. The relationship between the Word and the hearer is much more intimate; it is vital assimilation. The hearer and the Word become one, with mind merged with the Word.

The Word is the central mystery that is situated in the very core of Reality; the Word is the soul, the vital principle of everything. 'It is the WORD that expresses itself as words of human languages. The Word being ultimate is the source of everything, and nothing exists apart from it.'

It is important to realize the difference between the name of a thing and the thing itself. The Word 'tree' is not tree. Nor the word 'fire' is fire otherwise it would burn the paper on which this word is written.

As Vivekananda puts it:

> "Merely to repeat the words 'Food, Food' will not remove hunger, nor calling 'Water, Water' quench thirst. Similarly recounting 'God, God' will not give us the experience of 'God'. We have to make effort for realising or seeing 'God'."

If one concentrates on a thought or a word, one has to dwell on the essential idea contained in the word with the aspiration to feel the thing which it expresses.

To acquire the energy of the Word one has to grasp not only its meaning but also its message and vibrations, the *spanda* — 'the dynamic recurrent and creative activity of the Absolute Spanda is the spontaneous and recurrent pulsation of the Absolute.'

Some modern philosophers too have given hints about the celestial sound, on hearing which the mind becomes calm and still.

'Hamsa — the sound of the *nauns* of swan, mythical golden swan which lives in Mansarover, was resonant with the silence of cosmos, and with the inbreathing and outbreathing of *prana* — the life force.'

'OM — as the total vowel sound in which there are no consonants — the Om sound which reverberates in the universe and in the caverns of the heart when all other sound has ended' (J. Krishnamurti).

As Peter Matthiessen observes in the Afterword to the "Circle of Life":

> 'A universal resonance comes forth from all around us and this universality, this sense of oneness — glimpsed only through close attention to the present moment,

moment after moment — is the simple, great secret of existence.'

Some others have observed:

'One can hear it outside too — more particularly while the streamlet ripples out the tale to the pebbles; dark ocean waves roar it to the rocks surf bound, scent laden breezes sing it to the vales and stately pines mysteriously whisper.'

'And from the fourfold manifested powers, a chant of love ariseth — from the flaming fire and flowing water, and from sweet-smelling earth and rushing wind.'

We may go over some more statements on the word OM:

"If you strike a bell it produces hum-m-m. From that eternal silence a hum starts and this hum is called OM. You may have heard of the glory of OM and the greatness of OM, that OM is everything and that from OM the creation comes and into OM the creation dissolves, that OM is the sustainer of life, that OM is the beginning and end of all creation. All this is OM."

"That hum, which is first silent sound, first silent wave that starts from that silent ocean of unmanifested life."

The absolute simplicity of 'OM' is not merely reductionism of the beautiful Reality. All the words (*sarva vak*) are held together by the sound Om:

Omkara idam sarvam: all this, the entire universe.

In the words of one Upanishad (BU):

the threefold offspring of Prajapati,
the *devas* (angels), men and *asuras* (devils) listening to the teachings of their Father, all alike said Om, yes.

Om is assent and fulfilment as another Upanishad (Chandogya) puts it:

This syllable is eternal Brahma
The sound Om is so simple, so inarticulate,
passing as it does into a complete silence.

Guru Nanak: "God has created all from the Word — OM: the entire creation has been churned out by it. The three modes—*Satvik, Rajas* and *Tamsik*—are also born out of it."

"OM has created Brahma, Vishnu, Mahesh (the Trinity)— there is no end to their further prolific, countless reproduction."

"On the land and in the sea there is endless variety of beings. It is from one OM that they all came into existence."

The sacred syllable 'OM' is uttered as a holy exclamation. It implies a solemn affirmation and respectful assent meaning 'so be it, amen, yes, all right' etc. It is the most sacred word, in the Hindu scriptures, of utmost potency, capable of sanctifying, spiritualizing and strengthening all the utterances that follow or precede it.

"This word is verily Brahman, the word is verily the highest. He, who knows this word, obtains verily whatever he desires" (Kathopanishad).

The Descent of Revelation:

Gurudeva Mahatma Mangat Ram's recorded *Vani* (God-inspired revelatory verses) in Granth Samata Prakash runs to thousands of verses. (A few of them have been quoted in this book.) The story of how such words came direct from 'nature' or 'Lord' is most enlightening and is reproduced from the writing of a co-disciple and dear friend of mine, Prof. Som Raj Gupta (Source — The Silent Logos).

It was in the month of June in the year 1938. Gurudeva had arrived at a tiny village, Nakhetra village (West Kashmir) situated at a height of 5,500 feet and surrounded by tall hills and mountains. The purpose was to select a solitary place for uninterrupted *tapas* — meditation. At a height of 8000 feet was a forest called Baragali, dark and thick, with no sign of human habitation for miles around. Towards the summit of the mountain, a small plain-like place, absolutely silent and remote from humanity, with forest covered mountainous landscape all round, was selected. A devotee Choudhary Ramditta (from village Nakhetra who was supplying ration to the forest-lessee there) got a hut built in a span of hardly two hours, with a hole dug in the earth for fire and two tree trunks so placed on the open side as to serve as a door. Even in that hot month of June, the place was severely cold.

Next day, the devotees who had accompanied Gurudeva for selection of the place, left, but for Bhagat Banarsi Dass — affectionately called 'Bhagatji' by co-disciples—who stayed on. He long pestered Gurudeva for permission to stay with him during the forthcoming *tapas*, and Gurudeva reluctantly conceded to his repeated entreaties. On the third day, however, Gurudeva asked him to go away, but Bhagatji refused to be thus put off. With folded hands he entreated that he might be allowed to serve Gurudeva during the *tapas*.

Gurudeva said, "Premi (O' Loved one), it is hard fare to stay in jungles. Occasions may arise when you'll have to go without food. Add to this the constant threat of the prowling beasts. You are still a boy and never had an occasion to stay with *faqirs*. Disabuse your mind if you think it a smooth affair — this staying with them. But stay if you must! God bless your noble resolve!"

After uttering these words, Gurudeva went into *samadhi* — the blessed state where consciousness just does not know anything — even does not know that it does not know anything, to paraphrase a saying of the Kenopanishad. Bhagatji went on gazing at that literally indescribable state. Gurudeva sat cross-legged near the fire-place — eyes closed and head quivering a little. The trunk stood erect and then bent forward a little. Streaks of crimson hue criss-crossed with the pale on the face which nevertheless had a sheen and glow one associates with velvet. The pale face that normally bore the expression of melancholy compassion became a riddle, an enigma — for no familiar human expression bore that visage. There was neither happiness there nor unhappiness, neither hope was there nor despair, neither an expression of understanding nor that of non-understanding. It was a face that 'spoke' neither of death nor of life. Even the face of the corpse has a face of 'human' expression, but that face had none which could be familiar to mortal man. One could see that the man behind that face was dead and only the Impersonal lived in his place. Or should we say that Existence had usurped the place of the existent?

Gurudeva remained rapt in *samadhi* for a long time and Bhagatji went on gazing at that long-familiar but forbidding presence. When Gurudeva came back to what we humans call normal state of consciousness, he remained silent for quite some time and then said, "Think out on your own what you have to do from morning till evening and from evening till morning. You'll have some trouble, no doubt, but things will get straightened out shortly. Do unto 'It' only what you are asked to do, never press 'Its' programme. At the mealtime, wait not for 'Its' coming back from *samadhi* just go down to have your meal and bring tea for 'It'."

Bhagatji accordingly chalked out his daily routine of activities. Early in the morning, he would walk over two and a half kilometres down to a fountain of water and would have a bath in ice-cold water. He would then collect a bucketful of water, wrap up the bucket in a piece of cloth to protect his head from its bitingly cold touch, and carry the bucket for Gurudeva's bath. After Gurudeva's bath, he would again walk down almost two kilometres to have his meal and prepare tea for Gurudeva. This tea was the sole meal for Gurudeva in twenty-four hours and consisted of one and a half quarter of a seer (equivalent 0.8 kg) of milk and an equal measure of water. The tea time was 9 a.m. After having tea Gurudeva often went into *samadhi* and Bhagatji went into the jungle to collect wood for fuel. When he returned, he would find Gurudeva lost in *samadhi*.

Bhagatji daily saw a real wonder — one should call it a miracle — during his stay in that solitude. He would see that Gurudeva, with eyes closed and apparently oblivious of the world, would often sing verses. Sometimes the verses flowed on for hours on end — without interruption and pause. Bhagatji had seen this phenomenon earlier also. Then it had struck him with wonder and amazement; but now he felt thrilled and elated. For five or six days, he was lost in the joy of listening; then, one day, he thought of reducing those verses to writing. At the next 'awakening', he said, "Permit me, Lord, to put the verses you have memorised to writing!"

Gurudeva smiled his unique, benign and soft smile and said, "This affair is even old, even new. This is the natural voice. 'It' never remembers what 'It' has uttered. The natural voice gets lost in the natural atmosphere. What do you think about these thoughts that flow out anew this wise?"

Bhagatji: I think you first compose these verses and then recite them from memory.

Gurudeva: O you innocent! 'This' is no poet. It is the sheer overflow of God-intoxication and divine ecstasy. It is completely and utterly spontaneous and unmeditated. Do not think that this utterance involves any thought or conscious 'making' on 'our' part. He who has reached this state, even though illiterate and unlettered, will sing unwearied, and with joy and love, the glory of the Lord. Whatever gets spoken here will be the word of wisdom — of revelation. As the verses (ayats) revealed themselves to Muhammad, or the Vedas descended on the *rishis*, so is this revelatory utterance gushing forth. You'll understand this in due course — but not now. Take every verse that manifests itself here as you take the verses of the Bhagavad Gita! Now things are getting out of 'our' control. The joy refuses to be confined within — it is coming out in these strains. Who knows what the Lord wills by prompting you to act as the scribe? God knows what a great many verses have escaped into the thin air in the midst of jungles all these years! 'It' is surprised by your persistence. 'It' tried 'Its' best to resist your will, but eventually it prevailed and 'It' is compelled to sojourn here. How little the *vani* (utterance) that Kabir uttered could be recorded? Kabir himself confessed:

Sixteen billion verses of knowledge
did I utter, and yet I kept the Logos
within! The Word, O Dharmdas,
would not get uttered! Verily I tell thee—again,
and yet again.

Thus Kabir himself admits that he uttered as many as sixteen billion verses. How little of it could come to be recorded! But serve the world — as much as you can! Maybe some beloved of the Lord will chance to read it and you may thus find some meaning in your life.

Now what do you think of this affair?

Bhagatji: I have come to understand that these verses are like the verses uttered by enlightened ones like Kabir and his likes. Now do I follow that they too must have uttered as the Lord does.

Twilight was slowly descending on the forests. The landscape around the hut was getting enveloped in darkness, Bhagatji fanned the fire into flames and a warm glow lit up the hut. Gurudeva asked Bhagatji to recite some 'composition' of some saintly poet. Bhagatji, in his sweet and sonorous voice, sang a few verses of Kabir, Sahajo Bai and

Daya Bai — saints of medieval India (the latter two were ladies). When he stopped singing, Gurudeva said, "If you want more of such verses, then write them down!"

Bhagatji immediately prepared an inkpot. He had a notebook, old with leaves torn. There was no light — neither an earthen nor a kerosene lamp. He, however, fed the fire with more fuel to burn in larger flames. Bhagatji hoped that the *vani* (utterance) would be dictated in a slow pace to coincide with his writing but that was not to be. Lost in *samadhi* Gurudeva spoke continuously and without pause. There was no hesitation, no deliberation, no brooding — no waiting for the 'right word'. As the water flows out continuous and uninterrupted from snow-fed spring so was the effusion of words — profuse and pauseless. Tried as he might, the pace of his writing could not synchronise itself with that of the utterance. His fingers got 'benumbed' after he had written only three or four verse-paragraphs. With a timid hesitation, he requested for a more natural speed of dictation. Gurudeva opened his eyes and found the *vani* rather poorly written.

Gurudeva then dictated with eyes open until Bhagatji picked up speed — which he did in the very short span of three days. On the third day itself, Bhagatji found, to his surprise, that his pen moved with ease and with the pace of *vani* that Gurudeva uttered rapt in *samadhi*. He would not, of course, care for vowels while writing, and would insert them only when he rewrote legibly at the time of leisure. The dictation would continue past midnight — often upto 1 a.m. At that time, the mountains wore a fearful look; they presented a series of dark outlines rearing their ominous heads into the depths of the sky. The oppressive silence of the landscape often got disturbed by the varied voice of winds that blowed now softly and now with terrible velocity. The landscape often shook with the roars of wild animals. Bhagatji could not make out whether they were leopards or tigers.

Often the sky got overcast with thick clouds — their lightning and thunder making the scene look all the more fearful. That was the time and that was the place the Silent Word had chosen to incarnate itself in human speech. When that current ceased to flow, Bhagatji would rub Gurudeva's legs—benumbed by continuous sitting for almost 24 hours, and in one position. Only then would he lie down for a few hours of much needed sleep. But Gurudeva even then would not go to sleep; he would keep sitting and would get lost into *samadhi*. Bhagatji says that whenever his sleep got disturbed with thunder or with roars of the beasts, he found Gurudeva lost in *samadhi*.

One evening, Gurudeva asked Bhagatji to go to bed rather early. That night the clouds had gathered into a thick blanket in the sky and rain fell in torrents interspersed with successive flashes of lightning and deafening peals of thunder. The clouds seemed to rain darkness on that remote landscape. That frightening look of the earth and the sky did not prevent sleep from sending the thoroughly tired Bhagatji into oblivion. He had slept hardly for two hours when he was awakened by the voice of Gurudeva asking him to feed up the fire.

Rubbing his eyes, he woke up and fed the fire into the bright and warm flames — a cosy contrast to the dark cold that rained down out on the mountains. When he was fully awake, Gurudeva said, "Take up your pen and take down the effusion of the Lord's rapture." Immediately, Gurudeva went into *samadhi* and the Word pealed into the following words (translated from Urdu):

> The Lord manifests Himself on His own in this my body, and manifests Himself in a form wondrous and playful.
>
> Here within the navel that burns like a flame,
> Opens out a treasure of gems that surpassing burn

and flash. Alive will he die and will turn away from the world—
he who but casts a glance on these burning gems.

There in the navel sounds the *nada* — that sounds not in time; and sounds unbound by the bounds of space.

And hither shines a splendour, undimmed and like that of the suns when they shine in their tens of millions.

High in the sky — in the head — lies hidden in a hole a well of nectar, where abides the Word Eternal and Infinite — the Word that bestows the joy that lives in the cessation of the becoming of the intentional mind.

Tunes that emanate from instruments of all kinds and shapes float there in profusion, but only he who has met the Sadguru — the true Guide — shall ever hear them, and with the hearing, find already done whatever he was born to do.

A soft tune of love hums on the Mount Sinai but only he who is cast in the rare heroic mould will ever behold glare of the burning bush.

He who dies alive into the *nada* — the sound eternal — will have his mental processes quieten themselves into a void, and his mind will get free from all pollutions.

Worship your Lord — the abode and giver of supreme blessedness, and propitiate Him in your own house alone — in this mortal frame!

The suffering that burnt you, life after life, will have its end when you behold the flame that burns within the navel.

The dazzling splendour that shines within the navel is bliss supreme—bliss that bestows itself only on those that are humble and lowly.

A fragrance emanates from within and sends a thrill in each and every pore of my body. I hear a sound without words that makes me go mad in ecstasy. For I am all blessed — blessed to have reached the very goal of life's pilgrimage.

Come out, you disputants,
you both Pandit and Qazi
and find out and explain
What is the nature of this inner treasure?

The Word of wondrous tunes
thunders out without pause and end
But who will force open the shop
that has this treasure?

The Word alone is the Essence,
The Word alone is the abode of joy—
The Word that thunders high on the Mountain top

But the Qazi, Mullah and the Pandit
do not know it—
the glory that shines within their
own mortal frame.

Only he who is exclusively guru-oriented knows It
he who treads the path reverse
shall hear the Word—
The Word that is one with Brahman,
The Absolute.
He loses himself unto himself
and sees that
that others see not.

Who will show the path
traversed by a bird?

Only he whose thoughts are solely
oriented towards the Guru
will find the secret of Nirvana.

The undying flame has appeared
in my mortal body;

He who sees it will have
his longings appeased for ever.

The Word vibrates in my body
telling a tale that can't be told.
The mind of the man
who sees the Truth Eternal
shall verily become stable
Thus says "Mangat".

The flow of words came to a stop and Gurudeva came back to what we, who seek to live in the phenomenal world, call or miscall 'normal consciousness'. He merely asked Bhagatji to go to bed and read out in the morning what he had taken down, and went into *samadhi*. That, Bhagatji soon found out, was his normal practice, to go into the silence of *samadhi* after the creative energy of revelatory words had spent itself out in utterance. Next day, however, he would ask Bhagatji to read out the verses just to satisfy his curiosity about the content of those verses — for during the time of dictation he was not conscious of what he uttered. In this respect, the following conversation is quite revealing.

Devotee: Lord, the divine utterance flows out mostly in Hindi, whereas you never learnt this language; you learnt only Urdu.

Gurudeva: Words come out as my God wills. 'We' ourselves are surprised whenever you read them out, for 'This' does not know when a particular verse was uttered, nor does 'It' know whether it was the 'right' sort of thing or not. Premi, 'It' has no choice or will of 'Its' own. Stern, indeed, is the command of my Lord! 'It' has to say what He wills 'It' to say. It is for the good of the living beings that the Eternal Word is revealing Itself in words. My Lord's grace manifests itself in accordance with the needs of time and place. It can descend as easily or spontaneously in Sanskrit or English as in Hindi. But 'It' has no option but to present unto you whatever is flowing out on its own. Preserve it if you like it! In the near future, the country will evolve this kind of simple language. The mixture of dialects that you find in the *vani* (utterance) is in accord with the ability of the common people. Seers always give instructions to people in the language they use and understand. And such seers are born in every time and clime. Do not think that Muhammad was the last prophet and the (Sikh) gurus were the last gurus. Divine glory will ever manifest whenever people give up righteousness and give themselves up to unrighteousness — whenever they come under the grip of *rajas* and *tamas*, of the desire to acquire and enjoy the pleasures of the world and get entangled in them. The voice of divine beings does not fail to reach the good people howsoever remote be the place they live in. For their voice intermingles with the atmosphere that envelops the earth and finds its way into the heart of the good—unobtrusively and without their conscious knowledge. And the good people, under its influence, do good to the world at large. The thought of *samata* (sameness) has reappeared in a new form in this *vani*. It will influence humanity in due course of time — not now. It is only those who are established in Truth that can awaken the world to righteousness. The country that deviates from *samata* will not survive nor will the laws that do not accord with the thought of *samata* do any good to humanity.

Another conversation regarding the manifestation of *vani* should also prove instructive.

Devotee: How is it, Lord, that when you utter the divine speech, you do it continuously and uninterruptedly, and in a few minutes speak out many verse-paragraphs, but while correcting a small mistake (I inadvertently commit while scribing it) you take as much as two or three minutes!

Gurudeva: When divine rapture pours itself out the intellect comes to be inoperative — does not think in terms of the dualities of right or wrong. In that state of wakefulness, no wrong word can possibly be uttered. Only your carelessness or inadvertence causes certain mistakes to creep in. Only he who has realized the blissful state within can know what that freedom from (right or wrong) thinking is. It is only when the intellect gets outwardly oriented and merges out of the state of oneness with-the-real that it starts thinking about linguistic or other problems. When the intellect is merged into the Word, right thoughts rise up spontaneously and without thought-activity, the revelatory words rush out on their own. Nothing remains concealed in that state — neither the world nor its Creator. Hidden secrets reveal themselves out — with absolute

> clarity...Only that thought that leads humanity to blessedness is revealed by those who become one with Truth...

'There the Eternal Word alone exists':

Gurudeva describes the state of Oneness absolutely free from all dualities; there the non-dual infinite Reality — the Eternal Word — alone exists. None but one who has experienced that wondrous state of spiritual ecstasy could reveal thus:

> "There neither is the earth nor the sky. Neither is there air nor water. Neither are there divine beings nor incarnations. Neither are there sacred scriptures nor the reflective knowledge. There is neither the meditator nor the meditation. There the Eternal Word alone exists.
>
> There is neither the light of the sun nor of the moon. Neither exists there perceptible nor concrete object.
>
> Neither is there the circuit of coming into being nor of passing away of being. There the Light of Nirvana alone exists.
>
> There is neither Brahma or Vishnu nor Mahesh. Neither is there Gauri or Ganesh nor Shesha. There is neither the speaker nor the one to whom one can speak. There the non-dual infinite Reality alone exists.
>
> There is neither the Lord nor the servant. Neither is there disciple nor the teacher (guru). Neither is there the whirlpool of one and two. There the Silent Word alone exists.
>
> There is neither the creator nor the created. Neither is there the seer nor the seen. There Reality as fullness alone is to be found. This gnosis of Nirvana alone is written there.
>
> There one contemplates without eyes. There one tastes Bliss without ecstasy. There the entire creation is seen one and the same. Those know it who have found it.

> There one neither has a friend nor an enemy. Neither is there profit nor loss. Neither is there anger nor attachment. Neither does there anyone grow or decrease.
>
> There exists not the difference between freedom and bondage. There neither is the agent who acts nor the crevices of Time. There the Sovereign and Pure Essence alone exists. There the unstruck non-dual Sound alone pervades.
>
> There is neither the front nor the behind. None is there either high or low. None is there either rich or poor. There esteem or honour exists not.
>
> There exists not the whirlpool of one and two. Fullness alone pervades there, "Mangat" recognized the Word— the ultimate state of Redemption."

('The Silent Logos')

More about the Word:

While concluding this section, I could not do better than quote a few statements of Mahatma Mangat Ram on the significance of the Word, its knowledge and attainment. Granth Samata Prakash is full of hundreds of verses on and about Shabad Braham — the Word, and *Nad* the celestial sound. Both are the same.

> The indwelling Word is known only to the knowers of the Self. All the sacred scriptures (of all religions) — the Vedas, the Quran and the Bible — sing praise and glory of the eternal sound.
>
> When the intellect deepens its interiority, it becomes aware of the Word, and through the knowledge it completely disassociates itself from the pleasures of sense organs.
>
> The immortal Word resounds in each pore of the body. One who regulates inhalation and exhalation, in a rhythm — smooth and soft — hears the unstruck sound within.

It is this mystical Verbum Divinum, the transcendent sound, which is the Reality.

मन को जब अत निर्मल किया। अवनाशी शबद का भेद तब लिया।।

When the mind is absolutely pure, the immortal Word is uncovered within.

अत निर्मल जब बुद्ध हुई, सकल कल्पना त्याग।
"मंगत" पाया नाद को, जो गत अत विस्माद।।

When the intellect becomes extremely pure, abandoning all thoughts, an utterly astounding 'sound' (*nad*) is heard within, observes "Mangat".

जब लग करम ना निर्मल होई। तब लग शबद ना परसे कोई।।

None can perceive the Word within
unless one's actions are rendered clean.

That eternal and imperishable Word alone illumines everything; by the knowing of which everything is known.

A mind established in itself tastes the secret essence of the Word.

साचे जतन को धार के जो खोजे देहका कोट।
"मंगत" नेहचल ध्यान में, पाये अखण्ड तत्त जोत।।

One who searches rightly inside the body frame, will, in steady contemplation, find the resplendent, indivisible Word, says "Mangat".

(Note: We shall briefly talk of the technique of search at the end of this chapter.)

अन्तर बाहर एक परीती, शबद अखण्ड किलकारी।
सत् साजन सब भेद पछाता, बिन मद रहे मतवारी।।

A godly person knows the secret — that of listening to the perfect Word's sound of joy with love — within and outside, and thus remaining intoxicated without wine.

अवनाशी शब्द पहचानया जो सरब शकत निधान।
"मंगत" तिस की सेव से जीव पाए कल्यान।।

On recognition of the immortal Word — the treasure of all power — and its contemplation, one attains blessedness, says "Mangat"

Meditation:

Meditation is an individual relationship of the soul with the Father.

Mahatma Mangat Ram whose whole life was one long uninterrupted meditation says:

"Meditation is to perceive God as causative of all actions, to meditate on Him with firm faith, to see all happenings and non-happenings in His will, from moment to moment, and to focus the mind within on the Absolute Life-force. In meditation the intellect perceiving the Absolute within the body, merges with the same."

"Watching the movement of the breath and recounting silently (without movement of lips or tongue) the true *Name,* along with it, one can perceive within the limitless everpresent, inner being in the form of resonant Word. Saying the rosary, counting the beads is not necessary. The life-force — without beginning and end, which is pure conscious radiance, ever detached from five-element body, mind and intellect — is the real object of remembrance and contemplation."

"From contemplation and unitive knowledge of this real self — in the form of the eternal Word — through pure intellect, bodily strength and true faith, spring supreme purity and peace."

(Samata Vilas)

We shall go over the Yoga of Samata and its technique, briefly, after a few general observations on meditation:

> Meditation involves a type of inner attention, that is quiet, concentrated and at the same time relaxed inner dimension.
>
> The state of consciousness in which 'i' (small) knows 'I' (big) is called meditation.
>
> Meditation is an inward way of fathoming all levels of consciousness.
>
> Meditation is life force aware of itself.
>
> Meditation opens the mind to grow by putting away curtains of ego.

"Meditation is a state of mind in which there is no concept or formula, and therefore total freedom. In this state there is complete peace, peace that has order, beauty and intensity...Meditation opens the way to the incalculable, the unlimited", as J. Krishnamurti puts it.

Some of his further highly inspiring words are:

> "To us, the little space made by thought around itself, which is the *me*, is extremely important, for this is all the mind knows, identifying itself with everything that is in that space.
>
> In this little space all our activities seem to take place: the daily living and the hidden struggle with contradictory desires and motives. In this little space the mind seeks freedom, and so it is always a prisoner of itself.
>
> Meditation is the ending of this little space. Meditation is action which comes when the mind has lost its little space. This vast space, which the mind, the I, cannot reach, is silence. The mind can never be silent within itself; it is silent only within the vast space which thought cannot touch. Meditation is this silence."

'Remember your Lord deep in your soul with humility and awe and without ostentation: (remember Him) morning and evening and do not be negligent', says the Quran. All time is meditation time. But both dawn and dusk — 'the junction periods' — according to the tradition of Yogis, when spiritual forces are particularly active in our planet's atmosphere, are the best times for meditation. The chief requisites for meditation are solitude, quietness, proper surroundings and healthy environment.

Even in our active life generally saints would advise 2½ hours a day to be given to meditation. (10% of time and 10% of income, they suggest, must be earmarked for meditation and charity, as a good rule of life.) While one must be regular in meditation and meditate for as long as one can find time, the number of hours spent on meditation is no proof of spiritual progress. 'It is proof of your progress when you no longer have to make an effort to meditate', says the Mother. It is the quality and not quantity of meditation that is important, though saints have advised spending of more and more time in meditation as we grow older. In my personal view remembering the Divine should not be done as a severe discipline or duty. Meditation is done for our own good and not for impressing other people. It must be a movement of love and joy; not as a matter of compulsion or mere routine. Then, very soon a stage will come when, if we do not feel the presence of Divine at every moment and during whatever we are doing, we feel at once lonely, sad and miserable.

Holy Mother, wife of Paramahansa Ramakrishna, says:

> 'To pray to God and meditate on Him for even two minutes with full concentration is better than doing so for long hours without it...Practise meditation and by and by your mind will be so calm and fixed that you will find it hard to keep away from meditation...A single utterance of the Lord's name is as effective as a million

> repetitions of it, if only you do it with a steady, concentrated mind. What is the use of repeating a million times with an absent mind? You must do this wholeheartedly. Then only can you deserve His grace.'

Ramana Maharishi preached: "Find out wherefrom the 'I' springs and merge it at its source, that is *tapas* (penance). Find out wherefrom the sound of the *mantra* (hymn) in *japa* (silent repetition) arises and merge there, that is *tapas*. When the mind is anchored in the heart, true *tapes* takes place.

> "Who am I? and whence am I?" should be a perennial self-enquiry, an end in itself which does not call for an answer."

Once we master the art of maintaining meditative mood it can be made to remain like that even when we go about our work. Only such thoughts as are essential to perform it occupy the mind; no residual thoughts are left after the act, the saint observes.

According to Shirdi Sai Baba: 'Real meditation is to lose one's false individuality into the ocean of cosmic Divine Personality. It is the feeling of a 'drop of life' as belonging to the 'ocean of existence'. When we truly meditate the 'I' just disappears.'

Meditation, according to Maharishi Mahesh Yogi, is a process to experience the subtle state of thought and arrive at the source of thought — the field of infinite energy and intelligence.

'Meditation is that technique which brings our mind from the surface of life to the depth of our Being.' He further says that 'Scientific research on Transcendental Meditation (TM) had revealed several important features of the nature of enlightenment and the process through which it is gained.'

It (TM), according to the Maharishi, is something real, natural and tangible and develops systematically in a continuous and progressive manner, on the basis of neurophysiological refinement or purification.

'Meditation helps the individual develop physically, intellectually and spiritually. It provides deep relaxation to the body and helps reduce stress and tension. Concentration increases mental abilities. Spiritually one gains insight into the meaning of life. It increases the functional integrity and the orderliness of one's body and mind, offers that knowledge and experience which develops stability, adaptability, integration, purification and growth on all four levels of life, physiological, psychological, sociological and ecological.'

Let us also remove a misconception. In meditation we do not try to get peace but we are trying to give up our ego-supports and most of our desires. Peace and happiness come only when we have shed the bondage of ego delusion.

On the question of object or idea for meditation, Shabad Braham is always the best object for meditation or concentration and the idea on which the mind should fix is that of God in all, all in God and all as God.

Shankaracharya says:

> 'The wise man should, at all times, meditate, attentively upon his own self which, though unseen, is yet the only reality and though manifest as the external universe, is yet of the nature of subjective consciousness.'

Mahatma Mangat Ram reiterates his observations in short pithy sentences like:

अपने आप में आप को चीना।

Perceived my real self in my own self.

अपना आप जाप पुनीत।

Meditate on the Self in your self.

Such deep lessons could not be stated in simpler words!

Here is another pungent Urdu verse from Dr. Iqbal regarding meditative search:

ڈھونڈتا پھرتا ہوں میں اقبال اپنے آپ کو
آپ ہی کھویا مسافر آپ ہی منزل ہوں میں

Dhundta phirta hun main Iqbal apne ap ko,
Ap he khoya musafir ap he manzil hun mein.

I am trying to search my own self, says Iqbal.
I am a lost traveller, while I myself am the destination.

A problem! Friends often ask how to get rid of thoughts which come, rather forcefully, while sitting in meditation. Vivekananda has suggested a nice way in Raja Yoga. He says:

> 'Look at the thoughts and just observe what is the nature of human mind as they show it but do not give any sanction and let them run down till they come to a standstill.'

To wrestle with the mind to make it quiet is not of much use. We can train the mind to be quiet by not involving itself in its thoughts, let it stand back, detach itself, let the thoughts pass, without identifying itself, without making them its own. It should become the witness mind watching the thoughts when necessary, but able to turn away from them.

A friend of mine, late Gumnam Sahib, used to say that he lets thoughts come and disposes them off quickly, one by one, requesting them to leave him alone. This was found very helpful. I have tried this and fairly successfully, also another method: just penning down, very briefly in the beginning, the ideas or thoughts that come (generally of persons to meet or things to do) in a little notebook, kept by the side. The thoughts thus get fixed up after taken note of (to be attended to after meditation). This helps; the thoughts no more disturb meditation.

'When one tries to meditate there is a pressure to go inside, in a deep inner consciousness. But at first the mind takes it as a pressure to go to sleep, since sleep is the only kind of inner consciousness to which it is accustomed. This difficulty can be overcome if one perseveres — then gradually sleep changes to an inner conscious state.'

Post-meditative hours:

While concluding these general statements on meditation I would like to quote Vivekananda again when he says:

> 'What good is it, if we acknowledge in our prayers that God is the Father of us all, and in our daily lives do not treat every man as our brother?'

And, late Sadhu T.L. Vaswani, a modern saint of great repute, observes:

> 'The Great God is in the procession of life. Greet Him there! You will not find Him in the temples of marble and stone. You will meet Him in the sweat and struggle of life, in the tears and tragedies in the person.'
>
> 'Do good, Be good, See Good.
> This is the way to God.'

Our general conduct is immensely important. Meditation must bring visible change in our mind and the way we conduct ourselves in our daily life. In fact meditation is no meditation unless it is able to bring a welcome influence on the mind and its working during our non-meditation hours. That atmosphere of bliss which one builds by meditation should remain with us the whole day to help us face the ups and downs of life without losing our balance.

The Yoga of Samata:

Based briefly and respectfully on Gurudev's recorded guidance in *sadhna* (spiritual practice):

The first step is that of *simran* — recollection or repetition of the Lord's Name; the second state, *bhajan*, is characterized by devotion and worship; the third state *dhyan* is towards concentration and absorption, and the fourth one leads to the state of *samadhi*, that is the state of unity with the

Divine. One who takes to *dhyan* direct without first being steadfast in *simran* cannot easily get settled in *dhyan*.

- **The first step** on the ladder of spirituality for the equipoise of intellect/mind, that is, absorption in the bliss of the Self, is *simran* — the recollection of the Name of the Lord, in the recesses of the heart, lips and tongue being tightly closed.

Concentration of mind is necessary for recollection; freedom from thought waves helps this process. A pure mind alone can attain this state. And to be pure in mind it is necessary to be pure in food, in behaviour and association.

Freedom from the phenomenal pain of unreal imagination shall not be there unless the mind orientates itself towards the recollection of the Name of the Lord. Peace manifests itself when the mind, by discarding the illusory names and forms of imagination, establishes itself, with hope and love, in the ever-existent Name.

The control of mind is essential. An uncontrolled mind shall never be able to attune itself to the Name. With absorption in the Name of the Lord, the mind moves from the love of objects towards the love of God, and thereby all activities are viewed from the perspective of selflessness.

When the state of selflessness is reached, the buds of pure devotion begin to sprout in the heart. Such a noble feeling only blesses life. One who is desirous of the state of blessedness must, before anything else, follow the path of recollection of the Name.

The method of recollection needs to be followed correctly. That is, some recollect the Name with the help of beads, some recite the Name in a high tone, whereas others sing the Name. All these methods do give some kind of mental satisfaction, but the real peace of mind can be realized through unwavering recollection, totally fixed within, in complete introversion. The method and effort both must be right. The real way of recollection is that which unites the mind and breath in perfect inhalation and exhalation.

One attains, through recollection of the Name, the Nameless State, that is, the state of immersion in the indivisible Word. It is, therefore, essential to have faith in the Name.

The perfected ones (sages and saints) have projected many Names concerning the Absolute — but for spiritual practice a single Name (Seed Word) is beneficial and effective (preferably the one received from a true Guru).

Gurudev has rightly advised to be beware of those who speak of inwardness (repeating what the *faqirs* have spoken) without experiencing this state, nor even endeavouring to realize the state of blessedness. Through their exhibitionism, they are interested only in spreading the tentacles of 'gurudom', he observes. 'Go unto them who are really men of God, for they shall bless you with right guidance.'

We must remember that 'the Ultimate Word' is One, its conditions or states are many. To the extent one passes through these conditions, to that extent the state of inwardness is intensified...'Concentrate on the Name with integrated mind and body. Give up your doership. See the presence of the Lord in everything and lovingly remember Him. It is this attitude that brings blessings in life. All the impurities of (even) past lives are washed away. A person given to such recollection experiences within the Word Absolute.'

- **The second state: Bhajan (devotion)**: It is the condition in which there is experience of the Absolute Word and the mind completely concentrates on it. In this state the nectar of God's love is drunk and the mind hankers not after worldly pleasures.

Withdrawing itself from the things of the world, the mind orientates itself towards the Eternal Word, experiencing its various dimensions and aspects. In this state everything is seen in terms of Divine Will, and there is negation of self-ego.

It is above the lower part of the body, at the root of nose, in the middle of forehead (between the eyebrows) that the intellect experiences the Word.

If a spiritual practitioner exposes this state or tries to show miracles, he shall be deprived of Divine Bliss.

To the extent stability in this spiritual practice is achieved, the luminosity of the Reality within is experienced progressively. With freedom from bodily wants, the soul remains merged in the love of God. A person of this state must cultivate such qualities as forgiveness, mercy, patience, humility, selflessness etc...Much time must be spent in remembrance of the Lord, with less of food, less of sleep and less of worldly business.

'Absorb in that bliss that results from devotion, move in the world with modesty, have more love in remembrance of God than in things of the world', advises Gurudev.

- **The third stage: Dhyan (contemplation)**: This is the state when the mind, leaving aside all concepts and designs, gets absorbed in the Absolute Word and experiences only the bliss supreme.

'Stabilised in the experience of the Absolute Word, one hears internally tunes of various types, sees lightning within, cuts oneself asunder from the world. All actions are surrendered to will of the Lord, maintains equanimity towards diverse fruits of action, and lives a very natural life, without desires.'

One established in this state is a *yogi*. He is a true knower. His mind is away from wants and plans; he stays with his real self. He envies none, rather loves all.

'With steadfastness in contemplation one hears within indivisible Word rather loudly. He sees the whole world as the reflection of the Supreme Light. Nothing attracts him except Name of the Lord.'

Contemplation of God is the real blessing. It comes on giving up all desires. There has to be complete surrender to

God's will...No one in this state should be inclined to show any miracle.

When longing for all actions (for self) dies, and one dedicates his life to helping others, considering the whole world as God's manifestation, himself with a sense of non-doership and stable in bliss, such a composed, patient person has reached the state of *Samadhi*.

- **The fourth stage: Samadhi (enstatis)**: In this state of concentration all consciousness of the outer world is transcended; the intellect immerses itself in the eternal Word of the Absolute and all the ego-related fantasies come to an end. It is a state of experience in which luminous Consciousness alone is known.

The one who has achieved this Transcendent state of being, experiences nothing but the Absolute. He is the knower of the Brahman, remains established in the eternal Sound of the Absolute. Sees the whole world as manifestation of the Lord.

He maintains perfect equanimity in all circumstances, above the polarity of pain and pleasure. Within him is total renunciation. It is the state in which one remains immersed in one's essence.

One who has, through *tapas* (penance), established firmly himself in the Lord and has, by going inward, ruptured all association with the objective world — such a person achieves the condition of non-duality that is characterized by pure luminosity.

That person alone finds himself established in the Sound Absolute who, all the time, perceives body to be perishable and who, having realized freedom from the desires of the body, remains engrossed in contemplation of Self.

Only that person will attain the state of enstatis who considers indivisible and imperishable Reality to be the substratum of everything.

Summary: Be selfless in your devotion to God. Be firm in your faith in God. Resolve that you will serve all creatures with a selfless mind. Give up the luxuries of the world. Recognize that everything belongs to God. With a firm mind engage in the recollection of the Lord. Those who follow such a path obtain real devotion, faith, concentration and *samadhi*. Therefore, lead a pure life so that, while living, you may be able to cut asunder the knots of bondage.

On Technique:

Meditation is an individual, rather personal, approach towards unity with God. One may select and adopt the best way, as suits one. However, scriptures, saints and sages have, directly and indirectly, laid down certain guidelines for facility of the seekers. Mahatma Mangat Ram, in direct communion with the Supreme Being from childhood, knew the way — simple and straight. He could show it precisely with unbelievable clarity and conviction. One has, however, to traverse oneself all the way, no short cuts or 'lifts' to the destination.

Gurudev has given several hints on the way to meditate as recorded in Granth Samata Prakash, especially its section Yog Chintamani. He has described the technique of meditation in some detail and clear terms, in his letters to his premier disciple, late Sant Rattan Das (associated lifetime with Kabir Panth).

Before moving to technique, let us go over a few general but precious bits of Gurudev's advice of preparatory nature:

> अनहुआ और जो हुआ, प्रभ आज्ञा में पेख।
> बुद्धि होवे सुतन्तर, सत सिमरन परसे लेख।।

> True remembrance of the Lord is possible when the intellect is free; it treats all that happens or does not happen, as the will of God.

जब आहार सूक्ष्म व शुद्ध, और व्यौहार शुद्ध मर्यादा युक्त, और संगत केवल सत्पुरुषों की, और स्वाध्याय केवल सत्पुरुषों के जीवन का धारण किया जाता है, तब एक नाम चिन्तन में दृढ़ता प्राप्त होती है।

Simple and pure food, clean and regulated conduct of life, society of pious persons, and study of the lives of the truly great ones, help in attaining steadfastness in contemplation of the Lord.

अधिक से अधिक समय जब नाम चिन्तन में ही दिया जाता है और तमाम लौकिक व्यौहार सूक्ष्म मर्यादा का धारण किया जाता है तब बुद्धि नाम परायण हो करके तमाम शारीरिक विकारों की आसक्ति से निर्बन्ध हो जाती है और अन्तर में सत् सरूप के बोध को प्राप्त होती है, ऐसी दृढ़ता को ही परम तपस्या कहा गया है।

When more and more time is devoted to the contemplation of the Lord and worldly dealings are restricted to the bare necessary level, the intellect anchored on (Lord's) Name gets out of the hold of all physical perversities. And, inwardly recognizes the presence of the True, the real Self. Such steadfastness alone is called great penance.

Based on Gurudev's advice and with his blessings, I am daring to share with readers very brief hints on the technique of meditation. They are requested to read this part rather seriously and with due reverence only if interested. The narration is not made with any intention to teach or propagate the technique. On the contrary it is just sharing, in utter humility, with dear co-aspirants — one in Atmān — something superbly sacred and extremely valuable.

- Sit (on the ground) on a simple *asan*, be it of shrub leaves, soft weeds or reeds, a clean carpet piece or any other pure spread. Sit in any pose you comfortably can. If you feel tired in sitting at a stretch in a particular pose, for an hour or so, you may change the posture but keep the back and chest straight, in any case.

- Breathe comfortably; inhale and exhale peacefully.
- Carry, along with the breath, the Name (of the Lord) from the tip of the nose to the centre of the navel gently, and after a small comfortable rest-pause there, do the same thing, repeating the Name in reverse syllables, on the return journey of the breath. The air we breathe in is fresh and cool, while the outgoing is warm.
- Do not puff up the belly unnecessarily with ingoing breath, nor strain yourself with the outgoing breath. Let it all be as natural a process as possible.
- Breath is the carrier of *prana,* the subtle life-force which pervades the whole body. Attention has to be focussed on this subtle element/essence, joining it with the Name, thus combining the three — the delicate *prana,* the complete *surat* (mindful attention) and the adopted Name. This triad — this sacred trinity — is the secret of Yoga. (In advanced state of meditation attention is focussed on the point between the two eyes, root of the nose.)
- This auspicious combination, when regularly practised, makes the movement of the breath balanced and deep, as well as sufficiently slow, without effort.
- When this practice becomes mature and firm, it leads to the opening of the Kundalini (rising of the latent force, coiled at the base of the spinal cord) automatically. One also overcomes sleep, indolence, appetite and thirst.

What is the experience like as per Gurudev's observations:

- Firstly the Word—*Shabad/Anahad* (unstruck heavenly sound) is heard internally, at the navel point (that is the beginning of *Simran*). It reaches the throat with practice (that is the beginning of *Bhajan*); later it resounds at *Trikuti* — centre point between the two eyes (then it is the starting of *Dhyana*)—leading to total contemplation in advanced stages of concentration. Last it gets dissolved in *Kapal*, top of the head. This is *Samadhi*. The intellect then gets absorbed in the *Braham* — the Divine in us. Complete void — *Shunia* or *Sunn* — prevails there. A deep, deep silence with its own sound and light! (This is enlightenment.)

While the sacred Name imparted by Gurudev is a sanctified secret — and can be disclosed only by a competent, spiritually realized and authorised person — Gurudev has observed that the Mahamantra (given in the beginning of the book and universally initiated) as revealed to him by God, is infused with tremendous spiritual force. Its remembrance can help anyone on the spiritual path. (We may draw a parallel here with Gayatri Mantra of Vedic origin which too is known for its great potency.)

The Mahamantra comprising thirteen sacred words — when recounted silently and devotedly in the depth of the heart — unfolds in the aspirant an untold treasure of spiritual wealth and ensures all-round achievement and success.

Given below are a few selected God-inspired verses from Granth Samata Prakash (Hindi) outlining valuable hints of Gurudev on the technique of meditation:

प्रथमे आसन सहजे बांधे। इन्द्री इस्थिर मनुआ सॉडे।।
मुख नैन जीभा को बांधे। साचा नाम हिये में साधे।।

Firstly sit straight as convenient,
and stabilize the mind and senses.
Keep mouth and eyes closed and tongue motionless,
recalling the true Name (seed Word) within.

धीरे धीरे पवन को पीवे। शुद्ध ध्यान में नाम जपीवे।।

The breathing should be as slow, steady and effortless as possible, and the sacred Name blended with the flow of breath in and out with unflickering concentration.

बारह सोलह पवन की गमता, सम कर पावे तत्त समता।

The movement ratio between outgoing and incoming breath is 12 and 16 (measurement in figures put together). Their balancing helps attain state of 'sameness'.

अन्तर जाये नाम के थाँइ। वहां से पलट बाहर को आँइ।।

While inhaling let the impulse — alongwith the name— go to the centre of the navel and the exhalation process will start from there.

मुल द्वार में पवन को बांधे। साचा नाम निरन्तर सांधे।।

Hold the breath (for a little while) at the navel centre, recalling the true Name, throughout.

स्वास सुरत जब एका होई। शबद ब्रहम तब घट प्रगटोई।।

When the breath and *surat* (conscious attention) are combined, that is the first experience of the Word (Primordial Sound).

स्वास सुरत मिल किया हलोल। नाभी अस्थान में पाई कलोल।।

When breath and *surat* are in conjunction, vibrations are generated and one experiences sensation of reverberating sound at the navel centre.

नाभ कंवल परगासया, शबद सुनी टंकोर।
"मंगत" चला निज धाम को, छोड़ कलपना शोर।।

The navel 'lotus' lights up and twang of the Word is heard. One starts on the journey to own real abode, leaving behind the uproar of thoughts/conceptions.

स्वास सुरत को पल पल जोड़े। अगम शब्द का चढ़े सरूरे।।

As one joins attention to the flow of breath from moment to moment, one experiences ecstasy of the Word (Radiant Resonance).

घर में स्वासा नित गुंजारे। भेद को बुझे उतरे पारे।।

The breath resounds within all the time. Understanding this secret leads to crossing over. (Success achieving/emancipation.)

ब्रह्म सरूपनी ये पवन विचार। ज्ञान ध्यान का पुरन भण्डार।।

The air we breathe is manifestation of *Braham* — the Supreme Being; indeed full treasure of spiritual knowledge and contemplation.

In part-conclusion:

स्वास गति की गत लखे, ध्याये नाम तत्तसार।
"मंगत" परगट पाइये, तब साखी शब्द आपार।।

Watch the movement of breath and repeat the Name (of the Lord) alongwith it. Then the Limitless, Everpresent/ Ever-witnessing will be perceived within.

स्वास सुरत एका भया, मनसा भई लवलीन।
"मंगत" शबद परगासया, कोट भान छबी चीन।।

When breath and attention are joined together and the mind merges with them, the resonant Word — with brilliance of billions of suns — shines within, says "Mangat".

बूझ शबद मन मगन समाए। होए निरास परम पद पाए।।
तिस ते परे न कोई योग। मन पवना शबद रस भोग।।

On hearing the Word, the mind is drowned in delight; rising above desires it achieves a state supreme. There is no Yoga beyond it; enjoy the essence arising from the togetherness of the mind, breath and the *Word.*

Ida, Pingala, Sukhmana, Chakras and Kundalini:

पवन की धारा में सुरत लगावे। नागन सोई सहज को जगावे।।

As one focusses attention on the track of breath within, the dormant coiled channel (Kundalini) is easily activated.

इड़ा पिंगला सुखमन नाली। तीनों मिले उपर तिरनाली।।

Ida, Pingala and Sukhmana (the right, left and central channels) meet above the point between the two eye-brows.*

इड़ा पिंगला मथकर लीजे। सुखमन माहीं पवन भरीजे।।

On stirring the exhalation and inhalation, the Sukhmana, the central channel, gets filled up with air.

**Note*: *Nadis* have been interpreted as psychic (astral) nerves in the subtle body. These have been compared by Indian medical doctors to the vagus nerves in the human body which control the voluntary and involuntary nervous systems.

Sushmna (Susumna or Sukhmana) is the main *nadi* in the very centre of the spine. It is the passage through which Kundalini Energy rises.

The two ganglionic chains — main *Nadis* — are on either side of the spinal cord: *Ida* on the left and *Pingala* on the right — also called *Chandra* (moon or cool) and *Surya* (sun or hot) *Nadi* respectively.

In the portion of the body below the throat — called *pind* — there are two types of currents, the incoming breath is cool while the outgoing is hot, their respective proportion being 16 and 12 'fingers' (a sort of measure). This indicates a pair of opposites which has to be balanced. (Control of breath is a science by itself.)

सुखमन नाली में पवन भरीजे। उमग नाद माया गढ़ छीजे।।

With the Sukhmana filled with air, the primordial Resonance will then rise up and break open the fort of illusion.

मन पवन जब मेला होए। सुखमन बोले गगन घर जाए।।

When the mind and breath mingle into one, the reverberating sound rises through the Sukhmana to the top of the head where it resounds.

षट चक्रन को नाद प्रभ छेदे। चढ़े आकास तिरकुटी को भेदे।।

The sound primordial while going up pierces through six *chakras* (plexuses), and passing through *trikuti* (the mid centre of the two eyes) it goes up the apex of head.

(Note: The six chakras mentioned here are: Muldhara, Swadisthan, Manipur, Anahata, Visudha, Ajna. For details please see Annexure II.)

Elixir:

नाभ कमल से अमरत झरया। सुखमन नाली में सो भरया।।

From the navel centre (likened to a lotus) elixir drops and gets filled in the *Sukhmana.*

उलट पवन का लंगर खेंचे। सोती नागन उठ अमरत सेंचे।।

When the breath is going out let it pull up the base (of spinal cord) squeezing the navel centre (comfortably), thus the dormant serpent power will get activated and release the flow of elixir.

अमरत कुमभ अगम घर फूटा।
अत परकाश जोत अनूपा।।

In the unfathomable interior burst 'the pot' containing elixir; (emitting) light of nonpareil brilliancy.

Note: At another place in the Granth there is mention of *amrit* (elixir) flowing:

वाह वाह अमरत झर रहा
कोई गुरमुख पान करे

Hail to the elixir flowing,
a rare guru-oriented person can drink it.

(Evidently there is a mysterious connection between the source, its pumping up, its storage and then its pouring down. It seems a symbolic description of something highly precious within us of which we are oblivious. Only a highly realized Yogi could possibly experience and explain it.)

सुखमन खुली शब्द घर जागा। साध सीख पाई बड़भागा।।

On opening of *Sukhmana* the Word awakens (becomes more perceptible) within. One is fortunate in achieving this state, following the advice of some Realized soul.

सहेस हजार दल कँवल परगासा। अखंड संग सुरत बिलासा।।

Thousands petalled lotus (top of the head) blooms up; *surat* (conscious attention) plays with *nad* (celestial sound).

A glimpse of the Final State of Bliss:

जाप अजपा होए दिन रात। अखण्ड नाद मन माहीं समात।।

The automatic reverberation of the unbroken primordial Divine Sound (*Nad*) within goes on day and night; it remains constantly perceptible, permeating the mind completely.

नाद निरत में सुरत समाई। भरम त्याग निर्वान पद पाई।।

Consciousness loses itself in the throb of primordial resonance and one attains emancipation, shedding off all illusions.

आसन धरती सुरत आकासे। लखे ज्ञान निरवानी।।
उपजे शब्द जोत दरसाये, सुरत भई अकलानी।।

While seated on earth, with *Surat* (conscious attention) focussed in the *Kapal* (the top of the head), one experiences knowledge of emancipation, as the Divine Word arises, and there is intense radiance. In this state the individual consciousness merges with the universal consciousness.

सुरत समाई शब्द में, चढ़ी सुन्न के देस।
"मंगत" नजरी आया आद पुरख जगदीश।।

Surat on absorption in Divine radiant resonance rises to the zone of dead silence (inside head). Then the Creator, Lord of the Universe, is visible, says "Mangat".

अन्तर शब्द पहचान के मनुआ शून समाई।
"मंगत" निज सरूप में, परम आनन्द को पाई।।

On recognizing the Word within, the mind enters the state of void — complete silence. Thus is our true-self, full of immense bliss, says "Mangat".

CHAPTER 8

Oneness — Theory and Practice

Samata (equality; sameness):

समता अखण्ड शान्ति कुल विघ्न दोख से न्यार।
"मंगत" रूप नारायण का तत्त्व समता विचार।।

'Samata is peace supreme — above all impediments and inflictions. Consider the essence of Samata as the very complexion of the Supreme Being', says "Mangat".

As the greatest exponent of *samata* — sameness, oneness — in recent times, Mahatma Mangat Ram has described it copiously in his two Granths (holy books) Samata Prakash and Samata Vilas. The God-inspired verses and prose sayings of this great saint of modern times admit us to the nature of being itself. We are enabled to see deeper than fractionalism and disharmony. Revelation and doctrine converge on a single focus: *samata* the point where differences and duality drop.

Samata: Oneness, single and undivided. A state where finite melts into infinite. This was the accomplishment of Mahatma Mangat Ram. And the way to it lies in his example: an exquisite humility, fearless and undesiring. A reverence for oneness that underlies all the apparent clutter of the many. This, and selflessness: wherever anguish, distress and poverty are to be found.

Samata, oneness, non-duality, refers to a state of peace, fullness, perfection and abiding happiness. This state is possible when one knows one's reality, the real Self. It is a condition beyond all modes and qualities, impassive, free and tranquil. In this state, as the Gita suggests, duality disappears; duality of all kinds: pleasure and pain, friend and foe, me and you, mine and thine, loss or gain. One treats all alike.

Let me share with the readers some of the sayings of Mahatma Mangat Ram on the state of *samata*, its significance and spread:

- Samata alone is bliss and every creature within is desirous of this state.
- The light of oneness shines in each and every being, but due to the ego-centred mind it remains hidden.
- The knowledge of oneness is achieved only on giving up the pride of the body as well as of action, that is doership.
- The real essence of oneness is experienced when there is complete rupture from the pleasure of sense objects.
- One who perceives oneness within, remains ever-absorbed in the bliss of oneness.
- Through the cognition of Samata—oneness—alone one achieves faith in God, God realization and absorption in God.
- Samata-gnosis is the underlying light of all religions. It is not the creed of a denomination or of a particular religion.
- Authentic meaning of life is to be found in reflection of *Samata Tattva* (the fundamental Truth).
- The real adoration of Samata-gnosis consists in

perceiving God as all-pervading...worshipping Him only and serving His creation taking it as His will.

Some more thoughts culled out of 'Samata Vilas':

- Life is nothing but the expression of oneness. That which gives up oneness ends in destruction.
- It is in oneness that the real self-autonomy exists precisely because it frees everyone from the bondage of becoming, and thereby enables them to be participants in the bliss supreme!
- Instruction in samata results in freedom from narrow religious dogmatism and from worldly quarrels.
- Samata is a timeless gnosis, which remains ever the same in each and every condition, and one who achieves it becomes like unto it.
- The knowledge of oneness results in freedom from the bondage of fruits of action, that is, it is a state of autonomy in which selflessness is realized.
- The state of samata-knowledge is reached when one treads on the path of right action, right thought, right diet, right faith, and right renunciation.
- A person who has attained the state of sameness, is endowed with these effulgent qualities: desirelessness, humility, selflessness, seriousness, restfulness, service to others and equanimity. The qualities are like the rays of supreme bliss.
- Actual meaning of oneness is that one should, in each and every condition, remain in the state of sameness, be redeemed from the desire of possession and of renunciation: this is the real devotion in God as well as redemption.
- The real adoration of samata-gnosis consists in perceiving God as all-pervading, in achieving free-

dom from envy, in becoming pure in conduct, in throwing off the impulses of selfishness, in maintaining faith in God alone, in worshipping God, in recollecting God's name, in obeying the will of the Father, and in serving God's creation.

- To remain steadfast in the sameness of Atman, in action as well as in non-action; to be free from desire for obtaining or abandoning anything—this is emancipated life.
- Feeling of Karmayoga (yoga of action) as well as Jnana Yoga (yoga of knowledge) exists in every realized person. On the strength of these feelings one's intellect gets over bodily perversions and rests in the real Self—immortal Atman. It is unwise to differentiate between the two yogas. In Samatavad both of them are considered salutary and most helpful in attaining the same state (of samata).

  One who walks on the path of selflessness, that is, one who leaves the fruit of every action unto God, who has crossed the duality of action-oriented results, who concentrates on the Name, such a great soul has realized the samata-state, and, by going inward, remains absorbed in the bliss of Atman. Being engrossed in the music of Atman, he remains free from the stains of desire. Such a person's life becomes a source of comfort for all creatures.

  'In everyone permeates His grandeur
  In all creation see His manifestation.'

  (Mangat)

Oneness demands of us to see divinity in everyone, give up all disputations, all sectarian playthings and move in the world in all humility. Dichotomy is nothing more than an artificial human contrivance. In answer to a question on this subject said Mahatma Mangat Ram in simple words: 'When nature does not differentiate why do you? Close-mindedness will not allow you to reach any height.'

Lord Krishna says in Gita: 'One who treats alike all living beings in the world, he is really a true believer in sameness.' Hazrat Muhammad, the founder of Islam, says the same thing in more homely terms: 'Whole creation is God's family. One who serves this family, he is near to God.'

One of Kabir's oft-quoted verses on oneness, included in Guru Granth Sahib (the Sikh scripture), translated in English says: 'God first created Light and out of it came all creatures. Since the whole world has come from one Light, whom could we call good or bad.'

اول اللہ نور اپایا قدرت دے سب بندے
ایک نور سے سب جگ اپجیا کون بھلے کون مندے

On oneness—sameness—let us recall what Swami Vivekananda said:

'All evils come relying on difference.
All good comes from faith in equality,
in the underlying sameness and oneness of things.'

And, Shirdi Sai Baba says:

घट में एकता की ज्योत जला।
जन्म जनमान्तर का अंधियारा मिट जाएगा।।

'Light the lamp of oneness (Samata) inside you, the darkness of ages will get dispelled.'

Swami Rama of the Himalayan International Institute of Yoga Science and Philosophy of the U.S.A. puts the idea of 'oneness' as: 'Equality is the law of Absolute, and the disparity is man's making.'

Highest excellence is the engagement and exercise of absolute equality. Brotherhood based on a sense of equality is the supreme goal to be attained by human society as a whole.

Commonality of Religions:

Religion is essentially a means of the individual's quest or yearning to establish a meaningful and satisfactory relationship between him and the Supreme Being.

All paths of different religions lead to the same goal, that is God. The reality is one and the same. The difference is in name and form. From the studies of all religious maxims, commandments, vows and precepts, it will be seen that each of them, although dressed in different garments (of language), preaches the same principles: tolerance, brotherhood, charity and love. It is over hundred years ago when Vivekananda asserted at the concluding session of the World's Parliament of Religions held at Chicago (September, 1893): "It has proved to the world that holiness, purity and charity are not exclusive phenomena of any church in the world and that every system has produced men and women of the most exalted character."

Advising Hindu youth years later, he said: 'We must show the spirituality of the Hindus, the mercifulness of Buddhists, the activity of the Christians and the brotherhood of Muslims by our practical lives.' Thus, alongwith similarity in the basics of all great religions, certain aspects of each one have become particularly prominent in practice. There is so much to learn from each other!

(See Annexure VII for Manu's Laws (Hindu), Buddha's Precepts, Christ's Commandments and Muhammad's Selected Teachings.)

Mahatma Mangat Ram sees similarity in the teachings of the founders of all religions the world over. They had only one aim—to redeem man from the transient world he is born in and enable him to realize the bliss that is true and real. He says:

सब रिषियन की सार सुन, अध्यातम विचार।
वस्तु एक ही पूजते, नाना जुगत मन धार।।

'Listen to the spiritual teachings as the essence of all saints and seers. They all suggest worship of one True Element, though the methods are diverse.' Those who realized Truth and merged into it had only one message to deliver (to mortal man) that he see, in this very frame of flesh, the Lord of the entire universe. Every religion, Gurudev emphasizes, points out the path of liberation—certain principles that would enable man to earn it. But the foolish would not care for the path, they prefer wasting life-time on disputations concerning the path itself; ultimately they leave this world in utter disappointment.

सब सिद्धन की सार सुन, सब गुनियाँ दा ज्ञान।
सत् सरूप प्रभ एक ही, सब में भया परवान।।

'One fundamental truth which all realized souls and all the awakened wise have preached is that the one Lord — the True Being — is present in all beings.'

(Mangat)

He adds that whoever loved the Lord in any way he chose, he would find Him. Prophets and saints enunciated certain principles according to the time and country they were born in. The treasure of their wisdom was available to all, without any distinction.

Mahatma Mangat Ram had great respect for all great souls. He, accordingly, advised study of their lives and teachings with reverence. He, however, cautioned against the futility of study if it was merely a mental preoccupation. He says: "The greatness of prophets and saints alone will not bring salvation unless their noble principles are actually adopted in life."

He refers to the basic commonality in the teachings of all saints, over and over again. Says he:

Founders of all religions the world over had only one aim—to enable man to realize the bliss that is true and real. It is the primary duty of everybody to seek the Truth.

All religions and faiths talk of the transient world and the importance of investigating into the Immortal Being which alone is true bliss.

The philosophy of Samata is like a thread in the rosary of all religions — Hindu and others. All castes and creeds, faiths and religions are like rivulets running towards the sea of Samata, the ocean of Supreme Enlightenment.

पंथ भेद का बाद तयागें, समता रसना खाएं।
पूरन सिमर के पूरन होवें, सब मन के दोख मिटाएं।।

Give up all disputations on differences among Faiths; rather relish the sweetness of Samata (Sameness). Remembrance of the Complete (the Whole — the Full) makes one *so* and blots out all the blemishes of the mind.

(Mangat)

According to Gurudev the founders of religions talked of truth, without distinction. Christ treated the Lord as Father and loved and worshipped Him as such. He distinguished life-force from the body, became oblivious of body, but happily conscious of the life-principle — free from likes, dislikes and desires, established in Truth.

Muhammad, the noble one, treated the Lord as friend, with full faith in Him, totally surrendered to His will, in utter humility.

Buddha, the great renunciate, regarded *Nirvana* (liberation) as the essence, fearless of time and death, established in stillness of mind, unmindful of pain and pleasure arising out of matter, established in the light of Truth, beyond anything else.

Rikhab Dev (founder of Jainism) looked for doing good to others, true spirituality, above all dualities. Far above is the sound celestial, unattached, indivisible; the intellect finds peace on merging into it.

Zoroaster, the founder of Parsi Faith, considered Fire as the manifestation of the Lord, that which burns all time and action and bestows beneficence on the intellect — a state of complete absorption in Brahman, in the form of sacred fire.

पूरब पच्छम का जीव जो होई।
कल्यान धरम सब एक लखोई।।

Whether one belongs to the East or West, benevolent *dharma* — religious righteousness — is common to all.

(Mangat)

सत पुरषों का है एक धरम, परमादी बहुरगें धार।
"मंगत" मिथ्या बाद में, नित डूब रहा संसार।।

All godly people have one *dharma;* the disputants only engage in divergences. The world is getting drowned constantly in sophism, says "Mangat".

Dharma is a Sanskrit word which we have already come across in some earlier chapters. It denotes real spiritual aspect of all religions — which is the worship of one True Element — and merger with it — though the methods are diverse. Mahatma Mangat Ram has vividly described *Dharma* as:

धरम का रूप न जीव कोए, न कोई मज़हब और पंथ।
"मंगत" जतन जो मुक्त का, सो धर्म कर बाचें ग्रंथ।।

Dharma (righteousness) has no shape or form, nor does it belong to a particular religion or sect. Scriptures describe *dharma* as the way which liberates (uniting one with the Source).

Dharma is very much more than religion. It is a method of understanding man and his world, and not a body of doctrines, or of presuppositions, concerning them.

Dharma means that which uplifts one and unites with the Supreme Being. In practice it implies imbibing attributes and inductions of such moral values in life through which our actions become the noblest and society enjoys peace and happiness. Dharma, inter alia, promotes moral health.

Moral health is very important to society. Some of the products of moral ill-health in society are: juvenile delinquency, drug addiction, alcoholism, prostitution etc. Another indication of moral degradation is the abundance of psycho-somatic diseases in society today.

A question is often raised, especially in India wedded as it is to secularism, about separation of 'religion' from politics. Unfortunately the term religion in this reference is generally misunderstood. It is not correct interpretation of *dharma* which is one for all, whatever religion one professes. Real Dharma and right politics have identical goals; comforting the oppressed and loving the entire world, says Mahatma Mangat Ram.

Gurudev further says, whosoever is following whichever religion or faith, one should try to adopt right principles in life and reach the state of eternal peace. That has been the intention of the founders of all faiths and religions.

All great saints and all religions teach two fundamental things:

Selfless action and faith in Supreme Being.

Also, punctuality in all worldly duties and all spiritual pursuits.

The essence of all religions as reflected in the lives of their great mystics and prophets is the same, always leading the sincere followers towards purity, strength and harmony.

No religion teaches to kill, to harm, to hate. All agree that parents should be honoured, promises kept, fellow human beings respected and the needy and destitute helped. By understanding the noble elements of all religions, we can make our lives richer and fuller. All religions hold before man the ideal of perfection. They stress moral purification and spiritual striving as the means for realizing the ideal.

हर इलमाही वाणी की तालीम एक सी होती है।

The essence of every supernal revelation is identical (love, service and unity are its objectives).

(Mangat)

A friend of mine, I.D. Mutreja, who is deeply interested in spirituality and reads a lot, has made a comparative study of various religions and has summarised for me their commonality in three important aspects — Happiness, Treatment with others, Charity — as under:

A. Happiness:

All religions in some form or the other promise joy, felicity, beatitude, and bliss to their followers.

(a) *Zoroastrianism*: Holiness, the best of all good, is also happiness. The man with perfect holiness is perfectly happy.

(b) *Judaism*: The presence of the LORD is full of everlasting joy.

(c) *Christianity*: In the Kingdom of God there is righteousness, peace and joy in the Holy Spirit.

(d) *Islam*: The believer in God, who desired union with God and Spiritual path, attains real happiness.

(e) *Buddhism*: One who practises charity, tranquillity and friendship to all beings, attains the state of abiding happiness.

(f) *Hinduism*: The Vedanta declares in the Upanishads: 'That one Supreme ruler, the Self of all beings, who makes His form manifold — those wise ones, who perceive HIM as existing in their own soul, to them belongs eternal happiness.'

Adds Bhagavad Gita: 'The yogi who has become perfectly tranquil and has quietened his passions; who is free from all impurities, attains with ease the infinite bliss of communion with the Supreme Spirit.'

B. Treatment of others:

Hinduism: This is the sum of duty: do naught to others which if done to thee, would cause thee pain.

Buddhism: Hurt not the other with that which pains yourself.

Islam: No one of you is a believer until he loves for his brother what he loves for himself.

Jainism: In happiness and suffering, in joy and grief, we would regard all creatures as we regard our own selves and should, therefore, refrain from inflicting upon others such injury as would appear undesirable to us if inflicted upon ourselves.

Christianity: All things whatsoever ye would that man should do to you, do ye even so to them; for this is the law and saying of the Prophets.

Sikhism: As thou deemest thyself so deem others, then shall thou become a partner in heaven.

Zoroastrianism: That nature alone is good when it shall not do unto another whatever is not good for its own self.

C. Charity:

"Anything given in charity is a loan lent to Allah."

— Holy Quran 57:18

"Blessed are those who give without expecting anything in return."

New Testament 20:35

"Charity lovingly offered is lovable and always rewarding."

Gita XVII

"Charity takes one nearer to God."

Buddhist Dhammapada 224

"Virtuous regard greed as a disease and charity its only cure."

Jain Sutra-Kritanga 1, 2, 3

"Charity is always there where virtue thrives."

Taoism, Tao-Te-King 38

"Giving makes one virtuous."

Zoroastrianism, Vendidat XVII:37-38

Plurality vs. Universality of Religion:

I had the good fortune of meeting Dr. M. Darrol Bryant during his visit to India (November, 1993). He is deeply involved in interfaith dynamics and movement. He appreciated the booklet I gave to him: 'Mahatma Mangat Ram, His Life and Teachings'. He was delighted to know that my Gurudev held the founders of all great religions in great esteem and highly admired their basic teachings.

Dr. Bryant gave me a copy of his book 'Religion — A New Key'. He believes in the importance of interfaith dialogues and the participants meeting one another in an atmosphere of mutual openness, ready to alter misrepresentations about the others and eager to appreciate the values of others.

While Dr. Bryant in his experience does not seem persuaded that "all religions are the same" or that "the differences are merely superficial", he does believe that we have more in common than we normally recognize. "It is our shared experience of believing, praying, meditating, and doing that we can, as religious pilgrims, meet one another, it is here that we discover our human unity as 'pilgrims'."

Role of women in Religion:

We have briefly noticed earlier that spirituality is above sex. Here we shall discuss it further. I was impressed with what Dr. Bryant has to say about the women's movement, a development that began in the West but has now touched our entire globe. The reference is to the role of women or women's experience of the Divine. 'We have all become aware that the story of the religious life of humankind has been skewed by a gender bias, that has failed to give women their proper due in the story', he writes.

Dr. Ursula King, Head of Theology and Religious Studies at the University of Bristol in Great Britain, in her study — 'Women and Spirituality, Voices of Protest and

Promise' — makes a crucial point that 'in listening to the voices of contemporary women we must first of all investigate the feminist challenge to traditional religion. We must also listen to women's claims about the nature and power of their own experience as well as those experiences from which they strive to be liberated.' She adds: '...the protest and promise of the women's movement opens up a new horizon of human development which touches the horizon of transcendence.' Dr. Bryant comments that as we begin to recover the voice of women in the religious life of mankind, we can move towards a richer apprehension of the spiritual 'life of mankind'.

In India woman has held, from ancient times, a very high position in spiritual life. Mother worship is the worship of God as the Divine Mother, with countless manifestations. Her glory is ineffable. Her splendour is indescribable. Her greatness is unfathomable. Scriptures sing her praise.

There have been many women saints. The names of Sita, Savitri and Gargi are like stars in India's spiritual firmament. Of recent times Meera Bai tops the list of women devotees, immersed in ecstasy of the Lord's name. Currently Gurumayi Chidvilasananda is heading an ancient lineage of *Siddhas* (saints). She delivers discourses on spirituality the world over.

Mahatma Mangat Ram has also observed: 'There have been great spiritually realized ladies — Gargi, Mandlasa, Sita, Savitri, Ansuya, Meera and many others. They all reached great heights through meditation and contemplation.' He says further: 'The very nature of ladies is service; they serve right from their childhood to the end of their lives.'

Referring particularly to Rabia Basri, born in Arabia, Gurudev says: 'How highly esteemed was she!'

Still it is true that woman generally has been accorded 'second position'. She can and will emerge from this position. Her place in the cosmos is that of 'handmaiden of the

Great Goddess, the Divine Mother'. Because of the Goddess, life renews itself. 'Women have been less vocal in spiritual dialogues. They must articulate their spiritual experience. Men must learn to listen to that experience in its own terms — and then both moving to a level of mutuality that would be ideal' (Ref. Religion — A New Key).

A Universal Religion:

'Religions of the world have become lifeless mockeries', declared Vivekananda over a hundred years ago. But it is, broadly speaking, as true even today as then. 'What the world wants is character.'

Vivekananda further stated: 'If there is ever to be a universal religion, it must be one which will have no location in place or time; which will be infinite like the God it will preach, and whose sun will shine upon the followers of Krishna and of Christ, on saints and sinners alike; which will not be Brahminic or Buddhistic, Christian or Islamic, but the sum total of all these, and still have infinite space for development; which in its catholocity will embrace in its infinite arms, and find a place for, every human being, from the lowest grovelling savage not far removed from the brute, to the highest man towering by the virtues of his head and heart almost above humanity, making society stand in awe of him and doubt his human nature. It will be a religion which will have no place for persecution or intolerance in its polity, which will recognize divinity in every man and woman, and whose whole scope, whose whole force, will be centred in aiding humanity to realize its own true, divine nature.'

It would indeed be a great boon if the seed of such a concept of religion, the 'Religion of Man', could be sown in the minds of our youth. No wonder the world may have one day a universal religion. For now and in foreseeable future we may work towards broadening the frontiers of the principal religions to include in each one of them the basic elements of Vivekananda's revolutionary vision. This would really reach to what Mahatma Mangat Ram has described as *Dharma* — one for all universe.

Love and Devotion:

साचा प्रेम प्रभ माहीं मिलाए।
प्रेम बिना नही काज सराए।।

True love and devotion unite one with God;
Not so, without love!

(Mangat)

Love is one of the great universal forces; it is a divine force. The spirit that endows all things with life.

In its essence, love is the joy of identity, of becoming one; it is an irresistible power of union. Consciously, it seeks for its manifestation and realization upon earth.

Love is an urge towards complete oneness. On the one hand there is the supreme power of attraction and on the other the irresistible need for absolute self-giving. Love leads us from suffering of division to the bliss of perfect union. To approach God by love is to prepare oneself for the greatest possible spiritual fulfilment.

In the life story of Lord Krishna, Radha is regarded as the personification of absolute love for the Divine, total and integral, in full parts of the being, from the highest spiritual to the physical, bringing absolute self-giving and total consecration of all being. She loved Krishna in full abundance and is celebrated by Hindus, who till today chant the two names together as Radha-Krishna. There is an interesting story of Radha's total love and complete surrender:

The mother of Krishna came to Radha saying, "Radha, Krishna has high fever. And he says that until the dust of Radha's feet is sprinkled on His forehead, He will not get well." "All I have, mother, belongs to Krishna" was Radha's simple reply. "Take the dust of my feet and without delay sprinkle on his forehead."

And the mother says to Radha: "Surely, you know the consequence of such an act. If the dust of your feet is sprinkled on the forehead of the Lord, you will have to pay the penalty of going to hell."

What is Radha's answer? It is the answer of every true lover — "A hundred thousand times would I willingly go to hell, if only to give some relief to my Beloved." So it is that Krishna himself said on one occasion: "Deep beyond words is my debt to Radha, for she has surrendered to me all she is and all she has — her body and her mind, her heart and her soul."

Meera, a sixteenth century woman-saint of Rajasthan, was a great devotee of Sri Krishna. Many of her songs of love and devotion form folklore. Reproduced below is one of them (translated from Hindi):

Fain would I renounce my hearth
and home, renounce the forest,
renounce the town and the townsmen,

And renounce as well the precincts
of the Bansibat (my favourite resort):
I would fight shy of none.
I can cast off this body and
quit my abode; but tell me how
can I forswear my affections
For the sake of my Beloved, I
would gladly put the robe of a mendicant.

The world itself has gone mad,
that they call me mad;
But I shall not prevent anyone
from calling me mad;
I would fain desert those who
expostulate with me, and would

gladly renounce my father and brother;

Oh God, I would rather desert
my mother, but I shall never
disown Kanhaiya (Sri Krishna).

There is another old story which reveals the real nature of love spiritual as against physical:

Yajnavalkya, a great Upanishadic sage, teaches his wife Maitreyi who is about to renounce the love of her husband for love of *Atman*: 'To love a person or a thing without transcending it in the very act of love, that is without loving *Atman* in it, would be idolatory, and ultimately it cannot satisfy either the lover or the beloved. Only love that is transparent — to the *Atman* — can be means of ascent, the way to liberation and immortality.' This was a great lesson and appreciating it Maitreyi gave up the idea of renouncing her love for her sage husband.

'True love is self-giving, free of demand, full of submission and surrender; it makes no claim, imposes no conditions, strikes no bargain, indulges in no violence or jealousy or pride or anger — for these are not in its composition.' J. Krishnamurti extends this idea to all relationships with others: 'a total, unvarying, constant and egoless kindness/ goodwill that will not expect any reward or gratitude or even any recognition.'

True love only knows giving, not expecting anything in return. One just loves because one loves. Any distortion that we see in love, among human beings, is because of human failing. Love is surrender, not possessiveness.

Distortions of this great and divine power come from obscurity, ignorance and selfishness on the part of those loving each other. True love has no clinging, no desire, no hunger for possession, no self-regarding attachment; it is, in its pure movement, the seeking for union of the self with the Divine.

O friend, attachment to *that* which is perishable, ends in
pain and not agape;
When, so says 'Mangat', false hope is negated
then the song of love is sung.

Loving God, the creator, and His creation are complementary acts. The following verse of a spiritual poet forcefully expresses the point:

'Since I love only You, O Lord,
it is You alone whom I love
in all and in each one;
and by dint of loving You in them,
I shall end up by
making them a little
conscious of You.'

Love is a mobilising principle, a cosmic strength controlling every form of motion and simultaneously a purifying strength. It is one of God's attributes, similarly as beauty is. 'Who finds in his heart also room for love of man and who perceives the beauty of the real world which is a result of an act of God's creation, a reflection of God Himself, he alone can encompass divine love and beauty', according to a great humanist.

Love is marvellous tenderness. Passion is not love; love should not be debased to the level of the beast. 'The Divine love is a Love that manifests here upon the physical earth, in matter, but it must be pure of human distortions, if it is to incarnate.'

Swami Chinmayananda regards AIDS as a punishment, inflicted by Nature on too much of senseless 'sex' scourge spreading in society. This he said in an interview at an American university—San Diago, California, in August 1993.

Love cannot be affection, for affection has attachment in it. Pure 'Love' has no attachments. Attachments create hate towards the idea that the people we are attached to might be lost (for there is fear in it).

In the words of Swami Rama:

> 'Love and attachments are two opposing principles. Attachment contracts the human personality, while love expands it...Love is great power that has liberating qualities.'

Love should mean more to us than anything else in the world. We were created to love God and to love one another.

True love accepts, approves of, believes in others, is patient, kind, never selfish or envious, never proud or seeking its own reward or way.

'To live in others as in oneself is love.' What a profound truth put by someone with startling simplicity! A question was asked of him 'How should a person be unto himself and to others?' The answer was 'Be yourself. Be in love.'

'Life finds its wealth by the claims of the world and its worth by the claims of love', says Tagore. When we have accomplished divine love, the love of all beings comes naturally. We then love all, serve all.

Let us be concerned with and connected in one sweet essence of Atman in all — quietly and gracefully. 'Make your life full of love in all aspects', says Mahatma Mangat Ram.

Christ sought redemption through Love. He does not argue science and philosophy. Love and devotion to Him are the only passport to Heaven. He marks down Love as the first adjunct to the human code even to settle the virtues of man's relation to man: 'Love thy neighbour as thyself.'

I give below these lines on love I have picked up from the Bible:

> 'Make every effort to supplement your faith with virtue, and virtue with knowledge, and knowledge with self-control, and self-control with steadfastness, and steadfastness with brotherly affection and brotherly affection with love...'

(Jesus Christ)

I would like to add here views of a few famous Indian saints:

Maharishi Ramana:

> 'See love, Hear love, Reach out
> And touch love, Eat love, sweet love,
> Smell love, for love is but
> The Self's awareness of itself.'

Late Kripal Singh — Founder of World Fellowship of Religions:

> Love is no love which arises out of body and ends in the body. Love that arises from the body and ends in the soul, that is love.
>
> Love knows service and sacrifice.
>
> If one cannot love those whom he sees, how can one love God whom he does not see.

Late Paramahansa Yogananda refers to the power of love thus:

> 'Conquering the hearts of others by the power of love is the greatest victory you can win in life. Always try to consider others first and you will find the whole world at your feet. That was the greatness of Jesus. He lived and died for all.'

Satya Sai Baba:

> Start the day with love
> Spend the day with love
> End the day with love
> For Love is God
> That is the way to God.

He adds: 'Develop love, scatter love, reap love, there is no religion higher than that.'

'Love is selflessness. Love is not an emotional state confined to whims and fancies, but a transcendent state

of consciousness which goes beyond the bodily forms.'
(Brahma Kumaris)

Swami Purna:

'Love is pure. It is selfless attitude of devotion to the unfolding and blossoming of Truth. Human beings need to love and be loved. They also need to transform selfish love into selfless love. It is through such transmutation of lower urges into higher longings that one is able to attain more profound fulfilment and eventual enlightenment and liberation.

In the story of Ruskhan, the Muslim, there is a lovely example of physical love turning into spiritual love. Khan had seen a picture of Krishna and he was convinced that he had hopelessly fallen in love with the Beautiful Boy. However, after some time he came into contact with the God; he learned to perceive Him beyond his own fantasies. By following Krishna's teachings and transforming his love from personal to universal, Khan became a saint.

That is what is meant by growing through love; the essence of love itself must change.'

To quote Swami Purna again:

Love is the life of the soul
creating peace and
happiness.
Love and doubt do not co-exist.
Love and doubt cannot co-exist.

The difference between love of a merely physical kind and spiritual love is that the former causes degeneration, the latter engenders growth.

'Love is a much misused word. We must certainly coin new words to indicate different types of love:

affection (parents); fascination (sex); satisfaction (objects)'

as someone has aptly remarked.

Arif Naqshabandi, a great Muslim Sufi, thus speaks of love:

'One loving glance can illuminate the darkest corner of the heart. The miracle that can melt the most cruel heart can only be performed by those men of God who consider each heart a temple and an abode for God. They consider that to give pain is the greatest sin and to erase pain is the only way to please God.'

'One glance of love,
Can fill with joyous colours
the dark hazy image of life
Can heal the wounds of soul
And, turn them into flowers.'

'We are human only because we love others or have the opportunity to do so.'

'But it is those who love, because they live,
those truly win, for they truly surrender.'

(Rabindra Nath Tagore)

Lest we mistake mere spurious, physical so-called love as against truly spiritual love, I would quote Gurudev on the nature of the latter:

अन्तर एको देखया, सो बाहर रहे रमनाई।
"मंगत" पुरन देख के, मनुआ प्रेम समाई।।

"Mangat" saw the One (God) within and the same permeating all around. On seeing the Full, the mind merges into Love, he says.

प्रेम सम ना बन्दगी, योग, तप और दान।
"मंगत" बिना प्रेम के मिले न निर्मल ज्ञान।।

No meditation, Yoga, penance and charity can equal love,
Even pure knowledge cannot be achieved without love, says "Mangat".

जगत सराये में आया, तू मुसाफिर मीत।
"मंगत" निर्मल ध्यान से, साची पालो प्रीत।।

You have come as a traveller in this *serai* of the world,
Experience true love here through pure contemplation,
says "Mangat".

Poverty — a spiritual shame and social slur

We endlessly talk of oneness, of One Divinity permeating all beings. We claim to be children of One God. But seldom do we take note of how our other brethren and sisters live. We are not seriously concerned with their poverty, illiteracy, ill health. Many of them go without food, without clothing and without adequate shelter. This bothers us the least. If at all, it touches us only marginally.

As Mr. R. Panikkar says in 'The Vedic Experience': "How can you be just an 'intellectual' concerned with truth, or just a 'spiritual' busy with goodness, when men desperately cry for food and justice? We must remember that sin and shame of the world is our sin and shame, for we are a part of it. We cannot lose ourselves in inner piety when the poor die at our door, naked and hungry." The Gita asks us to live in the world and serve. That is 'spirituality'. Mahatma Mangat Ram advises us to serve others selflessly with body, mind and wealth.

In the words of the well-known English Poet W.H. Auden: 'We must recognize that man is basically an animal and until his immediate material and economic needs are satisfied, he cannot develop further...People cannot grow until they are happy; and even when their material needs have been satisfied, they still need many other things. They want to be liked and like other people; to feel valuable; to feel free and feel respected and above all not to feel lonely and isolated.'

Let us cross-examine ourselves. Are we doing enough as individuals, as members of a society, as nationals of a country or as inhabitants of this world for amelioration of the conditions of our less fortunate brethren and sisters? Surely not!

We are likely to have a sense of superiority if we do help the under-privileged in any way. Here Vivekananda has a right warning for us:

> 'You cannot help anyone, you can only serve the children of the Lord, serve the Lord himself if you can have the privilege. Blessed you are that privilege was given to you when others had it not. Do it (serve others) only as a worship.'

Unfortunately the gap between the poor and the rich, between the 'haves' and 'have-nots' continues to grow despite all the material progress the world has made. Despite all the religions we belong to or read about, all the spirituality we speak of, maldistribution of economic gains is responsible for the flagrant inequities. Years ago Bertrand Russell, the well-known educator philosopher, observed so aptly:

> 'Everybody could have as much of this world's goods as is necessary for the happiness of sensible people. With the problem of poverty and destitution eliminated, men could devote themselves more to the constructive arts of civilization — to the progress of science, the diminution of disease, the postponement of death, and the liberation of impulses that make for joy.'

Some so-called spiritual people, especially in India, will tell you: 'Those poor ones are under punishment from God for their *Karma* (actions in past life).' What a way to avoid the responsibility by those who are better off! *That silly excuse is offered only as an escape,* thus suffering or supporting a social and economic system which is too individualistic. In saying this I am not putting forward a plea for political acceptance of any particular socialist creed. We know how socialism, in its extreme form, communism, has crumbled in recent years.

As a reaction, an excessive emphasis is now placed on free market economy. Freedom in every reasonable sense is all right. But what about the handicapped members of society who, for any reasons, have remained behind? Our words of 'equality' and 'fraternity' fall flat on them. We talk endlessly of 'Peace' and 'Progress' for all, while we actually encourage growth and advancement of a few.

Many would talk of the next world or the life to come, simply to justify their disregard of the present untenable inequities and prevalent injustice marring the face of this beautiful world. I would like to recall here a pertinent para from Harold J. Laski, the famous political thinker of his time even if we may not totally agree with him:

> 'The churches have been enemies of reason in thought and of justice in social arrangements. Their concentration upon the life to come — for the reality of which I see no evidence — has, it seems to me, done more than most factors in history to deflect the attention of men from the relations of our life here and now. The result of that deflection has always been to the interest of those who live by privilege.'

The word 'churches' used by Laski is evidently in its general sense, referring to all established religious institutions.

The relations with our fellow beings and with our environment right in this life and in this very world are more important than anything else imagined rightly or wrongly. Laski is quite reasonable when he says that it is the people living by privilege — political, social or economic — who have been dinning into the ears of others that this life or this world is of not much consequence. With this view given weight, poor people particularly tended to remain poor taking it as part of their destiny and not a situation which they should resolutely correct. When one is spiritually awake and confident of the fact that the divine power is sustaining, guiding and supporting him, one would not take things lying down. A great change would thus come in the world as a result of proper understanding of spirituality. It would result in the improvement of quality of life of people generally and will not mean flight or escape from life.

Though intolerance is an evil but sometimes one has to be intolerant of what is not correct. Youngmen particularly should be prepared to defend what they believe to be right. We have to be prepared at times to accept responsibility of our convictions. There have been instances in history when saints and other noble souls had to undergo many hardships for the sake of their convictions. They would go all the way in defence of truth. To tolerate injustice, inequity or inhumanity is not right. Krishna while talking to Arjuna in the battlefield advises him to fight for a cause valiantly and not to give it up as Arjuna was inclined to do. We have similarly to take up a 'war' against injustice of any kind. The rampant poverty — wherever it exists in the world — is a grave social injustice.

I have seen during my life-time some saints and other good people who talked of and preached spirituality and also lived very simply, sharing with others what little they possessed or procured. I have also met and seen others who live in great style — rich and luxurious — with only lip sympathy for the poor.

Kabir, the greatest saint of his time, begs of God to give him only that much which is bare enough for removing his hunger and for feeding any hungry person coming to him for food.

'So long as even a single dog in my country is without food, my whole religion will be to feed it', said Vivekananda.

Mahatma Mangat Ram advises us to minimise our needs and serve others with the savings we can thus make. He says in strong words:

> 'He who is bereft of the spirit of service is bereft of humanity, a victim of demonic passions of greed, in-

fatuation, pride and jealousy, he ever remains in a state of unrest — this is like living in hell.'

Incidentally while defining scope and spread of Sangat Samatavad, Gurudev says: 'Consider the whole world as Sangat Samatavad (members of one human family).' He did not want his disciples or devotees to consider themselves yet another religion, faith or creed. Samata—equality—is a way of thinking as well as living. It does not believe in fractionalism.

Iqbal, the celebrated Urdu poet, has expressed himself remarkably on this subject, in the following couplets:

یہ حکمت ملکوتی یہ علم لاہوتی
حرم کے درد کی درماں نہیں تو کچھ بھی نہیں

یہ ذکر نیم شبی یہ مراقبہ یہ سرور
تیری خودی کے نگہباں نہیں تو کچھ بھی نہیں

Yeh hikmat-e-malakuti yeh ilm-i-lahuti
Haram ke dard ke draman naheen to kuchh bhi naheen
Yeh zikr-i-neem shabi yeh maraqbe yeh suroor
Teri khudi ke nigihban naheen to kuchh bhi naheen.

This celestial wisdom
and this divine knowledge
are worthless if they do not provide
a remedy for the agony of the people.
This invocation at midnight,
this meditation and this ecstasy
are valueless if they are not protectors
of your (man's) self-respect.

There has been tremendous transformation of agricultural and industrial production; the breakthrough in all branches of science, especially medicine and surgery; the communications revolution, the astounding adventure into space.

However, with all the wealth and technology, two thirds of the human race today lives below what can be considered a satisfactory standard of living and one third are in fact below the poverty line. Millions of children go to sleep hungry, their bodies stunted, their minds distorted by malnutrition and lack of medical facilities. 'Ten days expenditure on ornaments can abolish hunger on this planet, but hundreds of billions of dollars, pounds, roubles and other currencies are poured into the manufacture of lethal weapons, while millions continue to go unfed, unhoused and uneducated.' Thus observed Dr. Karan Singh (1986). This expenditure on arms race has, no doubt, gone down somewhat, but the condition of the millions as described has not improved. Their poverty is as grim as ever, possibly a little worse with inflation having gone full speed all over.

Let us be determined to do something for the material well-being, self-respect, and spiritual uplift of others too while working for our all-round advancement. As children of one God we shall please HIM if we did that. Let His power work, through us, to this end.

'Hard it is to understand: By giving away our food, we get more strength, by bestowing clothing on others, we gain more beauty; by founding abodes of purity and truth, we acquire great treasures' (Buddha).

World leaders pledge to fight poverty:

The first-ever Summit for Social Development held in March, 1994, adopted a declaration and programme of action aimed at eradicating poverty, fighting unemployment and narrowing the gap between the world's rich and poor. Most of presidents, prime ministers and other top leaders from some 120 countries signed the declaration. The summit, the biggest in history so far, did successfully shift the world attention from poverty alleviation to poverty eradication for the first time, following the initiative taken by India and other Group of 77 developing countries.

In the declaration, the participants pledged to pursue decisive national and international action plans to fight poverty, empower women, assist the poorest countries and to hold a special UN General Assembly session in the year 2000 to assess overall outcome of the summit. UN has also been called to declare the ten years from 1997 a decade for the eradication of poverty.

Let us hope effective, wide-ranging anti-poverty programmes are really undertaken with special zeal and spiritual devotion to bring relief to the 1.2 billion poor around the globe.

The Philippine President Fidel Ramos called poverty 'a tyranny against which we must wage the moral equivalent of war'. India's Prime Minister Narasimha Rao hinted at the significance of social development based on spirituality—oneness of human beings. Will India, through its practical example, show the way to the world as our Rishis did in the past?

CHAPTER 9

Development—An Integral View

> 'The well-being of society is to be promoted both by *Santi* (tranquillity) which purifies one's own mind and *Sakti* (power) which is required for the progress of the society.'
>
> (Maharishi Ramana)

Let us develop ideology, the basic concepts and corollaries of which would purify and advance human life in every direction. Real development is one that leads to peace and progress.

Progress:

Man really needs all-round development: economic, educational, moral and spiritual. One does not live by bread alone; body certainly has its own minimum needs. The mind and the spirit also need to be nourished and developed. Healthy body, sound mind and awakened spirit make an ideal combination. It is comparatively easy to develop intellectually. What is really difficult to attain, and lies at the root of real progress, is the moral stamina of a person. It is not just the intellect but a dedicated will which puts energy into life and leads people and nations to heights of glory. It is qualities like faith, unity, industry, discipline, justice, courage and cooperation which act as spurs in progress.

Just social and economic systems must take care of people's minimum needs of food, shelter, clothing, health and education. As contemporary history of many new nations shows political freedom without social emancipation and economic progress has little meaning.

Side by side, there has to be fair distribution of the fruits of development. The gap between poverty and plenty must be bridged progressively. Real spirituality, in action, would expect the world to act as a big family; the exploitation of one country or nation by another country or people must end. If we really believe we are all children of God, as we profess, how can some of us live rather extravagantly while others die of hunger, disease and other unfortunate handicaps or happenings. World peace, based on equal or fair opportunities for progress by all, can be obtained when we recognize all creation as one family of God. Even from the pure economic point of view the unjust inequity that divides mankind must end, in the interests of all.

On personal level too, we must understand that true progressive evolution, an evolution which can lead man to his rightful happiness, can come only through a deep inner process of individual self-perfection. According to a theosophical writing: 'Grow as the flower grows, unconsciously but eagerly anxious to open its soul to the air. So must you press forward to open your soul to the Eternal. But it must be the eternal that draws forth your strength and beauty, not desire of growth.'

Man is not merely a conglomeration of animalcules, as in terms of material analysis. He looks beyond the house to the dweller in the house, beyond the parts to the force that holds the parts together. That is the Principle of Life, the universal and all-pervading ocean of *Prana* of which the most important manifestation in man is Breath; as we have discussed earlier. That is the force of the Brahman, nay Brahman itself, as some describe.

It seems incredible, but it is a fact that we ignore 'ourselves' to lavish all our love and care on the flesh. We do not give due share of attention to the animating part of our corporeal bodies.

In our times we find progress everywhere around us, but no serious attempt is being made to improve the man, to help him tune himself up. In this sad and tragic neglect lies the miserable cause for the mounting sense of dissatisfaction and discontent, which in their turn force youngmen to be brutal, immoral, addicts and criminals. The peaceful life of the society gets shattered. The cultural harmony in the community of man becomes broken. Disaffection spreads. Hatred increases. From local disturbances to brawls, riots, strikes, confrontation, battles and wars all fan out, blistering the fair face of peaceful prosperity.

How best can we help our brethren to be successful and happy? No doubt we know the theory, and it is no closely guarded secret. We do successfully practise it in our factories and farms, in offices and in Governments. But we never think of applying them in our own life, says Swami Chinmayananda.

As M.M. Sharief, author of 'A History of Muslim Philosophy', says there are certain tendencies which may adversely affect solid progress:

- Blind imitation of the superficial ways of life, superficial mimicry—even irreligion and scepticism.
- Oppositely clinging to the stone-wall of conformism.

Extremist tendencies must be shed off. Even the Quran describes the Muslims as people of the middle path (Ummat-al-waste), he says. Buddha, as we know, advised on Golden Mean — the Middle Path. So have all other prophets and many saints.

Mr. Sharief further says: 'Lop-sided material progress of the West was unethical and unspiritual, so the religiosity of the East was a hollow and life-thwarting force. The realm of spirit had to be rediscovered by the East as well as the West. A good deal of science and technology of the West was valuable and East was to learn it and adopt it to eliminate poverty, squalor and disease, but the East must not make the mistake of worshipping material power as an end in itself. Physical sciences and the tremendous forces they have unleashed must be harnessed to ethical and spiritual aims.

'Fossilized religious dogmatism could not generate an outlook that would lead individuals and communities to self-realization.'

There are also innumerable distractions, petty problems and seductive desires encountered throughout any individual's lifetime. 'They are all part of Maya's Magical Picture Show—a trap to prevent one's growth out of infantile fantasies and into resplendent consciousness.'

If we use the tools of intellect and mind to reason mindfully, we can advance our own growth.

To achieve the highest, to merge with the highest, we must become like the highest — infinite intelligence and infinite wisdom.

In order to grow integrally one needs self-confidence, faith and devotion.

> पूर्ण दृढ़ता और सत् विश्वास से ही सफलता प्राप्त होती है।
>
> Success can be achieved with will which is firm and faith which is true. (Mangat)

In this type of growth skilful performance of duty can be raised to the level of a spiritual phenomenon (Yoga). The doer must unite himself with his task. The concept of social duty is replaced by divine obligation. And finally, as Gurudev remarks:

'Self-improvement leads to improvement of others, too.'

Environment:

Humankind and the natural environment share a symbiotic relationship—both constantly influencing and affecting each other. Man draws heavily from nature and in turn his every action influences nature — in recent times increasingly adversely.

People have suddenly woken up, during the past few years, to a frightening scenario of deteriorating environment of this planet on which life has evolved in the myriad facets over some billion years. There is reason to be dismayed at the cumulative effect of man's depredation of the environment over the centuries and its impact on the nature of human race. Thus writes my friend, Mr. H.D. Shourie, in his esteemed journal 'Common Cause'. He refers to a telling book on this subject entitled 'The End of Nature' by Bill Mckblin of the USA. There is no doubt that mankind has defiled this planet to a degree that it is already affecting the quality of life everywhere. No wonder that the environmental crisis is engaging the world's attention as never before, says Shourie.

Deep concern is being shared among nations about a worsening of poverty, hunger, ill health, illiteracy, and the continuing deterioration of ecosystems on which we depend for our well-being.

Harmony with Nature:

It is quite appropriate for humans to feel harmony with nature, especially when seeking higher, natural growth. Nature is our inspiration and our mother. Throughout the ages *sadhaks* (spiritual aspirants) and sages dedicated their lives to living in harmony with the natural forces within themselves and in their environment. In Vedic times some trees were revered as if they were high beings. They were appreciated for their uplifting influence, and higher teaching was often given in their midst. It is a scientifically proven fact that trees create a change in the atmosphere (known as negative ionization) which affects the brainwave pattern of humans causing the alpha state, which one experiences in the first stages of meditation. It is easy to understand how wise men like Rabindranath Tagore, having no 'institute' as such, began teaching in the openness of nature where there were no walls to limit growth nor boundaries to enclose the imagination. Dance, music, writing, philosophy — all went on under the trees.

Mahatma Mangat Ram spent most of his time amid trees, on river banks or under open starry sky. He had great reverence for all life including that in plants. Once, he was noticed talking to a tree in which a big nail had been inserted by his devotees who had done so to tie a rope of the tent being fixed for the saint at Kelaghat (Dehradun). He expressed apology for the injury caused to the tree, for his sake.

Gurudev encouraged plantation of shady trees at the Ashrams set up by his devotees. Tapobhumi at Rajpur (Dehradun) is an ideal meditative place full of thousands of plants and trees.

He was against plucking of flowers too. Never allowed anybody to garland him or otherwise offer flowers. He saw no reason why the flowers should be destroyed for worshipping imaginary divinities. He quotes Kabir who has rightly said:

> 'Brahma is the root, Vishnu is the branch and Shiva the flower.
> By breaking the three (divinities) whom do you worship?'

Vedas refer to prevalence of God in the entire Universe — in water, in plants, in trees. Obeisance is paid to Nature's bounties in most worshipped terms, as:

'May, the Waters, the mothers purify us!'

'I venerate this mighty earth, the golden breasted upon

whom the trees, lords of forests stand firm, unshakable in every place.'

'Breather, O! wind your healing breeze, you are the medicine of this whole world, the messenger of Gods!'

Here is a saying, also a small story pertaining to sanctity of plants and trees:

Rabbi Yohanan ben Zakkai used to say, "If there be a plant in your hand when they say to you behold the Messiah! Go and plant the plant and afterwards go out and greet him."

Rajah Koranya had a king banyan tree called Steadfast and the shade of its widespread branches was cool and lovely. Its shelter broadened to twelve leagues. None guarded its fruit and none hurt another for its fruit. Now there came a man who ate his fill of fruit, broke down a branch, and went his way. Thought the spirit dwelling in that tree:

"How amazing, how astonishing it is, that a man should be so evil as to break off a branch of the tree, after eating his fill. Suppose the tree were to bear no more fruit." And the tree bore no more fruit.

The Quran says: 'Remember Allah frowns at those who corrupt the earth by making mischief.' If we remember this we will not do any harm to mother earth. Anything anti-environment and anti-ecology is disrespect of earth, is in a sense corrupting the earth.

It would be appropriate to conclude this section with a prayer which Indian scriptures enjoin on humanity:

To the heavens be peace, to the sky
to the waters be peace, to plants and all trees
to the Gods be peace, to Brahman be peace,
to all men be peace, again and again,
peace also to me.'

Harmony and Peace:

Live in complete harmony with Nature, experience the grace of God in the splendour of the universe.

> Be blessed by God's reassuring love,
> The sweet dawn will sweeten your soul,
> The dazzling mid-day will set your
> hearts aflutter,
> And the serene music of your soul will guide you towards peace and prosperity.
> And when the day's task is over
> you will sleep in the lap of Mother Nature,
> All the deities will be favourable to you.
>
> (Yajur Veda)

There is boundless ocean of peace and harmony within us.

There is harmony in nature, a harmony so complete that it is life — a melody, one note merging into the other creating an enchanting effect. The prickly bush, the delicate flower, the gigantic tree, the lowly grass—all co-exist. Everyone has a place in this universe.

'There is harmony in the spiritual teachings of all saints and seers', says Mahatma Mangat Ram. He further observes:

> 'A man who is at peace with himself will make others also be at peace with themselves. And, the way to collective peace is the way of restraint — restraint of the passions of desire, anger, greed, stupidity and egoity. Restraint, in fact, constitutes good conduct, and unbridled indulgence evil conduct.
>
> 'Social peace, goodwill and harmony depend on the way the rulers (now the politicians in power) live and conduct themselves.'

Harmony means a total movement of life in which there is no fragmentation. In the words of J. Krishnamurti: 'The most important thing in life or rather one of the most important for each human being, surely, is to live in order, in harmony with all things around him—even with the noise of the great towns, even with something that is ugly, vulgar without letting it affect or alter the course of one's life, alter or distort the order in which one is living.'

Further, as Dr. Kapila Vatsyayan, Secretary, Indira Gandhi International Centre for Arts, says in her revealing book 'Concepts of Space: Ancient and Modern': 'Today man is more than ever before aware of a loss of totality, wholeness and harmony. Whether scientists or philosophers, artists or men of inner experience, all are concerned about the fragmentation and alienation of Man at all levels, individual, societal, physical, psychical and cosmic. Disharmony and confrontation arise out of this lack of wholeness. Yet when man looks within and at the core of most of civilisations and cultures, he discovers ways and means of reintegration, of creating harmony between men and men, and universe.' Dr. Vatsyayan further refers, very aptly, to the inner life of reflection and the outer of movement and action, the interrelation of the two, and the theme of wholeness.

'The harmony of the outer life with the inner values of the Being should be maintained and then all avenues of outer life will be much more glorious. Will be worthwhile.' This is Aurobindo's view again emphasising integral harmony between matter and spirit.

Glorifying the outer values of life by the light of the inner self; bringing more spiritual lustre to material glories of life...That is the type of harmony we humans, especially the youth, could create and develop.

There are two well-known, oft-quoted sayings from Bible in which a known interpreter of Chinese life, Mr. Lin Yutang, would wittingly suggest a welcome change in order to promote much needed peace and harmony among nations. The words suggested by him are:

Instead of 'Thou shall not covet thy neighbour's goods':

'Thou shall not covet thy neighbour's territory'.

Further, 'Thou shall not kill' can be considerably improved:

'Thou shall not kill, not even people of a different country'.

'The most desired is peace—peace of mind, peace in society and peace between communities and nations.

If there is uprightness in the contemporary world, in the heart, there will be beauty in the character.

If there is beauty in the character, there will be harmony in the house

If there is harmony in the house, there will be order in the nation

If there is order in the nation, there will be peace in the world.'

(Confucius)

Mother Teresa's strength—prayer to peace—comes from her simple, uncomplicated beliefs which she has on her visiting card:

The fruit of Silence is Prayer
The fruit of Prayer is Faith
The fruit of Faith is Love
The fruit of Love is Service
The fruit of Service is Peace

Peace of the individual is the unit of world peace. The spiritual masters teach the attainment of inner peace through meditation and the realization of the oneness of all humanity ultimately can lead to outer peace on this planet. Through God-awareness, we experience balance and equilibrium. We feel lighter, brighter, more energetic, more mentally clear and more purposeful — happy, joyous and peaceful. The more we live with thought of God, the more fulfilled we will be. Paramahansa Yogananda said, "He is wisest who seeks God. He is most successful who has realized God." If we bring peace in our individual spheres the effect will be cumulative. Each one of us can make our contribution by imbibing a spirit of commitment.

How does disharmony arise on individual level? Usually the fault is on both sides. On our side we have a tendency to too harsh judgment of others, a readiness to see and stress the faults, defects, weak side of others and not to see enough of their good sides. This prevents the kindliness of outlook which should be there and gives an impression of harshness and critical severity and creates a tendency to contrariety and revolt which even when it is not there in the minds of the others, acts through their subconscious and creates all these discordant movements. To take advantage of what is good in others, keeping one's eye always on that, and to deal tactfully with their mistakes, faults and defects is the best way; it does not exclude firmness and maintenance of discipline, even severity when severity is due; but the latter should be rare and the others should not feel it.

To have peace in one's soul is the greatest happiness. 'Grant yourself a moment of peace and you will understand how foolishly you have hurried about' is an old Chinese saying.

> वाहिरमुख रचना माहीं पल पल जीव भरमाए।
> "मंगत" अन्तर सोझी बिना, कभूं ठौर नहीं पाए।।

> One who is always looking outside is caught in delusion, without understanding one's 'inside' one is never at peace, says "Mangat".

> ओढक तत्त विचारिया, शान्त रूप भगवन्त।
> घट घट आनन्द मूरत, नित नित नाम जपन्त।।

> As ultimate hypothesis, God is perfect tranquillity; He is present in everyone as Bliss incarnate. Remember His Name all the time.

Whether one be householder or a mendicant, real peace can be had only by reorienting life towards the Spirit. 'It is a peace which transcends the (dialectic) of joy and sorrow', says Mahatma Mangat Ram. Some more of his observations on real peace are reproduced below:

> 'आन्तरिक चाहना हर जीव की निर्भय शांति की है लेकिन यतन गलत होने के कारण शांति की बजाय अशांति को प्राप्त कर लेता है।'

> In the heart of hearts every individual desires peace without fear. There is, however, unrest because of incorrect effort towards peace.
>
> Inner peace can be realized only through self-endeavour...No one has realized or experienced the essence of Reality without right effort.
>
> Atman alone is the embodiment of everlasting peace.
>
> The realization of inner peace is possible only when the intellect, by divesting itself from the influence of objects, engages in meditation of the Self.
>
> One can achieve peace and bliss by cultivating good character, that is by restraining passions of desire, anger, greed, attachment, ego etc.
>
> One shall not be blessed with beatitude and peace unless one experiences Truth.
>
> Blessed, indeed, are the knowers of the Self, for they attain the bliss of eternal peace.
>
> Man may succeed in bringing under control the elemental forces of nature — the sun, the moon, the air or the water etc. but that will not relieve him from inner anxiety and restlessness.
>
> Thus research on outside elements in pursuit of sensual pleasures will lead to more and more unrest and fear, instead of bringing peace. No doubt about it.
>
> Let man investigate into life-force, for peace within and peace outside.
>
> Materialism or extreme attachment to the pleasures of the body leads to destruction. When common people

become blinded by addiction to sense pleasures, then the very intensity of their expanding desires gives rise to disturbances and violence which eventually prove suicidal.

The nature of unrest and turmoil in case of the life of an individual and that of society is similar. Until the basic principle of realization of Truth is determinedly adopted, the individual life, family life, social life and political life will never be in peace and harmony.

The real peace is within rather than in things of the world and to be desireless is the highest form of peace, emphasises Mahatma Mangat Ram. In answer to a question how can real peace be attained? he says: 'Real peace shall be attained when one, with great endeavour, surrenders at the feet of the Lord...The best and real means for the attainment of real peace is to give up all forms of selfishness, and thereby serve all beings selflessly and in accordance with one's ability.'

Sant Kripal Singh says that 'the attainment of inner peace through meditation and the realization of the oneness of all humanity ultimately can lead to outer peace on this planet.'

Maharishi Mahesh Yogi observes:

'Meditation establishes a man on that status whereby he becomes the embodiment of harmony. From him emanate the vibrations of peace and harmony, and without his knowledge, he is helping the whole universe derive from him all help.'

Sai Baba says:

'The world can achieve prosperity and peace only through such people whose hearts are pure and whose minds are free of prejudice and passion, lust and greed, anger and envy.'

We are living in an age of science. While making

material progress through advance of science, we have to ensure that it contributes to peace and harmony. Modern scientists have been looking for new methods to spiritualize the conclusions of physical sciences. To bring about a state of peace, there has to be ultimately a happy marriage of spirituality and science. True spiritual teachings show how to use matter yet not to be enslaved by it.

Let our mind turn to this prayer as soon as we wake up in the morning: "*Sarvesham Swastir Bhavatu, Sarvesham Shantir Bhavatu, Sarvesham Purnam Bhavatu, Sarvesham Mangalam Bhavatu.*" This means: "May there be auspiciousness or goodness for all; may there be peace for all; may there be happiness for all; may no one suffer!"

Science and Spirituality:

> 'Can there be an honest understanding between the outlook of science and the inlook of spirituality? This is a question not easy to appreciate.
>
> 'Spirituality can, and must help curb the destructive and narcissistic materialism of modern science and the naked consumerism it has so monstrously generated.'
>
> (Samata Vilas)

Enquiry, curiosity, search—call what you like—humanity has always had the desire to know and fathom both working of its own being and of the physical world around.

Concepts have been devised and methods have been invented to understand and control the world of matter. The desire to understand the physical world generally has been termed science.

Quantum physics has clearly shown us the link between matter and energy—how particles are nothing but fluctuations in a universal energy field. Everything that happens in the body of a living being is the expression of that energy pattern.

In terms of physical body what is a man, a puny little thing on this planet. And what is our planet—only a small mass of earth and water compared to an average size star. In spirit, however, an individual too can be as vast and big as the universe. That is only when the self merges into the Self.

Let us have a view of the universe from the following facts gathered by Science for us:

Universe: A mention of Universe was made briefly in Chapter 3. Let us talk a little more about it. A galaxy is a band of millions of stars. The number of galaxies of the type of our own milky way is not exactly known. Some billions of them is a meagre estimate. Some of them are billions or trillions of kms away from us and across each other.

It is estimated that cosmic distance stretches from us such that light would need 6 billions years to travel at a speed of 1,86,000 miles (2,99,275 km) per second and that much distance in the opposite direction too. We can say that the known cosmos is 12 billion light years wide. We have so much journeying to do; yet, so much to know, so much to see, so much to discover and still there may be much more to find. 'Supernova' — a star in our neighbouring galaxy blasted out into space debris to create 1 million planets of the size of our earth and shone as intensely as 250 millions of our sun put together. Light of this blast reached us just in February, 1982, after travelling 1,70,000 light years across space.

It is also not unlikely that in the near future scientists may get clues of some extra-terrestrial intelligence or civilisation like ours or even better than ours. Many mysteries that baffle us now may get untangled then.

Basically science is the means of attaining knowledge for the betterment of human life. True science always has the welfare of humanity as its central motive. Einstein, the great scientist, said: 'Science for peace' should be the motto and practical conviction of the powers.

Science has made wonderful progress. However, it can be put to both good and bad uses. In reality, slavery to any perishable material, including our own body is dangerous. Science, like fire, is a good servant but can be a bad master.

Calm dignity of master: Modern science and technology with their tremendous inventiveness have given man mastery over nature, far beyond what we could dream in the past. Surprisingly, however, man himself is feeling increasingly helpless and fearful, forgetting that he is the master of, and not slave to, the newly created 'power', in one form or the other. We should be conscious of our position as master and not behave as slave in respect of any power whatsoever. Bertrand Russell has beautifully expressed this sentiment thus:

> 'If we are to profit by our new-won mastery over nature, we must acquire a more lordly psychology; instead of the cringing and resentful terror of the slave, we must learn to feel calm dignity of the master.'

As confident and dignified masters we can make wise use of, and not be foolishly used as slaves by, any power placed in our hands by science, technology or any other faculty or phenomenon, material or spiritual.

Atomic energy has given man a new source to meet the ever-growing need for generation of power for industrial application. It is also a handy source of working plants and machinery in remote and inaccessible areas, such as polar ice-caps. There are hundreds of other applications to which atomic power can be put to use for peaceful purposes, but alas, the wickedness in the mind of man can utilize it for destruction, too.

The use of nuclear power for human happiness, or for bringing doomsday nearer for entire humanity, lies entirely in the hands of those in possession of political power. As Martin Luther King, a great religious revolutionary, boldly observed in 1963:

> 'The means by which we live have outdistanced the ends for which we live. Our scientific power has outrun our spiritual power. We have guided missiles and misguided men.'

In the words of Bertrand Russell:

> 'The effect of science upon our view of man's place in the universe has been of two opposite kinds: it has at once degraded and exalted him. It has degraded him from the standpoint of contemplation, and exalted him from that of action. The latter effect has gradually come to outweigh the former, but both have been important.'

Science in service of Society:

Historically, scientific discoveries have been made with the avowed objective of their utilization in fruitful and gainsome application for improving the standard of living of the people. But without proper wedding between science and spirituality there can be a big dilemma. The curve of the history of human civilization has a peculiar graph. It creates and by its own destroys as well. Spirit and matter have often found themselves at variance with each other, but one has not crushed the other as much as helped life. Both have, with each other's guidance and assistance, gone forward with the world along the way.

We cannot just curse materialism/science outright. It has helped extend curiosity, intellectual rectitude and power of knowledge to various fields. Not only has it, with an unexampled force and richness of invention, brought and put in our hands for much evil, but also for much good, discoveries, instruments, practical powers, conveniences which—howsoever we may declare their insufficiency for our higher interests—yet few of us would care to relinquish. It has also, paradoxical as that at first sight may seem, strengthened man's idealism.

Science and life:

In this scientific age, attention is focussed all over the world on science and technology and there is a general tendency to relegate philosophical studies to the background. But as full appreciation of true spiritual values and an overall view of life are as essential for a healthy society as science and technology, conscious effort is being made in many countries to counteract this unhealthy tendency. Philosophical societies are becoming active.

I would like to quote Mr. Sharief again. Says he:

> 'Let us have an organic view of life and existence in which heaven embraces earth, intuition and faith are reconciled with universal reason, science ceases to be antagonistic to religion and religion does not rebuke science, and infinity informs and animates finitude. This would amount to organic unity of all aspects of Being which creeds, philosophies and sciences have sundered by analytic thinking.'

Happily even the greatest scientists have not denied existence of God. It is Einstein again who is credited with the statement: 'Science without religion was lame and religion without science was blind.' Happily again some of the epic narratives of contemporary science, including the birth of our species, do lend themselves to religious interpretation. According to them a universe predisposed to create life seems more likely a product of divine design. With a little effort, some of the eminent scientists say, you can see the hand of God behind this design. Paul Davies, the physicist and writer who has done the most to advance this view (in 'God and the New Physics', 'The Cosmic Blueprint' and 'The Mind of God'), puts it this way: "The very fact that the universe is creative, and that the laws have permitted complex structures to emerge and develop to the point of consciousness—in other words, that the universe has organized its own self-awareness—is for me powerful evidence that there is 'something going on' behind it all. The impression of design is overwhelming."

This view is reminiscent of deism, the doctrine that attracted some of America's Founding Fathers, including Washington, Jefferson and Franklin. Deists believed in a clockmaker God; he built the universe, wound it up and let it run. They also believed we could sense this God through reason alone, by inspecting his handiwork—the universe and its laws.

Science and Yoga are not divergent but very closely associated. Both have much more in common than in variance...Both need to be yoked together. Truth spans both — macrocosm and microcosm. The mystics, in contrast to the scientists, arrive at truth by their intuitive methods of enquiry.

Complementary roles:

In general, science has its limitations for the questions of "Why?" though it can solve questions related to "How" and "What". Further, the knowledge of God and soul or metaphysics, knowledge of world(s) beyond the physical world of galaxies, of stars, and the knowledge of transmigration of souls in this world drama and so on, all these fall beyond the domain of science. Science deals in the realm of sense perceptions. It cannot explain the mysteries of the self. 'Science is the religion of the known and religion is the science of unknown.'

A proper synthesis of science and spirituality may lead to the highest sense which is complete in all respects; in the sense that nothing more remains to be known, and which in turn becomes partly the instrument of future attainment. Such a complete science will have to be soul science. Integration of science and spirituality will prove a potent means to bring about peace and enlightenment.

Science, in a sense, itself, is a spiritual power. In other words, we as human beings have within ourselves a basic urge to know. This is part of life. We have analysed and looked in every direction, our senses have multiplied a million times. We can see the stars and inside the atoms, we can hear what is happening on the other side of the globe, our minds have been multiplied by computer. However, there is one great responsibility of science and those using it to see that it does not serve killing and annihilation of man—nature's most remarkable species—and annihilation of this incredibly beautiful planet of which we are a part. Certainly the complementary roles of science and spirituality can add to human happiness. Science and love of God beautifully blend. This is reflected in a prayer which astronaut Edwin E. Eldrin carried in his pocket on his historic trip to Moon. It reads thus:

> 'The light of God surrounds me
> The love of God enfloods me
> The power of God protects me
> The presence of God watches over me—
> wherever I am, God is.'

Vision of a new world:

Can we look forward to a world of real peace and progress, development and democracy, dignity and divinity, harmony and happiness? Yes, it is possible if we, its inhabitants, firmly believe in the validity of these objectives and resolutely work to achieve them.

In a highly interesting and educative book 'Only One World' written by a friend of mine Dr. Gerard Piel, Founder-Publisher of Scientific American, the subtitle of which reads 'Our own to make and keep', some highly pertinent issues have been discussed most scientifically and imaginatively. Dr. Piel has particularly addressed himself to two basic questions: Environment and Development. With the end of cold war time has indeed come to work out wholeheartedly and honestly towards their solution, he suggests.

'The world population now is 5 billion. 750 millions are without access to safe water and their daily calorie intake falls 10% short of minimum requirements. Of the world's one billion poorest people, 500 million live north and south of the Himalayas and in East Asia. India is home still of 250 million of the world poorest' (Dr. Gerard Piel).

'The quality of future life on Earth will depend to a high degree on the size of stable world population that is likely to be reached sometime in the next century, and on the speed of the demographic transition in the pre-industrial world', says Maurice F. Strong, Secretary General, United Nations Conference on Environment and Development, in his Foreword to Dr. Piel's book.

One could not but agree with Dr. Piel's observation that economic development has proved to be the surest mode of population control. As such it is the ultimate environmental protection measure. To that end, a massive transfer of technology and economic assistance from rich nations to the poor nations is imperative. (The most portable technologies of industrial revolution—sanitation, medicine, popular education—have reached the pre-industrial world first.)

To make our planet one world again, Dr. Piel concludes: 'Common humanity must heal in time the estrangement in which for so long some people have lived rich and most have died poor! To keep this only one world, the exploiter of nature must become steward.'

In this brilliant presentation, Dr. Piel has explained, recalling the experience of developed nations, that industrial development has invariably been accompanied by the slowing and then halting of the growth of population. Hazards to environments laid by industrial technology, it has been shown, are subject to cure by technology, he says.

The world is described in Marshall McLuhan's phrase 'Global Village', or in Ninian Smart's phrase 'global city'—as our planet grows smaller due to modern means of communications and travel. It is increasingly imperative that we understand one another if we are to live together in relative peace and harmony.

The tremendous resources of modern mass media must be pressed into service so that the vision of a new world can become a reality. Simultaneously, governments and non-official agencies need to be increasingly involved, thus setting up a worldwide network linking the hundreds of groups and millions of people all over the world in the best interests of 'our own world to make and keep', to borrow Dr. Piel's phrase.

A new global consciousness:

'All individual souls are linked and supported by a vast, diffused spirituality whose limits perhaps coincide with those of cosmos itself', says Jules Romais, well-known as one of the world's leading literary figures.

'With the progress of Science and Technology, and with revival of interest in spirituality, mankind is at crucial evolutionary crossroads and is groping for a new model, a new philosophy, a new paradigm, a new global consciousness', observes Dr. Karan Singh, a ruler turned politician and a human integralist, quoted earlier too. (I happen to know him personally from the time he was a little boy. I was then serving the state of Jammu & Kashmir in India, under his father late Maharaja Hari Singh.)

For this, he says, we must draw on many of mankind's traditions—both religious and of secular mode—and also upon latest insights of man. 'In the Vedas we have ideals that are startling in their contemporary relevance. Such concepts as the spiritual unity of all that exists, mankind as a single family — *Vasudhaiva Kutumbakam*—, the harmony of religions, the welfare of all sections of society, for example, provide an ideological framework for the new consciousness.'

This new consciousness could happily combine 'active outer involvement' and 'intense inner living'—which happens to be the major theme of this book. I would like to quote Dr. Karan Singh again when he says: 'Life is a movement towards maturity, and the more challenging the outer situation, the greater are the opportunities for inner growth.' He further says: 'Neither materialistic denial nor ascetic refusal would help human race in creation of a new quality of life and aesthetically and ecologically balanced human environment...What is needed is a delicate balance between tradition and modernity, our ancient wisdom and emerging scientific and technological advancement.'

Power concept: wealth creation:

Let us briefly talk of 'power' in the sense the word is commonly used. Mr. Alvin Toffler, author of 'Powershift' (Bantam Books) who has also authored world-famed 'The Future Shock of the Third World' and 'Stunning Vision of the Future', refers to a new system of wealth creation based on individualism, innovation and information. Speed is the bye-word in all walks of life. A hunger for knowing is the urge. Power, according to him, is the most basic of social phenomenon, and it is linked with the very nature of universe.

He also refers to the emerging global power game in the decades ahead which cannot be understood without taking into account the rising power of Islam, Catholicism and other religions—or of global conflicts and holy wars among them. (Let us hope to the contrary there would be better interfaith understanding of which a mention has been made in the earlier pages.)

Drug Menace:

'Religions are not the only forces rising up to challenge the power of nation-states as such.' In his massive examination of the global narcotics business, James Miller writes: '... The Underground Empire today has more power, wealth and status than many nations. It flies no flag on the terrace of the United Nations, but it has larger armies, more capable intelligence agencies, more influential diplomatic services than many countries do.'

Illicit drug consumption, production and trafficking continue to rise in many parts of the world. This trend is both cause and effect of the global rise in crime, the spread of HIV-AIDS and the decay in family values.

According to estimates (as quoted by Secretary General United Nations in his message in June, 1994) at least 40 million people throughout the world regularly abuse drugs. Drug abuse and drug trafficking are dreaded scourges of the present-day world. They not only undermine the social system, jeopardise peace and harmony, breed corruption and destroy families, but also create severe health problems. Drugs have also definite link with terrorism. It is thus a multi-dimensional problem. It is imperative that comprehensive multi-disciplinary strategies continue to be adopted to fight the menace with vigour and dedication. We owe it not only to the present generation but to future generations of the world too.

The 'Power Unlimited' we are talking about is to be directed, inter alia, towards establishment of a society in which there is harmony among religions and a holy war against the 'power cocaine' which is marring the lives of many of our youths.

Years back, when I was young—freshly come out of the University in early forties—a question was asked by someone from Gurudev on Communism, which, it was then generally believed, would be the future world order. The sage-thinker replied:

> 'If communism is accompanied by spirituality it would in fact be manifestation of God (on this earth). If based on selfishness—which is scene of the present so-called

enlightenment—it amounts to devilishness.' (The maximum life of the then prevalent communism, he said, would be fifty years. This has come out true.)

'Just as different parts of the body perform different functions but are coordinated and treated equal by the intellect, so should different sections of society be treated by the ruling power: performing allotted duties according to their merits, but receiving equality in treatment. As in the body, any part getting into trouble gets attention of the intellect—other parts cooperating in the process—so should be the position of people forming a community or society. Nature itself represents communism, rather perfect socialism, in action.' (Gurudev often gave the instance of sun, moon and air, serving all as duty, without distinction.)

To me, it seems, to be real citizens of the modern world and to build a new world order we shall have to appreciate and promote spiritual values of life—not religiosity but oneness (Samata). Modern youth is our future hope. Let us hear what late Swami Chinmayananda has to say on this:

'In order to be a real citizen
of the modern world,
the people must develop and grow
into a new stature,
into a new consciousness,
a new awareness.

When we say that the modern youth
has no faith at all
we are only insulting him
and maligning him.

The fact is not that he has no religion
but the religion that is available at this
moment to him
is not capable of catering
to his demands or to his problems at all.'

Future:

I would like to record here an optimistic note quoting again my learned and spiritually awakened friend, late Gopi Krishna (of Kashmir) who was highly hopeful of future of the world. Says he in his book 'Higher Consciousness':

> 'With the growing knowledge of evolutionary mechanism, a larger and larger number of spiritual geniuses will be born in all parts of the world to aid the leaders in every field of human endeavour.
>
> 'They will build a tension-free, harmonious world in which everyone is provided with basic needs and has an equal opportunity to perfect himself (or herself).
>
> 'The life of our progeny will be so full of charm and beauty, harmony and music, love and romance, adventure and exploit in space (both inner and outer) wonders and marvels, that no imaginative thinker has so far been able to frame a picture of it...It is to be gained not in hypothetical heaven but here on earth in the organic frame of man. It is the sublime state of beatitude that is promised in every holy scripture of mankind.'

Tagore had a vision of India which can as well be vision of the world. His poem reads as under:

> Where the mind is without fear
> and head is held high,
> Where knowledge is free
> Where the world has not broken
> up into fragments by narrow domestic walls;
> Where words come out from the
> depth of truth,
> Where tireless stirring
> stretches its arms towards perfection,
> Where the clear stream of reason,
> has not lost its way into the
> dreary desert sand of dead habit,

Where the mind is led forward
by Thee into ever-widening
thought and action—
Into that heaven of freedom
my Father,
let my country awake.

The words of spiritually awakened rare people—as Tagore—apply to all humanity, to the whole world. The country of birth is merely an accident. As Socrates declared:

'I am a citizen
Not of Athens
or Greece
But of the World.'

So all great philosophers and spiritually realized people rightly feel as citizens of the world, nay of the whole universe. May more and more people think that way! And, the dream of a growing global consciousness come true. We can indeed make this world a happier, freer and better world in every way.

CHAPTER 10

Power Unlimited

We started this book with a very important question — the purpose of life. Real happiness, we have noticed, does not inhere in the gratification of senses, but is linked with knowing the 'Reality' in us, our inner being, a state of godhood. Life, indeed, can be so fulfilling when we decide to make a commitment in understanding our relationship with God, deepening that understanding, and then applying what we learn to our world. That is the spiritual path we have been talking about in the previous chapters.

The Spiritual Path:

Let us have a quick summary of the important steps and stages in the spiritual way of life we have talked about so far.

Real purpose and good of life is served when the real nature of temporal life is properly grasped.

The body is the first and obvious reality.
The mind is the relative reality.
The Self is the Ultimate Reality.

Human body is an opportunity for emancipation. Devotion to the Lord drives away doubts and delusion.

Worthy of knowledge is One God's existence;
Worthy of remembrance is One Name of God;
Worthy of renunciation is 'ego'.

Those who always remember God can understand the dignity and value of man in the true sense of the word.

मानुष तन को पाये के, सत मारग ज्ञान विचार।
"मंगत" समता शान्ति, तत्त खोज परम पद सार।।

Having been born as a human being, deliberate over the true path of knowledge (gnosis).
The state of oneness according to 'Mangat' is the real bliss; one should seek this supreme state.

By keeping the presence of God in mind, one thereby remains pure in thought, word and action.

अवनाशी तत्त परगट भयो, जब देह अन्तर मीत।
"मंगत" मन तब मानया, नित सिमरे नाम पुनीत।।

On perception of the 'immortal element' (the Word) within the body, the mind will be convinced of (Lord's) Presence and repeatedly remember the sacred Name, says "Mangat".

'Be not carried away by the glitter of the things of the world; be not deluded by the glaze of objects. Free the mind from the delusion of attachment...'

When the mind rushes out, recognising a world-of-objects, it runs wild among them, rejecting things that are not conducive, and pursuing things that are imagined to be conducive to its happiness...the ego strives and struggles; pants and suffers; this is bondage.

An intellect that functions through ego can never lead to peace.

One who is very proud of having read many religious books and has not purified himself from his imperfections, such an educated person can be likened to one who jumps into a well with a light in his hands, thus wasting his life.

(Mangat)

Truth is not something far away from us or our life. We are 'truth'. It is here, there and everywhere, all pervading, all embracing. We have to seek nothing to know. What seeks in us is to be sought after. What thinks in us is to be thought over.

मानुष जनम को धार के, सत मारग ज्ञान विचार।
"मंगत" भरमन सब मिटे, घर पाये शबद निरंकार।।

Having been born as a human being, ponder over the knowledge of the way to Truth. You will be free from all that fetters you and experience within you the Word beyond form, says Mangat.

तमाम लमयी संसार चेतन सत्ता प्रकाश के आधार पर ही स्थिर है।

The whole world of matter exists on the basis of conscious radiant Force, says Mangat.

Science is high knowledge it cannot be denied. Such knowledge being a part of total wisdom is essential to a clear approach towards deep Truth behind. If by the power of science clear truth is not perceptible, that is so much the defect of rational thinking of man.

"The West turned to outer discovery, in their dialogue with Nature. Out of this emerged very significant truths concerning science and technology. India also has had a dialogue with Nature, but it was of a different order — the understanding of Self, of the Universe, of the Highest Principle...the most significant pursuit."

(Mrs. Jayakar)

(We need both — science and spirituality.)

> Seekers after comfort and romance (alone) will be sadly disappointed on the spiritual path.
>
> (Samata Prakash)

> **Q:** How shall man be redeemed?
>
> **Ans:** Man can, within a short period of life, be god-like if he keeps the following three norms constantly in mind:
>
> 1) Belief in, and reflection upon, the Divine;
> 2) Awareness of death; and
> 3) Selfless service.
>
> (Gurudev)

Service of others:

Let us not worry about the result of our well-intentioned effort, in any field, but thank God He has given us the chance of service. We have discussed about service to others under Chapter 4. I would, however, like to touch on this subject again here since we are going to talk of the support of Nature one gets in overcoming even moral deficiencies through selfless service. It should be of special interest to youngmen to know how to overcome the oft-quoted five moral weaknesses or psycho-physical deficiencies through self-giving. Here again I am drawing on the enlightening observations and inspiring guidance of my Gurudev Mahatma Mangat Ram:

> Each entity of Nature has the tendency of functioning in such a manner as to cause comfort to other entities. That is the law of self-giving. The sun, the moon, planets, rivers, fire, air etc. — all of them work for the good of others. Your life shall, indeed, be like unto God's, nay, full of glory, if you always think good of others.
>
> Nature shall extend its support to you and you will experience the expansion of spiritual delight.

दुनिया में दूसरे का भला चाहने वाला पुरुष ही हमेशा खुश रहता है।

One who wishes well of others is really ever happy.

(Mangat)

Five moral defects or psycho-physical deficiencies—lust, anger, greed, attachment and ego—can be overcome by faith in God, and selfless service.

Anger ceases to be when love, in equal measure, is directed towards all. Both greed and ego are abandoned when all are served with concern. Attachment and lust both are destroyed when the Lord is seen as real of the Real.

The single method by use of which freedom from all the five 'enemies' can be attained is to put the body, mind and wealth in the service of others. Service to others is a supreme spiritual act.

(Samata Vilas)

We can learn the spiritual selfless service from Nature. Rivers don't drink their own water, trees don't eat their own fruits; nor do the clouds devour the drops (their rain's produce). The affluence of the good ones is for philanthropy only.

(Taru Manjari)

In today's seemingly fast-moving world, have we ever stopped for a moment and asked ourselves what it takes to be truly dedicated on the spiritual path, to know each day that we are consciously working with God as our companion in all that we do? Or more appropriately as instruments of God. Surrender each deed unto Divine Will, think of ourselves as His instruments engaged in action without sense of doership.

In being dedicated on the spiritual path, our first commitment is to understand our relationship to God and ourselves. There is only one power in this world that controls and regulates the universe — God's power — and we can enter into a working relationship with it. How can we do this? First, we can know we are worthy of it; we can have a positive self-image. Secondly, if necessary, we can change our mental attitude — know that we are winners and achievers instead of someone who is presently immobile. Open the mental windows of your mind to Life's creative energies. If you like, enter into a process of creative imagination but do so with strong intent and deep feeling. All of us have an ideal picture of ourselves — an image that is held in our minds "to become that person someday". That someday is present now.

In the words of Aldous Huxley: 'The phenomenal world of matter and of individualized consciousness — the world of things and animals and men and even gods — is the manifestation of the Divine Ground within which all patrial realities have their being, and apart from which they would be non-existent.'

It is a well-established truth that the Power which is behind all things of the world, the conscious and the unconscious, is a central Principle which mediates between the opposites and holds them in balance. It is common to the moving and the unmoving alike. Unseen outside, it constitutes the very core of every object and of every change. It is present in the inmost being of everything in an immeasurable degree. We too are living beings impregnated with that power. A realization of this will open up a vista of revealing truth. For verily, the microcosm is an expression of the macrocosm. The cosmic force expanded in the latter lies imprisoned in the former. The macrocosm is the universe; the microcosm is the body. The knower of this truth — the omnipresence of the Brahman (Supreme Being) — attains the highest, says the Taittiriya Upanishad.

An unseen dimension of human being:

As stated in the introduction:

अनन्त शक्त सत रूप को, बारम बार चितार।
"मंगत" सो निज रूप है, जल थल में भ्रतार।।

'Unlimited energy is one's true form,
Recall this again and again
This, Mangat's own true form,
roams at will both earth and ocean.'

Having realized our real self as the all Powerful, the Eternal, the Immutable — we are advised to remember *IT* over and over again, and feel its presence everywhere — on land, in water and in space.

Let us go over some more highly inspiring words of Gurudev:

पूरन शक्त सरब समाई। पूरन भेद खोज सुखदाई।।

Perfect Power is all-pervading.
Find out this beatific secret.

अनन्त शक्त प्रभ एक है, जो सर्ब जियां आधार।
"मंगत" गुरमुख विरले घट जानी निर्मल सार।।

God is the power unlimited behind all life.
Mangat says: This pure truth is understood by the rare God-oriented souls.

That, indeed, is the greatest discovery. Firmly established, the image of God in us expresses itself — in the infinite capacity of self-transcendence. As Dr. Radhakrishnan briefly puts it: "When we are emptied of our self (our ego), God takes possession of us.'

Only if we can lift up to a new amplitude of consciousness in ourselves, then alone we can become mightier and stronger. When we are mightier and stronger, the problems of the world are no more problems to us.

Inexhaustible source of Energy:

'There is a boundless source of energy and a boundless domination of freedom within every heart because we are essentially the Self. One can touch the source of all things — the limitless energy by receding one's consciousness to vast depth', says J. Krishnamurti.

Once discovered the tremendous source of energy is never exhausted. It is the energy that can be described as spirituality, received from the all-powerful, in and around us. 'Behold your power and your glory', says the Bible.

Clairvoyance, clairaudience and prevision psychometry — and evidences thereof—are only a partial, infinitesimal power within us. Released into the cosmic consciousness, man's spirit can become one with God, one self with the Spirit of the Universe or rise with Light and Vastness that transcends the universe; his nature can become one dynamic power with universal Nature or one Light with a transcendental Gnosis.

J. Krishnamurti refers to emptiness of mind — when there is not thought. 'It is the emptiness, that brings power ' — he says. 'Not the power we know, the power of money, the power of position, the power of husband over wife. This pure power is like that in a dynamo.' Stillness of mind, as experience would show, does make one aware of the divinity within. There is no power greater than that of the Divine's presence felt within.

Mahatma Mangat Ram has equated stillness of mind to godhood. The feeling and the fact of Divine presence within lends one a power which is great yet non-assertive, strong yet self-giving, full of knowledge yet humble. Guru Nanak warns against that power which breeds tyranny. Says he:

Conceit is the ruin of the soul,
Slander darkens the mind,
Power breeds tyranny.

The tender-hearted are pure,
They who have knowledge are humble.

'As you advance on the path of devotion, you develop the attitude that God is guiding you, that He is the reality. You begin to feel that you do not exist to be confined to the 'I' and 'mine' but that you exist to surrender this 'I' and 'mine' for the sake of God who dwells in everyone' (Swami Jyotirmayananda).

Swami Vivekananda, the greatest of the youthful leaders of his time in the world, says:

> 'All powers of the world are ours. We have shut our eyes with our hands, and complain that there is darkness around.
> You have in you the unlimited power — Anant Shakti — and ocean of peace.
> Self-confidence is the greatest power. Are you aware of your immense hidden powers?'

Here surely he is not talking of power which emphasizes the importance of oneself, breeds ruthlessness or self-expansive aggressiveness. But of power that leads to perfection, creativity, selfless service and sense of fulfilment.

Divine Power operating in us:

Sai Baba says: Man will cooperate with God and become the vehicle of Divine Power, if he has acquired the two qualities: Truth and Love. Saints like him do demonstrate the Divine Power working through them. (Though showing of miracles or performing of supernatural acts is not favoured by certain saints including Mahatma Mangat Ram.) However, Sai Baba calls miracles as his 'visiting card' only.

St. Paul wrote: "Now glory be to God who by *His mighty power* at work *within us* is able to do far more than we could ever dare to ask or even dream of — infinitely beyond our highest prayers, desires, thoughts, or hopes."

It is God who does the work in us, and it makes sense that the more we trust in Him, the more He is able to do.

Trust in God flourishes best in a childlike innocent heart. Then it is He who thinks in us. Years back I read the following lines in the Foreword to "Zen" in the Art of Archery, by D.T. Suzuki:

> 'Man is a thinking reed but his great works are done when he is not calculating and thinking. "Childlikeness" has to be restored after long years of training in the art of self-forgetfulness. When this is attained, man thinks — yet he does not think. He thinks like the showers coming down from the sky; he thinks like the waves rolling on the ocean; he thinks like the stars illuminating the mighty heavens; he thinks like the green foliage shooting forth in the relaxing Spring breeze. Indeed, he is the showers, the ocean, the stars, the foliage.'

We shall thirst for some sublime God-inspired endeavour as our sights soar higher, gazing into possibilities of a greater and a loftier purpose in life. It is then we glide into a richness of the treasures that are already within us.

'We must bring out these wonderful powers that are placed now in our keeping and pour them forth for the benefit of the world around. Not only the Lord has given us each an explosive magazine of power, but also in us are the faculties to wield it rightly.'

Let alone other faculties, our brain power itself is enormous. But few of us bother to learn about it and even fewer utilize it adequately. Modern science and any number of psychologists would confirm this fact.

Men of God, Faith and Action:

The great poet of East, Iqbal has also expressed his deep appreciation and reverence to men of God, truly spiritual people and paid such homage to them which is rare and unmatched in literature. What can be a better description praising an honest, spiritual person and man of God!

کوئی اندازہ کر سکتا ہے اس کے زورِ بازو کا
نگاہ مردِ مومن سے بدل جاتی ہیں تقدیریں

"No one can ever assess
The power of his strength
For one glance from the man of God (Momin)
Can change destinies, and reverse."

He has also forcefully described ammunition for the struggle of life:

عمل پیہم یقیں محکم محبت فاتح عالم
جہادِ زندگانی میں ہیں یہ مردوں کی شمشیریں

"The firm belief, constant strife
Love in your heart, conquering worlds
These are the weapons of men
In the crusade of life."

About the pleasures of faith, which is the essence of Sufism, he says:

"Neither swords nor scheming
Can help break, the chains of slavery
Only with firm faith in heart
Can you break free."

(Translated from Urdu)

After listening to saints, philosophers and poets on the subject of spiritual powers and their use let us see again what Dr. Wayne Dyer, a prominent writer on modern management (quoted earlier too), has to say in his book 'The Sky's the Limit':

'Each person on this planet is inherently, intrinsically capable of attaining dizzying heights of happiness and fulfilment.'

'Anyone can achieve a high level of human development, can in effect become a 'self-achieved', non-limit person, if he or she works at it.'

For self-development, for professional competence, for spiritual achievement, in fact for any type of excellence we must recognize that within each one of us there lies a vast potential of energy and power which, when properly understood and directed, will lead to previously unimagined heights of perception and awareness. No goal will then be too difficult to achieve.

Will-power:

An enlightened intellect is not necessarily a dedicated will.

Will is a tremendous factor in life. Indomitable will-power is a sine qua non for success in the life of every human being.

'Man's will-power is the great generator of energy.' It is through will-power that we are able to draw quickly on the infinite store of inner strength. It is the power by which we can reach even the heights of God-realization.

Paramahansa Yogananda tells us that 'You revolve that (thinking) will around a problem of health or of finances or of controlling a habit, or around the desire to know God. If you will and act until victory, then you have obtained dynamic will.' He adds: 'When you make up your mind to do good things, you will accomplish them if you use your dynamic will-power to follow through. If you go on trying, God will create the means by which your will shall find its proper reward.'

We can have two commendable aspirations:

—worldly prosperity and well being,
—spiritual illumination and freedom.

In both cases righteousness must be the basis. The

former should be directed and subordinated to the latter. The degree of success in life is evidently commensurate with the degree of one's will-power.

All the movements and achievements of men in the world in different spheres including science are manifestations of the will of man.

As Swami Budhananda of Advaita Ashram, Calcutta, writes in his book 'Will-Power and its Development':

> 'Many of us have no idea how much of goodness, strength and greatness cry within us for self-manifestation. We have mostly known only the weaker side of ourselves, which in fact belongs to the not-self, according to Vedanta. It is the basic tragedy of our daily life that effectively prevents a real encounter with our true self. Therefore, it is important for every person to know how to avoid the failure of will. The only way to do it is to cultivate the will-power.'
>
> 'Incredible though it may appear, many of us do not have even the will to develop the will-power! We seem to think it is big botheration, too exacting a responsibility to be carrying about all the time. But when we know for certain that within ourselves is unlimited power, that we are not these puny things as we appear to be, that we are not weak reeds worthy only to be broken anytime — then we develop the mind to manifest that power in our life by sharply cutting out all delusions and illusions which are to the contrary.'

How do we assert the divine within us? If we want to assert the divine, we must not do two things: we must not be cowards and we must not be hypocrites. We must be brave, take courage in both hands and follow the truth to its logical conclusion. Go with truth wherever it takes us, this should be our motto.

Two things will oppose this creative move within us:

(1) our regrets about the past, and
(2) our worry about the future.

Both of these are detrimental to the cultivation of will-power, because they successfully undercut all forward-looking, creative, positive movements within our minds. They are also wholly unnecessary performances. Exaggerated regrets for our past and overmuch worry about the future will only damage our present, weaken our minds and injure our future also.

Physical energy is conserved by living a moral life of purity and moderation. In moderation is suppleness, in suppleness is strength.

There is however one important point to be noted in the development of will-power: the will must be given a right direction. All the notorious evil geniuses in history who inflicted on humanity unspeakable suffering, also had a kind of powerful will. We are not talking of that kind of malevolent will-power.

Our soul has infinite resources, and our mind draws these resources from the soul. The mind can be either positive or negative; it can either use energy or misuse it. Even though everyone has the same potentiality of immense energy, most people do not equally utilize their inner resources.

Swami Jyotirmayananda thus advises on the question of developing will-power:

> 'You should develop will-power not for petty things but for tuning yourself to God. To the extent that you do this, you begin to discover immense power of will within yourself. Your mind becomes a reservoir of energy, and your good thoughts uplift countless people. You realize you are not a limited personality because you have discovered universality within yourself. This is the goal of developing will-power.'

Despite will-power we may face adversities. What should be our attitude? Here again the Swami advises:

> 'Welcome tests given by God. Saints say: When there is adversity, develop the spirit of austerity. Think of it like this: you are given adversities because God wants you to be qualified for something great. For example, when you want to test the value of a metal such as gold, you have to give it a harsh test. You might subject it to intense heat to melt it down a little, or you might treat it ruthlessly with chemicals to determine if it has any value. The same applies to the metal in your personality. If the gold within your personality is to shine forth, nature must give you severe tests. The greater the severity of these "tests", the shinier will become the metal within your personality.'

Concentration and controlled attention:

When asked by a well-known author Napoleon Hill to explain the sources of ideas, Dr. Gates (see his background under 'Creative Thinking' a little ahead) said: The sources of all ideas are:

1. Knowledge stored in the subconscious mind and acquired through individual experience, observation and education.
2. Knowledge accomplished by others through the same media which may be communicated by telepathy.
3. The great universal storehouse of Infinite Intelligence, wherein is stored all knowledge and all facts, and which may be contacted through the subconscious section of the mind.

A story concerning concentration oft-related in India tells of the spiritual test given by the great king Janaka to his would-be disciple, Sukadeva. To test the young devotee before accepting him for spiritual training, Janaka required Sukadeva to tour the royal palace while carrying in the palm of his hand an oil lamp filled to the brim. The condition of passing the test was that Sukadeva was to observe minutely (and subsequently report to the king) every item and detail in each palatial room, without spilling even a drop of oil from the brimful lamp. The meaning of the test is that the spiritual aspirant must learn to keep his attention centred in God, not allowing his thoughts to wander from Him for a moment, lest the oil of divine communion be spilled, while at the same time he performs accurately to the last detail his duties in the world.

The human form is the highest product on the plane of existence, manifesting divinity more vividly and actively than in any other life. We must find through concentration and controlled attention in the depth of our being that which carries in it the sense of universality, limitless expansion and unbroken continuity.

'God', says Henry Thomas Humblin, the Saint of Sussex, 'He is not afar. His abode is not on some distant mountain peak or in unreachable starry heaven.' Dr. Radhakrishnan expresses the same idea in the following words: 'The Supreme is not a 'god' who sleeps in serene abstention while hearts heavy laden cry out for help but a saving God of love believed and experienced as such by the devotee. He is by you, with you, within you. There is no place where He is not, not a place He has left untouched, not an atom where His presence does not shine...'

When the little operates as a part of the whole, then the little is limitless. When it acts separately, it is limited. Let us be united with vastness around; let the Light and Power and Presence envelop us and protect and cherish and foster, till all our inner and outer existence is one movement and an expression of its peace and strength and bliss.

Power of Prayer:

We may again talk briefly of the power of prayer. (This subject was discussed earlier in Chapter 6). Man is considered as the most perfect manifestation of God. He, according to Sufi saints, combines in himself all the divine attributes and perspectives. Most of the perspectives are, however, *virtual* and can become *actual* through spiritual exertion. Through contemplation, meditation and devotion, man can achieve a perception of divinity and unlimited power by reunion with the Almighty.

> निमख निमख अराधिए, एको नाम भगवन्त।
> "मंगत" भरमन सब मिटे, घर परसें शक्त अनन्त।।

> From moment to moment worship it;
> One Supreme Being's Name
> Thus efface all confusion and
> perceive power unlimited within, says 'Mangat'.

Man can be whatever he wants to be, says Yogananda. Man can change his outer and inner nature by concentration. A person of strong mind can be whatever he wants to be. The limited human personality can be greatly expanded by meditation.

It has been scientifically proved that effective prayer does perform miracles in human personality, observes Robert H. Schuller, a well-known writer on management. Dr. Alexis Carrell, a Nobel prize winning medical doctor, wrote in a posthumously published work:

> 'Prayer is not only worship. It is also an invisible emanation of man's worshipping spirit. The most perfect form of energy that one can generate. The influence of prayer upon the human mind and body is as demonstrable as that of any secreting gland. Its results can be measured in terms of increased physical buoyancy, greater intellectual vigour, moral stamina and a deeper

understanding of realities that underline human relationships. In fact, I would say that true prayer is a way of life, the truest life is literally a prayer.'

He prayeth best who loveth best
All things both great and small;
For the dear God who loveth us,
He made and loveth all.
(Coleridge)

"May the ineffable mystery of the Lord of the universe be revealed in my heart. May I expand into His limitless vastness, shedding all the dead might of mundane awareness."

It would be appropriate to quote Rigveda here:

"O Lord!
While you are with us,
With our words of prayer
All challenges of life we answer,
You are ours and we are verily yours."

That would be the right realization of the Power Unlimited in and around us, and its right utilization for our good and good of the world.

Positive thinking:

Thoughts make us what we are. Many saints as well as modern management experts are equally emphatic about the importance of positive thinking. All deprecate negative thinking. Calm positive thinking is revivifying. There would be hardly anyone who has not experienced this sometime or the other.

Over 2500 years ago Buddha said in one of his precepts:

'Opposite a negative wave of thought with a positive wave of thought.'

Swami Jyotirmayananda of Yoga Research Foundation

Mission (USA) has much to tell in his book 'The Art of Positive Thinking'. He says: 'Positive thinking implies keeping one's mind free from sadness, dejection, worry and tension, and negative sentiments such as anger, hate, greed and pride. In positive terms, a mind that entertains thoughts of joy and goodwill, thoughts ready to forget and forgive, to harmonise and to promote peace is a positive mind.'

When we begin to realize the amazing influence of positive thoughts not only on our body but on our circumstances, that is the beginning of a divine process, the Swami says, that will lead us to self-realization which is the goal of all positive thinking.

'Making strong positive suggestion, the suggestion to yourself, does not imply that you are hypnotising yourself, it is rather a process of self-awakening.' He advises:

> "Learn the art of giving positive suggestions to yourself. Instead of sustaining weak thoughts in your mind, give positive suggestions:
>
> 'I am the architect of my own destiny.'
> 'I have infinite resources of spirit within me.'
> 'I am gaining more will-power day by day.'
> 'I am experiencing peace and fulfilment.'
> 'I am the master of my mind, intellect and senses.'
> 'I am abiding in God who is all-blissful.'
> 'I am essentially Sat Chit Ananda — Existence, Knowledge and Bliss.'
> 'I am the supremely free Atman — the Self.' "

We should not permit our mind to be disturbed by a failure. Instead we should be unruffled and summon courage. With an optimistic disposition, by thinking and acting in a positive, constructive way we can overcome any unpleasant situation.

'I am hated, misunderstood and deceived by others — one who harbours such thoughts in one's mind can never be free from the causes which inflict destructiveness upon oneself' (Buddha).

Mahatma Mangat Ram advises that it is only at a certain stage of spiritual development *Jnana Yoga,* when one rises above body-consciousness, and arises in the Atman (our real self), shedding the feeling of 'I am the body', 'I am the doer' — that one can say to himself: 'I am the Atman above the body and its senses...I as Atman am pure consciousness... fearless...above duality and desires...immortal...sachida-nanda...bliss...I as Atman am the Life, the Witness of all.'

In the philosophy of Samatavad that he advocates both Karma Yoga or Bhakti Yoga and Jnana Yoga co-exist, the sentiments behind both are helpful in attaining the highest goal of life — the self-realization.

We may now briefly see how 'positive thinking' is viewed by those whose advice can be helpful, particularly in modern working life.

'Failure will never overtake you if your determination to succeed is strong', says O.G. Mandino, author of the highly popular book 'The Greatest Salesman in the World'. Some of his 'secret lessons' in positive thinking are:

'Today I begin a new life.'
'I will greet this day with love in my heart.'
'I will persist until I succeed.'
'I will act now (This is the time. This is the place. I am the man).'

Evidently, it is vital that we develop a strong belief in our ability to succeed. Need not be timid, tired or tense, says Robert H. Schuller in his book 'Self-Love'. 'Dedicate your success to the service of God and your fellowmen. Put a soul in your goal. Surround your dream for success with the trinity of faith, hope and love.

Faith stimulates success
Hope sustains success,
Love sanctifies success.'

Again Robert H. Schuller in his book 'Move Ahead with

Positive Thinking' recommends, among many other good ideas:

> Stop thinking of reasons why something won't work and start thinking of ways in which we can make it work.
>
> Begin each day with a positive seed thought and hold it there.
>
> Talk yourself into possibility thinking.
>
> Use your imagination to become what you really want to be.

'I can do all things through Christ which strengthens me.' This passage, from the 'New Testament', was favourite of Norman Vincent Peale, author of the two well-known books: 'The Power of Positive Thinking' and 'Positive Imaging'. He extends the same sentiments in the following words:

> 'Let God be your partner (It is surprising the load he will take off you).'

The concept of imaging, according to him, is a form of mental activity. It consists of vividly picturing, in our conscious mind, a desired goal or objective, and holding that image until it sinks into the subconscious mind, where it releases great untapped energies. He narrates the concept of belief in three pithy sentences:

> 'I believe that I am always divinely guided.'
>
> 'I believe that I will always take the right turn as the Right.'
>
> 'I believe that God will make way where there is no way.'

Norman Vincent Peale suggests use of powerful imaging technique that consists of just three words: 'Act as if...' In his book 'Positive Imaging' he further says:

> 'See yourself always as a child of God.'
>
> 'What is imaged in your mind tends to actualize. (Knock the letter 't' from 'can't'.)'

'Practise what you do well; draw strength and confidence from your success.'

'Condition your unconscious mind with spiritual power/principles.'

'Sensitize yourself to the beauty, variety and excitement of living.'

Napoleon Hiller & W. Clement Steve offer, in their famous book 'Success through a Positive Mental Attitude', some highly precious thoughts:

Man's greatest power lies in the power of the prayer.

Loving people and serving is the greatest value in life.

To remove several mental cobwebs: negative feelings, emotions...beliefs and prejudices.

Day by day in every way through the grace of God, I am becoming better (a good positive feeling).

You can do if you believe you can.

'If you are sincerely seeking growth, you will assert yourself positively in every aspect of your life. To become pure and positive, one should think, act and speak, even eat in a pure and positive manner. Do not confine yourself behind a wall of negative manifestation like anger, hatred, greed, envy and prejudice, but lift yourself above that. "I am everything, I am the cosmos and the cosmos is within me; whatever is pure and positive I am That!" Remove the negative aspects, the obsessions and neurosis from the sphere of existence. Break the boundaries of limited mind and body. Experience bliss throughout yourself and around yourself. Find yourself in the Ultimate...you are above, in the highest state of consciousness. It is possible to live outside the law of matter' (Swami Purna).

Creative thinking:

'Your Creative Power' and 'Applied Imagination' by

Alex F. Osborn have inspired hundreds of thousands of people in the West, especially the USA, to be engaged in creative thinking. Many people have been motivated to positive, constructive action.

Osborn, like so many creative thinkers, used a notebook and a pencil as favourite working tools — for jotting down whenever an idea occurred. (My friend P.L. Tandon, a well-known Marketing Economist, does the same. I learnt it from him.)

Dr. Elmer Gates was, in his time, a great American teacher, philosopher, psychologist, scientist and inventor who developed hundreds of inventions and discoveries in the various arts and sciences. He did his creative thinking by "sitting for ideas" in a small soundproof room — having a plain table and a chair. On the table were pads of paper, several pencils, and push-button to turn the lights off and on.

"What is good in people — and consequently in the world — is their insistence on creation, their belief in friendship, in loyalty for its own sake" (E.M. Forster). A good combination of positive qualities!

He also says: "The people I admire most are those who are sensitive and want to create something or discover something and don't see life in terms of power."

When we are talking of the Power Unlimited in us, surely it is not meant to be used in the ordinary sense of the 'power' but creatively and usefully for good of the people. Sensitivity, creativity and selfless service go together and make life purposeful.

Intuition:

Each one of us must have experienced that logical and vertical thinking does not always give us all the answers and certainly not the great ones. It is no wonder, therefore, that Einstein (on the theory of Relativity) said: 'The really valuable factor was intuition.' It is the power of obtaining knowledge that cannot be acquired either by inference or observation, by reason or experience. It is a sort of seeing with the eye of the mind; it is instinctive knowledge.

Intuition is not just a hunch; it is not wishful thinking; it is not hope and it is not pure guess work.

Intuition can bring about discovery, creativity, prediction (precognition ability) and ultimately illumination.

'Nature does not rest content with merely the calculated efforts of human minds. Most of the great discoveries in the past were stimulated by flashes of sudden insight in those whose brains were already in tune. But for this extraordinary phenomenon, human progress would have never been possible' (Gopi Krishna in 'Higher Consciousness').

'Learning of many things does not teach insight' (Heraclitus).

Intuition can and must be developed. Meditation is closely linked with intuition: 'Brain-skilling practice can give us power to select at will from the subconscious and unconscious states. One must be prepared at all times to be overtaken by intuition. We have just to internalise and to introspect. We hardly do that and mostly live on the surface of our being.

'Deep in the depths of all of us there is a secret longing, a silent impulse, a soaring ambition to do something beautifully great, spectacularly noble, and surely enduring. This is a divine summons from the deeper Pressure in us, to take off from the decaying levels of mediocrity into Voiceless Heights of spontaneity and perfection. We must hark to these indisputable intimations divine, too sacred to ignore; too cruel, if we should reject.

'These are the calls commanding us to marshal all our facilities and powers and march out to conquer. When so enlarged in our outlook on life and in our vision of God, we learn to obey its biddings — there then comes that experience — that miraculous unfoldment in ourselves. Thereafter, we are no more satisfied with our commonplace living and its routine activities, but must then demand from ourselves nobler exertions, greater achievements' (Aurobindo).

Miracles:

People often confuse miraculous powers and paranormal activities with spirituality. As we see in the history of most primitive societies, no distinction was made between magic and faith. The deities worshipped, whether in the form of idols, natural objects, or forces of nature, were all deemed to have magical powers. People would undertake various practices and disciplines for worshipping and propitiating them, regarding these as methods for acquisition of magical properties. The shaman, the witch doctor, the oracle or the magician were regarded with awe and fear.

The primitive practice of investing a holy man — the prophet, the mystic and the Yogi — with supernatural powers continues, with some modifications though, to this day.

'Most of these beliefs are based on superstition. Expecting miraculous intercession for one's own spiritual or temporal needs...exhibits lack of self-confidence and dependence on others for the solution of one's problem.'

As Gopi Krishna observes in his book 'Higher Consciousness':

> 'It is no wonder then that the miracle-working Yogi exercises a tremendous influence and draws enormous crowds of admirers and followers.'
>
> 'True there have been isolated miracles, some paranormal phenomenon and small scale magical feats, often intermingled with fraud and self deception but no widespread or significant victories over nature. Whatever good or everlasting improvements have been effected have all been due to the power of intellect applied by talented men and women, believing in their own efforts and skills, without reliance on the super-

natural or the occult. Even the powers of healing displayed by some psychics today are not possible of universal application.'

No doubt that certain gifted individuals, mystics, saints or adepts have sometimes shown miraculous powers. But there are limits to their displays. All these phenomena, no doubt, provide an interesting subject for study and investigation. I have often suggested in my discourses with spiritual friends that a university should be set up somewhere at the foothills of Himalayas where selected saints and Yogis from all over should be brought in for scientific study and experimentation of their miraculous powers and how, if at all, these can be developed for the good of the people in general.

The phenomenon of life is itself a visible, conclusive proof of the inter-dependence and mutual harmony of the physical and superphysical laws. However, we need not place too much reliance on the miraculous and the supernatural or to reject them altogether. The more rational attitude would be to investigate them thoroughly and sympathetically without undue bias towards either side.

We must guard against the so-called *mantra* specialists and miracle-workers, and the stories of instantaneous self-realization. Wrong and delusive notions, concerning the Divine and the miraculous, unfortunately continue to grow.

Extraordinary things sometimes do happen enroute spiritual growth—some sort of psychic achievements, some miraculous powers. But we need not pay attention to them lest we become sidetracked.

'If you have some spiritual experience, spiritual powers within, people hover around you: some want a child; some want worldly fame, some want sickness removed...If we start sharing our experience there is always a danger of becoming a victim to performing miracles because the ego inflates.' "I can do this and I can do that", says Maharaj

Charan Singh. He advises not to become rival of the Lord by performing miracles.

Mahatma Mangat Ram also advises against 'miracles'. The greatest miracle is the human body itself. He warns against superstition, running after miracle-mongers, belief in magic, charlatans and so on. Self-realization is a process of personal endeavour. Even when a saint shows the path, based on his/her experience, we have to walk ourselves. There is no short-cut to the Divine. It is dire devotion, indepth interiority, and sincere sustained efforts that lead one to the understanding of one's divine nature and for mind to merge into that state. There is no wonder, no miracle, no power bigger than that. Let that be our goal, rather than being dragged in the sidewalks of superstition or running after exhibition of miracles.

In answer to a question from a disciple who was curious about *sidhis* (thaumaturgic power) Shri Ramana Maharishi said: 'Do not fix your attention on changing things of life, death and other phenomena. Do not think of even the actual act—seeing or perceiving them — but only of that which is responsible for it all. It is inside yourself. The results of this concentration will be seen in all sorts of involuntary clair-voyance, in peace of mind, in power to deal with troubles, in power all round, yet always involuntary power.'

The stories and life histories of saints and Yogis written by their disciples especially abound in miraculous anecdotes and tales. A Persian proverb very aptly says: 'Spiritual teachers do not fly in the air. It is their disciples who make them fly.'

There is no mention of the word 'miracle' in Gita, most popular of Indian scriptures. Not one of the great modern Indian saints and sages — Sri Ramakrishna, Maharishi Ramana, Sri Aurobindo, Swami Dayananda, Mahatma Mangat Ram— endorse the exhibition of psychic gifts or the working of miracles, even if endowed with such powers.

Spirituality and Modern Management:

There has been considerable interest in recent years in spirituality as applicable to modern management. There have been seminars and workshops on this subject.

This is a healthy trend. A common mistaken notion of spirituality is that it is a flight or escape from life. That it is very much related to management of human affairs too is a happy recognition of the multi-purpose potential of spirituality. Introduction of spiritual values in all walks of life certainly ennobles its purpose as well as contributes to its practical success.

Let us briefly go over a few aspects of spirituality and modern management:

Honesty, truth and integrity are as much qualities of a spiritual person as attributes of a successful manager.

Politeness, consideration and respect of others, mean not only good public relations in the modern sense, these are a must for a spiritual person for he/she sees the Supreme Being residing in each frame of flesh, God in everyone. (See Annexures VIII and IX.)

Humility, of course, is a virtue. But it should not mean callousness or insensitivity. True spirituality makes one highly enthusiastic and super-sensitive, qualities also necessary for good management.

Spirituality teaches us: Be a Witness; learn the art of detachment. Detachment when correctly understood should not give us the idea of becoming cold and indifferent to the problems of others. Rather, detachment would endow us with spiritual charm.

Scriptures, Gita in particular, advocate *action,* selfless action, with the objective of helping others. The modern corporate concept is also service of society — the consumers as well as shareholders. As we know, there is now a growing recognition of social responsibilities of business.

Work without attachment to the fruit, the spiritual principle, when applied to business and management ennobles the quality of our effort. Work for work sake should mean deeper devotion, not dilution or diminishing of interest.

Putting of 'head, heart and soul' in a lawful and worthwhile activity is nothing but application of spirituality in that activity. The result is obvious. I have, in my own experience, seen how great craftsmen do that when engaged in producing things of rare beauty.

Knowing one's real self, and drawing power from that unlimited resource, adds to one's will-power so necessary to make success of any big job, meet any challenge, overcome any obstacle.

Power of prayer, will-power and positive thinking — which we have briefly discussed earlier — are three great forces common to practitioners of spiritual advancement and successful modern management.

We are a family. This spiritual fact when applied to a group of people one manages, works wonderfully. The Japanese experience in applying this concept to business and industry has worked so well.

Spirituality supports harmony between thought, word and deed. Such a harmony pays its dividends in management. A person possessing and demonstrating this harmony commands real respect of people he/she works with.

Spirituality, from all angles, means skilful performance of duty, equanimity under all circumstances — success or failure—helping oneself by helping others, praying to God for guidance and His Grace which would lend dignity and success to any good-intentioned activity or enterprise.

Towards Perfection:

There are three ways to reach the goal of perfection — that is being possessed by God and allowing HIM to work through us:

— knowledge of Reality (*jnana*),

— by adoration and love (*bhakti*) of the Supreme, or

— by the subjection of the will to the Divine purpose (*karma*).

These are distinguished on account of the distribution of emphasis on the theoretical, emotional and practical aspects. Men are of different types — reflective, emotional or active — but they are not exclusively so. At the end knowledge, love, action mingle together.

Knowledge is power, this is a common saying. It is perfectibility man has eternally sought from the meandering paths of knowledge. Marquis de Condorcet, a great French spiritualist, has very aptly remarked at a place, "No bounds have been fixed to the improvement of human faculties, the perfectibility of man is absolutely indefinite; the progress of this perfection henceforth above the control of every power that would impede it, has no other limit than the duration of the globe upon which nature has placed us."

Why should we say that we are too weak to walk the path of perfection? Can we not see this weakness is only limitation of power? We are responsible for placing this limitation on ourselves by ourselves, while the stable, the unchanging, the deathless, the all-powerful is always there, right within us and outside. Self-knowledge, self-reverence and self-control — these three will lead man to sovereign power. 'Keep the thought in your mind that the Divinity is within you and that you have endless possibilities. Nothing is impossible for you to achieve by Divine Grace', thus advises Swami Jyotirmayananda.

For Youth specially:

We have talked of spirituality — the role and power of the spirit — throughout this book. We have also seen that fundamentals of all religions emphasize existence of one God, His all-pervasiveness, the life energy and bliss flowing from Him.

The question arises why many people, especially the younger ones, are not attracted towards religion. The obvious answer is that the religion available today does not generally answer their demands. The old religions have to modify themselves to meet the aspirations of the younger generation and to convince them of their efficacy in enabling them to recognize within them the vast source of energy, intelligence and awareness.

Need of a new religious outlook:

'In case the modern man can be explained in terms of his own modern science, the nuclear science of the outer world and the modern developing science of psychology, if he is taught that the psychological and emotional entity in Him is the expression of something deeper, something vaster, and something higher than all-supermental; if he can know that beyond the mind there is a mighty source in each one of us, and lead him where he can realise and experience that dimension in himself, then that path would be the modern religion fit for the modern man' (Swami Chinmayananda).

I was recently reading a book 'Islam' by Fazlur Rahman. Being impressed with his views on God and religion, which would appeal to youngmen, I reproduce some of them briefly:

> 'God has ingrained in the human soul a discernment of good and evil.'
>
> 'Religion should not be considered as incurable enemy of reason. There should also be no conflict with modern science.'
>
> 'Although faith and reason operate in different spheres, they must not only not conflict but must positively cooperate in human advancement.'
>
> 'No religion can claim proprietary rights over truth or divine guidance.'

'The Quran enjoins upon man to think intelligently and to study nature — God's creation as the 'signs' of God.'

'The fundamental concern of the religions should be to restate their basic ideas in such a way as to open the doors for influence of new ideas and for acquisition of modern knowledge in general.'

'The medieval content of religions must be developed to meet the needs of modern society. Excessive stress on the external disciplines of religion merely creates religious fossils.'

Society has to be taken out of the moral and spiritual debris consisting of superstition, miracle mongering and charlatanism. Social change is inevitable and trends that have already set in are irreversible. They have simply to be channelized suitably. There is need for constructive and bold humanism, a revival of human values, a recognition of God as the source of all power, a conviction that each one of us is divine and can manifest that divinity in all movements of life.

Abstention from all evil, performance of good acts, and purification of one's mind — this is the doctrine of the Buddha. Following it in word and spirit would be manifestation of spirituality in life.

Advice of Gandhi and Nehru:

Having known and come in close contact with Mahatma Gandhi (known as Father of Indian Nation) in my young days, and having worked as a young civil servant in Pandit Jawaharlal Nehru's regime (he was India's Prime Minister for 18 years) I would like to share some of their thoughts which impressed me intensely and which should be of special interest to youth. One was a spiritual politician, the other an intellectual statesman. (Incidentally Gandhi regarded Nehru as his political inheritor.)

Gandhi:

Begin your day with prayer and make it so soulful that

it may remain with you until the evening. Close the day with prayer so that you may make a peaceful night, free from dreams and nightmares.

Prayer is not asking. It is longing of the soul. It is a daily admission of one's weaknesses.

It is better in prayer to have a heart without words than words without heart.

Speak the truth and remain non-violent at any cost.

I do not want my house to be walled in all sides and my windows to be stuffed. I want the culture of all lands to be blown about my house as freely as possible. But I refuse to be blown off my feet by any one of them.

Mine is not a religion of prison house. It has the room for the least among God's creation, but it is proof against insolent pride of race, religion and colour.

Nehru:

Greatness comes from vision, the tolerance of the spirit, compassion and an even temper which is not ruffled by ill fortune or good fortune.

Let us think not so much of what we have done but what we have left undone and what we have done wrongly.

I do not think that a person who ignores the small things, the small truths, the small decisions, the small politeness, the small graciousness, can take anything big in a big way.

You cannot talk of God to a starving person, you must give him food.

You cannot make all men equal but we must at least give them equality of opportunity.

It is dangerous and harmful to be guided in our life's course by hatreds and aversions, for they are wasteful of energy and limit and twist the mind and prevent it from perceiving the truth.

Violence for Gandhi was opposite of truth and he therefore preached to us against violence, not only of the hand but of the mind and heart, as well.

Self-discipline:

Man's nature, especially his mental nature, has a spontaneous tendency to give a favourable explanation for everything he thinks, feels, says and does. It is only by observing the movements that occur in us — many impulses, reactions and conflicting views that drive us to action — with great care, by bringing them, as it were, before the tribunal of our highest ideal with a sincere will to submit to its judgment, that we can hope to form in ourselves a discernment that never errs.

True Discipline
can never be imposed
it must spring
from the Heart...
spontaneously

(Swami Purna)

Beyond a wholesome discipline, we must be gentle with ourselves. This is one of the lessons I had access to. Years back (1968-70) when I was posted in Jamaica on a UN assignment, connected with marketing and management, one day a missionary left with me a paper — "Desiderata' by Max Ehrmann. It provided me as a young executive with spiritual leanings, rich food for thought. I have tried to follow fairly successfully quite a few of the suggestions given in the paper — copy of which forms Annexure X of this book. I would recommend its perusal especially by the young readers. Maybe they find the reading fruitful. For those who have already read this — as also any other quotations and references given in the book — my presentation may be treated by them as happy revision and an opportunity for appraisal of the knowledge applied in practical life.

The Holy Mother says:

'Prayer and meditation, or pilgrimage, or even earning money, all these should be done during the earlier part of one's life.

'In old age, one's physical and mental strength is weakened.

'Your prayers and meditations must be accomplished now, in your youth.'

'It cannot be that in the old age one may begin to serve and fulfil life's four ends of *dharma, artha, kama* and *moksha*. It is proper, therefore, to strive for their fulfilment right from the beginning of youth' (Taru Manjari).

Infinite possibilities:

'Individual mind is a wave of Cosmic Mind. Thus one can allow his mind to tune itself with the Cosmic Mind by rising beyond the limitations caused by ignorance and egoism. In doing so, he can draw unimaginable energy from the Cosmic Source and effect wondrous changes in the world of matter.'

'There are infinite possibilities in each one of us', says Swami Chinmayananda. He adds: 'We must learn the art of tapping these mighty resources within. The only way to explore these unknown veins of power and strength, efficiency and ability, success and glory, is to put forth our sincere efforts into the work in hand, more diligently, more industriously. Let us keep very high visions of achievements; they, by themselves, will come to serve as intimations of what we can be; they will summon us to larger and more earnest efforts.'

Our strength should perennially cascade from our realization of the immense resources in ourselves. The Lord, the Omnipotent, resides ever in our heart. "To Him alone you go, in all conditions", says Gita. Therefore, let us carry ourselves confidently; success shall be ours, and, in fact, failure can only be "success delayed" to every prompt servant of the Lord.

In the present crisis of world history, it matters profoundly what view is taken of the value of the human individual. Only if we are intellectually convinced that it extends beyond the limits of ordinary consciousness and reaches out to that for which the ordinary name is God, can the purpose of human society be secured. From the nature of the personality of man springs the possibility of the mystical Divine union, the promise of limitless inheritance, and the realization of power unlimited in him.

Late Gumnam Sahib (quoted earlier, too) used to say:

سبق سیکھا ہے ہم نے اہل حق سے خود شناسی کا
خدا کا جاننے والا خدا سے کم نہیں ہوتا

Self-realization is the lesson imparted to us by all Men of God. One who really knows the Self — God — is no less than God, they say.

Mahatma Mangat Ram says:

'Seek the Light, with holy determination, which is the source of the physical journey. This inner Light has been spoken of as the Self, Truth, Bliss, Eternal, God and so on.'

सब से बड़ी ताकत अपना मन है जो ईश्वर के स्वरूप
में स्थित हो जावे तो वह खुद देवता है।

The greatest power is our mind, which when settled in God, becomes itself god-like, says Gurudev.

अनन्त शक्त प्रभ एक है, जो सरब जियां आधार।
"मंगत" गुरमुख विरले घट जानी निर्मल सार।।

God alone is Power Unlimited;
He is the source and sustainer of all.
Rare are the spiritually-oriented ones,

who understand this unadulterated truth,
says "Mangat".

Let us go deep into ourselves and find within the source of all power, as Mahatma Mangat Ram did:

अन्तरगत में सूझया, अनन्त शक्त भण्डार।
"मंगत" तिसका खेल है, सरब जगत बिस्तार।।

Perceived within, the treasure of unlimited power — energy unbounded. The whole wide universe is the expression of its play (manifestation), says "Mangat".

Recognizing *That* source within us and feeling *Its* presence all the time — in whatever we think, say or do — is, in brief, the main lesson of the journey we have had together through the pages of this book.

OM SHANTI — AMEN!

Annexure I

Wrong religious notions, beliefs and superstitions:

Mahatma Mangat Ram advises against wrong religious beliefs, blind beliefs and superstitions. To start with he would wish us to adore ideals of saints and other great persons, not their idols. It is their noble thoughts and deeds which should inspire us.

In the devotional path, respect for any figurative representation of the worshipped great souls is meaningful only if it acts as reminder of their qualities and inspires the devotees to inculcate those in their lives. Mere worship of their pictures or idols will not lead us anywhere. On the contrary it may plunge us into darkness.

Any worship which produces superstition, fear and greed is faulty. So is the worship which promotes pride, treachery, cleverness, jealousy and selfishness.

Worship of various gods and goddesses and stars/ planets seeking fulfilment of desires, fetters us further to darkness. Any worship which does not lead to enlightenment is not right.

No god and goddess can rid us of facing the result of our Karma (action). Righteousness alone can relieve and lead us on the right path.

To ignore the One Supreme Being residing in us — whose Grace can do anything for us — and to worship numerous gods, goddesses for fulfilment of our desires is sheer folly amounting almost to atheism.

A believer in Samata has faith in Atman, is always ready to serve others, and does not worship a book, a stone or a burial place.

Cursed is human/animal sacrifice to please any god or goddess. So also offering of meat, wine, etc. to them for their appeasement.

On religious falsehood:

There are people who shave their heads, or remain naked or stand in water, or remain near burning fire, or allow their hair to grow or adopt other exhibitionistic methods. Such so-called religious people suffer from much more attachment than is to be found among the worldly people. They want to be worshipped. Beware of them!

On pilgrimage:

Natural scenery and flowing water alone do not make a place sacred or place of pilgrimage unless God's glory is sung and propagated there.

Any place of birth, stay, penance, or death of a truly godly person—or where there has been a war for righteousness—is place of pilgrimage.

Visiting such a place, however, has merit if it is for learning something from the lives of the celebrated souls. To bathe there for washing away one's sins or undergo certain rituals designed by clever priests is meaningless. There is much falsehood and sacrilege in the name of religion at places of pilgrimage!

The holiest pilgrimage is knowledge of Atman, our true self. The Atman is all-pervading. This knowledge will remove all mental agony.

Faith in God is the prime pilgrimage. Without this one cannot have peace of mind, which is the outcome of true and selfless action, notwithstanding any number of visits to places of pilgrimage.

To lovingly serve one's parents, elders and neighbours is a really great pilgrimage.

On ghosts, dead and deified ancestors:

All existence in the world is combination of spirit and matter. Matter is made of certain basic elements, which in various combinations make all forms of life. Their disintegration is death.

'Ghosts and 'spirits' of dead people have no form; it is mere whim of the mind. It is the fear born out of sinful actions which assumes imaginary dreadful forms...'

'Imaginary are the tales people have woven concerning the existence of ghosts...' The assertion of communication with them is pure charlatanism. Living for long in forests and cremation grounds, which were fearsome, Gurudev never experienced any ghost. He says: 'In order to make an easy living, the clever ones cheat the simple folk (by making false assertions).'

Annexure II

A student of philosophy meets Mahatma Mangat Ram:

Dev Raj, then a student of philosophy (later Prof. and Principal), met Gurudev in 1948. He was feeling very lonely and sad, with practically no interest in life. He was even thinking of suicide.

At the end of Satsang (a spiritual discourse) Gurudev, as usual, asked those present to ask any questions. Dev Raj just briefly mentioned his agony. On this Gurudev told him in a very soft smiling manner: "If you had put in half the effort on this (God-realization) side, of how much you have struggled on the other (worldly) side, you would have won the battle of life. Even now there is time. Do not be obstinate." Dev Raj got the message.

Next day Dev Raj again went to him. Gurudev had the serious demeanour of a highly contemplative philosopher. The discourse revealed to Dev Raj the depth of Gurudev's understanding of life. Dev Raj, who had read works of eminent philosophers like Hegel, could never imagine that a simple *faqir* as Gurudev, not much educated in the formal sense, had simple and straight solutions to offer for life's most difficult riddles.

A letter from Gurudev:

It would be interesting to reproduce here a letter written by Gurudev to Professor Dev Raj some time later, in reply to certain points raised by him. Incidentally, Dev Raj is author's co-disciple and his understanding as well as exposition of Samata philosophy is just superb!

Describing his normal attitude towards life, he wrote to Gurudev in his letter that he felt, intensely and immediately, that the world was a transitory appearance with no substantiality and that when this mood got deep, he felt, not sad but disinclined to interest himself in the affairs of the world.

Gurudev's letter as reply translated from Urdu (Source: The Silent Logos) reads:

It is, indeed, a noble wisdom that sees and feels the perishable nature of the phenomenal world but a more mature wisdom will have the same feeling with regard to the body. When the determinating faculty—the intellect—comes to acquire a clear-eyed view of man's mortality, it self-submits itself to the Reality. When man gets convinced that the entire world of names and forms is transient and perishable, he ceases to entertain any attachments and aversions that he may happen to have for the things of the world: the pleasant no longer interest him and the unpleasant repel him. This freedom from attachments and aversions is the ideal disposition to have towards the world.

Man should keep an alert and careful watch on his morality and purge his mind of all desires for the pleasures of the senses. Let him withdraw his mind from the objects of the senses and his intellect from all thoughts, and fix them, exclusively and undeviatingly, on the Name. This kind of exclusive and one-pointed meditation will put to end all thoughts, and the determinating faculty, emancipated from the primal dualities of the doer, actions and their fruits, will then lose its ego-bound identity to become one with Reality.

The determinating faculty is afflicted with a (primal) malady for embodied existence. Even when it realizes that the world is ephemeral, it would not get disillusioned with its pleasures—their spell will continue to bewitch it as before. It would not, that is to say, face the truth of the mortality of the body. Nor would it care to get rid of its passions for embodied existence. It is, indeed, very hard for man to get out of the net of his infatuations. The only way out of the maze of this ignorance lies in realizing, intensely and immediately and each and every moment, that the body is not to last for long, and in getting free from desires for sense-pleasures, and, when this kind of dispassion is attained, in surrendering one's mind and intellect to the One Name. That verily is the way to get established, with no fear of a fall, in the Supreme Reality.

Establishment in truth and yoga means establishment in the Eternal Word, which is of the nature of eternal bliss. This gets accomplished only when man comes to be indifferent to the pleasures of the world and concentrates, time and again, his intellect on the Name and surrenders the dualities that every living creature reaps by way of the fruits of his action, and ceases to think about what happens or does not happen. So dear seeker! Concentrate your mind on the Name and leave your joys, desires and attachments. That is the way to liberate yourself from this harsh world. Therefore, let not your mind get dispersed in philosophical thoughts, but concentrate it on the Name. That will give rise, in you, to true faith and true devotion—the two requisites for putting to end one's desire for embodied existence. Whenever the flow of mind tends to get deviated into deep thoughts, think of them as vain and false and give your attention, entire and undivided, to the Name. This kind of continuous and uninterrupted meditation will one day still the intellect into an undeviating stability and it will 'hear', in the void of that stillness, the Word that is nothing else than its own real being. It is, therefore, imperative that the mind be oriented towards the Name rather than towards philosophical thinking.

Try, therefore, to be innocent of this unreal world and entertain no thoughts about it. If man adopts the right means, he will succeed in extinguishing his mind with comparative ease. His determinating faculty will get dis-associated from the needs and passions of the body—from attachments of the ten sense and motor organs—and will give itself entirely up to the Name until its own reality, the Eternal Word, reveals Itself to purge it of all pollutions—to establish it in the Supreme Abode, the pure immovable consciousness.

When the intellect posits (by way of spiritual discipline) the Self to be the doer, when, that is to say, it surrenders, each and every moment, each and every action to the will of God, it gets liberated from all attachments and aversions and gets established in the Eternal Word, the Abode of Reality. This kind of mental disposition is called *karmayoga*—the disposition to surrender all dualities that actions bear by way of their fruits. When the intellect, through this kind of discipline, gets purified of its passion for embodied existence, it loses its determinating nature and realizes itself as the non-doer, action-free, infinite and desireless Self—the Witness and the *Nirvana*. This state of realization is called *jnanayoga*. In truth, there is no difference between these two states of *Karmayoga* and *Jnanayoga* if one takes into consideration their essential truth and purpose. As long, however, as the intellect is afflicted with 'I-am-the body' sense and passions for embodied existence, it will do man good if he resorts to *Karmayoga*—the disposition that surrenders the fruit of each and every action to the will of God. This yoga is also called *Bhaktiyoga*—the yoga of devotion.

Think of these matters with care and try to do the right kind of effort so that the mind may get purified of all pollutions and you may realize within yourself your own infinite and peaceful reality. Do not think, dear seeker, the realization of the transitory nature of the world will alone lead you to the state of real peace. Nor should you think that this realization will ever stay with you. With the passage of time, it may get usurped by worldly attachments. Therefore, equipped with this thought of the transience of the world, devote all your energies to the realization of the Reality within. That way alone lies one's good—that is, in concentrating both mind and intellect on the Name.

Note: Although the above letter was addressed by Gurudev to a particular devoted disciple, years back, its message is immensely and ever meaningful for all those interested in spirituality. It throws light on a perennial Reality which we are likely to forget.

Annexure III

Elements and their Offshoots:

The five primordial elements constituting the entire nature are: Earth, Water, Fire, Air, Sky (Space). The five sensuous psychic pollutions (passions)—lust, anger, greed, attachment and pride—are born out of them, as stated below:

Elements	Organ of Knowledge	Function	Passions	Organ of Action
Prithvi (Earth)	Nose	Smell	Greed	Anus
Jal (Water)	Tongue	Taste	Lust	Phallus
Agni (Fire)	Eyes	Sight	Anger	Hands
Vayu (Air)	Skin	Touch	Attachment	Legs
Akas (Sky)	Ears	Hearing	Pride	Speech

Shown below are also the five organs each of knowledge and action, with their corresponding functions and 'perversions'.

The five elements are causative of following 25 modifications of nature; each element in the body in five forms:

Sky	Grief	delusion	shame	fear	glory
Air	Jumping	running	expansion	contraction	stiffness
Fire	Hunger	thirst	sleep	indolence	splendour
Water	Saliva	blood	perspiration	urine	semen
Earth	Skin	hair	flesh	marrow	bones

According to an ancient philosophy — prevalent in South India specially — NA-MA-SI-VA-YA makes up the five-lettered Panchakshara. These letters stand for the five elements that constitute the world: Earth, Water, Fire, Air and Sky respectively. A particular colour is also associated with each of them—yellow for Earth, white for Water, red for Fire, green for Air and black for sky.

The five elements were invested with five geometrical forms by the Supreme Creator (so say the ancients). They are as follows:

Earth is represented by a square □

Water is represented by a crescent ◡

Fire is represented by a triangle △

Air is represented by a double triangle ✡

Sky is represented by a sphere ○

Annexure IV

Kundalini Yoga with a note on sex:

Literally translated the Sanskrit word Kundalini means 'of a spiral nature'— 'coiled up'. The implication is that of a double spiral moved up into three dimensions. Such a spiral has its origin and end in the opposite poles of a central axis on which each point of intersection, metaphorically termed *chakras* (wheel) and pictured as lotus petals, is suggestive of horizontal planes which yet remain dynamic regimes permitting energy exchange and ensuring evolutionary progression. To achieve greater awareness is what Kundalini is all about.

Technically speaking Kundalini refers to the divine energy that, according to Hindu belief, is lying coiled up and asleep at the base of the spinal column of every conscious being. Sometimes this energy has been called serpent power. In the individual the pathway of the divine energy lies through the spinal column to the brain, and it is said that when it reaches the brain, then the person becomes thoroughly illumined.

'The Kundalini Energy properly handled and controlled, it is believed, can become a powerful tool in one's life. It makes its presence felt most of the time accidentally or only in a limited way as clairvoyance, clairaudience or personal magnetism' (Swami Sivananda Radha).

Gopi Krishna, born in Kashmir in 1903, and whom the author had the privilege of knowing personally, had done much research on Kundalini. He has written a number of books. In his 'The Dawn of a New Science', he says that Kundalini is a process of evolution. 'It is the natural device for the spiritual unfoldment of man.'

He describes it further as the union of individual soul with the Divine; the self is forgotten in the intensity of the experience. On the arousal of Kundalini, he claims, the whole area of perception of an awakened individual undergoes a transformation. 'A new man with a different pattern of consciousness is born. There is inwardly an exhaustless mine of wonder and joy, conscious of his openness with the deathless infinite ocean of life.'

The arousal of Kundalini force does have perceptible effects on human body. Various signs and symptoms that occurred within on the awakening, as mentioned by those who experienced it, include:

a) the phenomenon of lights such as a still candle flame; cool, blue shine of diamond; the lustre of the moon; the radiance of the sun; the dazzling flash of lightning, or the glow of fire,
b) the variety of sounds heard, likening them to thunder, humming of bees, roaring of waterfalls, or the pealing of bells.

Further, the psychic power reservoir when activated presents a marvellous picture of extraordinary nervous activity in all tissues and fibres.

Like the atom, every organic cell in a living body is a mighty store of psychic energy. We do not generally take cognizance of this fact, when we reflect on the mechanism of life.

Chakras: The *chakras* (nerve plexuses or clusters) generally accepted to be seven in number, are all situated in vital spots of the body, five of them on the cerebrospinal axis (plus two above) commanding the organs of reproduction, elimination, digestion, blood circulation, respiration, ideation, and the modalities of consciousness. These are:

1. Muladhara— a) Pelvic plexus (Prostate gland)
   b) Sacral plexus (Parasympathetic system)

   This is the base where the Kundalini energy is in slumber like a three-coiled serpent.
2. Swadisthan — Aortic plexus, below the navel
3. Manipur (Nabhi) — Solar plexus near the navel below the diaphragm
4. Anahata — Cardiac plexus
5. Visudha — Cervical plexus (Thyroid)
6. Ajna or frontal between the eyebrows, thalamus plexus
7. Sahasrara — in the bony cavity of the head

Each of the Chakras is in control of one of the senses, therefore, each chakra is and should be affected by what is going on in the others.

According to Gopi Krishna (reference his book Higher Consciousness): 'The descriptions of hypothetical lotuses beginning with 4 lotus petals (associated with Muladhara) and going upto 1000 petals (as in case of Sahasrara) and *Shaktis* or goddesses, associated with the chakras, are easy to understand in the light of the religious beliefs and elementary knowledge of human physiology at the time. But we can be sure about the basic fact that these descriptions are intended to signify the involvement of all the important organs of the body in the process of transformation set in motion by this (Kundalini) divine energy.'

The main *Nadi* in the very centre of the spine is called Sushumna. It is the passage through which the Kundalini energy rises. Sushumna connects all the *chakras.*

The two ganglionic chains on either side of the spinal cord are called Ida (on the left) and Pingala (on the right) *Nadis.* Ida is suggestive of coolness or moon; Pingala means hot or sun. There are 72,000 *Nadis* (astral nerves) in the human body. Of these 24 are important. They are situated in Muladhara. These *Nadis* with manifold powers are separated and unified in the Muladhara and are utilized by the Kundalini Energy according to its needs as the main force. Of the above 24 *Nadis*, 10 are most important and out of these 10 *Nadis* three are fundamental, viz. Ida, Pingala and Sushumna, mentioned above. Ida is the breath which flows (incoming and going) through the left nostril, Pingala through the right nostril and Sushumna is the path in which energy can move freely. These are also called as Chandra (moon) *Nadi*, Surya (sun) *Nadi* and *Agni* (fire) *Nadi* respectively.

There is, it seems, a real biological basis for this extraordinary power centre of latent energy—called the Kundalini—within the human body. This force is evolutionary, both in its expression of the procreative urge and its internal union within the body, opening the door to the inspired consciousness that guides the progress of human race through sages, saints, scientists, geniuses and artists.

Powers of chakras:

Certain qualities and powers are attributed to each of the chakras by various preceptors and writers (or, they claim so). These are summarised as under:

1. *Muladhara*: Innocence. Eternal knowledge. Wisdom. Power of speech.
2. *Swadisthan*: Creativity. Ability of well reasoned discourse, prose or verse. Freedom from enemies (including enemies within). Power of seeing beyond.
3. *Manipur*: Virtue. Right behaviour. Protection. Wealth, welfare, well being. Power to create and destroy. One can atomise oneself, it is claimed.
4. *Anahata*: Promises the hearing of the cosmic sound (AUM) with the inner ear. Harmony and happi-

ness. Dutiful life. Rendering oneself invisible. One can also project an image of oneself at a distance. Entering another body (so they say).

5. *Visudha*: Freedom from worldly desires. The gateway of liberation. Knowledge of the past, present and future. Concealment. Destruction of danger. Power of healing people from any distance.
6. *Ajna*: Forgiveness, beneficence. Leave the body at will.
7. *Sahasrara*: Identification with the Supreme. Pure intellect. Collective consciousness. Integration. Silence. Cool vibration.

The above is a very brief summary of what one hears from knowledgeable and experienced people, or reads in the books on Kundalini and the chakras. On the royal road to self-realization through meditation, one may notice or just cross over these stations. The objective should be the ultimate integration of the soul (consciousness) with Supreme Being (the universal consciousness), the source of all power: truth-consciousness-bliss.

'Because tradition emphasized the direct teaching from Guru to disciple, Kundalini has remained mysterious and thereby created much speculation and confusion. It is unfortunate that today when there is a great deal of interest and discussion about Kundalini Energy, it is very often linked to only one aspect—sex. In the West, particularly, it has now become a word and a concept that serves as an excuse for many things', as Swami Sivananda Radha observes in her book 'Kundalini Yoga'. The Swami says: 'It is not indulgence in sex that the Kundalini Energy encourages. However beautiful sex may be, it does not open the door to higher consciousness.' She rightly suggests: 'On the spiritual path..., it needs to be understood that Kundalini is not for the person for whom life is the continuous seeking of (worldly) pleasure or the achievement of success in name and fame.'

On sex:

Since 'sex' has come into focus in the foregoing narration let us briefly talk about it and the Female and Male Principles as postulated in ancient Indian philosophy.

Masculine and feminine principles are not narrowly limited, but are inseparable elements of Energy giving birth to whirling worlds, from the tiny atom to millions of galaxies — richness in mystical varieties expressing life itself.

Shakti (the female principle) and *Shakta* (the male principle) are one. They are inseparable. Shakti is the primal force of life that underlies all existence, as one cannot separate heat from fire. *Shakta* is the male principle of Cosmic Energy. In spirituality there is no gender. The worship of Divine Mother means the acceptance of all creations.

Shiva/Shakti — an expression often used in Indian mythology—is neither male nor female (nor neuter), but existence, consciousness, bliss (Sat-chit-ananda). Symbolically the union of Shiva and Shakti is presented in one body, or as two bodies united. Lord Shiva ultimately becomes half-man and half-woman, indicating that power and its manifestation are inseparable.

Sex, no doubt, is a significant force. Because of the overemphasis on sex in modern life it is important to give consideration to certain aspects of it.

The most precious energy that is able to bring another human being into existence must not be scattered senselessly and uselessly. Those who defend sex for pleasure do not realize the consequences on different levels, says Swami Sivananda Radha. 'We must look at sex, besides being a procreative force, in its psychic connotations', she suggests. 'When there is attachment to sex, then liberation cannot be achieved.'

'Regard the sex impulse not as something sinful and horrible and attractive at the same time. Reject it not by struggling with it, but by withdrawing back from it', advises the Mother. She adds: 'Look at it as something not your own but imposed on you by a force of Nature outside you. Refuse consent to the imposition. The sex trouble is serious only when it can get the consent of the mind and the vital will... The one thing to do is to separate oneself from these movements to find one's inner self and to live in it.'

The cultivation and developing quality in regard to sex has to reach a level of refinement where neither partner becomes sex-demanding. Additional offspring can be a great hindrance at a certain point for married persons interested in spiritual life. *Brahmacharya* (celibacy) is recommended not so much as a moral issue but as a matter of intelligent choice. This path is not easy. But spiritual practice does help in securing freedom from unnecessary pressure of senses, as well as of sex impulse.

Annexure V

How I overcame fear of death:

Years ago, I was on board a Dakota plane from Jammu to Delhi. It was a cloudy day. Soon after taking off, the plane got into extremely rough weather over the hills. Despite the pilot's best efforts, it seemed, he could not control the aircraft which was being tossed about by the fierce storm — threatening winds and thick dark clouds with frequent lightning. It was feared the plane might crash any moment against a hill. The passengers were given a danger signal. The lady passengers and children were crying aloud. Some elderly persons, who out of fear could not control themselves, were seen rushing to the bathroom not minding the constantly on 'Fasten belts' sign. There was terrible confusion and chaos in the plane. I, too, feared I might face death along with others any moment in the apprehended plane crash.

Spontaneously, I opened at random the little book SAMATA VIGYAN YOG — which I always carried with me on tours—prayed and contemplated over what my Spiritual Master, Mahatma Mangat Ram, had to say. The inspiring words of wisdom (rendered into Hindi from Urdu and translated into English) are:

काल के भय में नित बन्धाए। एक पलक नहीं शान्त पाए।।
छिनभंगुर सब क्रिया भई। तिसके ताप में नित तपेई।।

उतपत परले का यह तमाशा। तिसका मोह देवे अत त्रासा।।
खोज करो नित अभयपद मीता। जां को परस पावें शान्त पुनीता।।
मंगलकारी तत्त रूप नारायन। भरम त्याग हो तिस चरन परायन।।
अखण्ड शान्त नित सत सरूप। तिसकी प्रीत हरे भ्रम कूप।।
नित प्रापत घट घट भरपूर। सरब का ठाकर परमानन्द हजूर।।
काल करम का संसा नास। जो चित आवे प्रभ अबनास।।
सकल व्याधि से जीया छूटे। काल करम का भय सब चूके।।
प्रभ आधार जीवन चित पाई। निर्भय धाम की लखी प्रभताई।।
जीवन भयो निहाल तब, जब सार जीवन की पाई।
"मंगत" अन्तरगत माहीं, तत्त चेतन शबद लखाई।।

- You are mortally afraid of death; without a moment of peace of mind.
- Everything would come to an end; that is what is worrying you.
- Watch the drama of life and death; it is attachment with life which is causing so much anguish.
- O friend, look within for the state of fearlessness. On perceiving it you will experience peace supreme.
- The Lord is merciful. Give up all apprehension. Depend upon HIM with unswerving faith.
- He is peace uninterrupted, a state of perfect tranquillity.
- Just love Him and overcome the utter confusion you are in.
- And, He is in you and in everyone else fully; all-permeating Supreme Being and Bliss Incarnate.

- You would overcome the fear of death (also time) and action, as you concentrate on the Immortal Lord within.
- You will overcome all infliction, and be absolutely free from fear of death and action.
- Do live with complete dependence on God, you will be blessed with the state of fearlessness.
- On understanding the essence (significance) of life, you will be blessed with real happiness and experience within the Word, the epitome of supreme consciousness.

As I prayed I was afraid of death no more. With God's Grace the plane got out of danger within a few minutes. We landed safely at Amritsar. I was moved to tears by the most appropriate lesson from my Master's book. It dawned on me then what power prayer has, why we fear death, and how can one achieve a state of fearlessness. (I wish I had continued that understanding and spiritual state of mind for good. However, I have never forgotten the impact of the story I am sharing with my readers.)

Annexure VI

Some selected common prayers:

Thou art my Father; Thou art my Mother,
My Friend and my Relative; Thou art my wealth;
Thou art my knowledge; Thou art my all,
O God of gods!
Thou art the All.'

(Gurustrotram)

O, Supreme Lord, the source of
Existence, Intelligence and Bliss!
The Creator of the Universe!
May we prove worthy of Thy choice and acceptance!
May we meet Thy Glorious Grace!
May Thou vouchsafe an unerring guidance to our intellects and may we follow Thy inspiring lead with Righteousness.

(Yajur Veda)

O God, grant us boon the best,
a mind to think and a smiling love
increase of wealth, a healthy body
speech that is winsome and days that are fair.

(Rig Veda)

From the unreal lead me to the Real
From darkness lead me to Light
From death lead me to Immortality.

(Brihadaranyaka Upanishad)

May our ears hear what is good, may our eyes see what is good. May we, what time we live, be blessed with healthy limbs and body, that we may glorify the Lord. May all the gods bless us. May our minds be at peace.

(Mandukya Upanishad)

Praise be to Allah:
Lord of the Worlds, the Compassionate,
The Merciful
Master of the Day of Judgment!
You alone are worship and to you alone
we look for help.

Guide us to straight path. The Path of those upon whom You bestowed favours, not those who have invited Your wrath, nor those who have gone astray.

(Quran)

Where there is hate, let me bring Love;
Where there is offence, let me bring Pardon;
Where there is discord, let me bring Union;
Where there is error, let me bring Truth;
Where there is darkness, let me bring Light;
Where there is sadness, let me bring Joy.

May it be, O Lord, that I seek not so much to be consoled as to console, to be understood as to understand, to be loved as to love, because it is in giving oneself that one receives; it is in forgetting oneself that one is found; it is in pardoning that one obtains pardon; it is in dying that one is raised up to eternal life.

(St. Francis of Assissi)

O God
Guide me;
protect me;
illumine the lamp,
of my heart;
and make me

a brilliant star.
Thou art the Mighty
and Powerful!

(Bahai Prayer)

Draw us closer to Thee
every moment of our life
until in us be reflected
Thy Grace
Thy Glory
Thy Wisdom
Thy Joy and
Thy Peace

(Hazrat Inayat Khan)

O Sweet Adorable Presence! the Glory of glories,
The Sun of suns, Light of lights, Deity of deities!
Remove the veil of ignorance that blurs my vision,
And grant me strength to realize my oneness with Thee.

(Swami Sivananda)

Light of all life, make every breath of mine
a string to sound your sweetness,
every particle that meets my eye
a mirror to reflect your face.

Grant that purity and placidity of life
in which your presence is felt ever and
everywhere as clearly, intimately and effortlessly
as my body feels the space and heart the
warmth of living.

Life of my life, grant me everlastingness
in that intimate awareness of yours
to be ever and ever yours.

(Swami Ishwarananda Giri)

"Dear God!

- Give me the courage to change the things that can and should be changed.

- Give me the strength to accept the things that cannot be changed.
- And, give me the wisdom to distinguish one from the other."

(Extract)

"LORD OF LORDS!
Grant me the good,
even though I may
not ask for it
And keep me away from
evils, even though I
ask for it."

(Anonymous)

"Salutation to you who are transcendental
and immanent;
You ever shine with bliss and are
the self with powers unlimited."

(Abhinavagupta)

Annexure VII

Manu's Laws, Buddha's Precepts, Christ's Commandments and Muhammad's Selected Teachings

Manu's ten-fold laws:

Firmness	Sense mastery
Forgiveness	Insight
Self control	Wisdom
No stealing	Truthfulness
Inner and outer purity	Meekness (Humility)

Buddha's 10 precepts and 10 Acts of Merit (advised):

Precepts	*Acts of Merit*
1. Do not kill.	1. Give charity to the deserving.
2. Do not steal.	2. Observe the precepts of morality.
3. Do not commit adultery.	3. Cultivate and develop good thoughts.
4. Do not tell lies.	4. Render service and attend on others.
5. Do not slander.	5. Honour and nurse parents and elders.
6. Do not speak harshly.	6. Give a share of your merits to others.
7. Do not engage in idle talk.	7. Accept the merits that others give you.

8. Do not covet others' property.
9. Do not show hatred.
10. Think righteously.

8. Hear the doctrine of righteousness.
9. Preach the doctrine of righteousness.
10. Rectify your faults.

Christ's 16 commandments (Sermon on the Mount):

1. Blessed are the poor in spirit: for theirs is the Kingdom of Heaven.
2. Blessed are they that mourn: for they shall be comforted.
3. Blessed are the meek: for they shall inherit the earth.
4. Blessed are they which do hunger and thirst for righteousness: for they shall be filled.
5. Blessed are the merciful: for they shall obtain mercy.
6. Blessed are the pure in heart: for they shall see God.
7. Blessed are the peace-makers: for they shall be called the children of God.
8. Blessed are they which are persecuted for righteousness' sake: for theirs is the Kingdom of Heaven.
9. Blessed are ye, when men shall revile you, and persecute you and shall say all manner of evil against you falsely, for my sake.
10. Rejoice and be exceedingly glad: for great is your reward in heaven: for so persecuted they the prophets which were before you.
11. Ye are the salt of the earth: but if the salt have lost its savour, wherewith shall it be salted? It is thenceforth good for nothing, but to be cast out, and to be trodden under foot of men.
12. You are the light of the world. A city that is set on a hill cannot be hid.
13. Neither do men light a candle, and put it under a bushel, but on a candlestick and it giveth light unto all that are in the house.

14. Let your light so shine before men, that they may see your good works, and glorify your Father which is in heaven.
15. Think not that I am come to destroy the law, or the prophets: I am not come to destroy, but to fulfil.
16. For verily I say unto you, till heaven and earth pass, one jot or one title shall in no wise pass from the law, till all be fulfilled.

Prophet Muhammad's selected teachings:
(as extracted from the Quran, Prophet's Life History and their commentaries)

1.	Faith	Belief in existence and unity of God. 'Allah is one, there is no god but Him.' Eternal, Self-Subsisting, Beneficent.
2.	Divine Worship	'total surrender to God'...'Allah desires your well being.'
3.	Prayer	'with regularity; and steadfastness, sincerity and devotion.'
4.	Purification	'purifying the individual moral character.' 'Beauty of character' ...'Adultery is evil.'
5.	Behaviour	'He is not a believer who commits adultery, or who steals, or who drinks liquor or who plunders, or who embezzles...beware beware.'
6.	Backbiting	'It is more grievous than adultery.'
7.	Righteousness	'The noblest of you in Allah's sight is the most righteous of you.'
8.	Patience	'Conduct yourself with perfect patience.' 'God is gentle and loves gentleness'...'Be not angry.'
9.	Envy	'Be on your guard against envying others; it eats up goodness as fire eats fuel.'

10.	Service to humanity	'The best of men is he from whom good accrues to humanity.'
11.	Love	'Do you love your Creator? Love your fellow-beings first.'
12.	Truth	'Be truthful. No secret of yours will remain hidden.'
13.	Charity	'Be charitable. Allah loves the charitable.'
14.	Kindness	'Feed the hungry and visit the sick, and free the captive if he be unjustly confined. Assist any person who is oppressed, whether Muslim or non-Muslim.'

Annexure VIII

Human Relations Checklist

1. Remember that appreciation and praise bring out the best in people, while criticism tends to bring out their worst side.
2. Pass on to other people any compliments which are paid to them by third parties.
3. Don't burden others with your problems. Remember that other people have their own problems, most of which you are completely unaware of.
4. Be a comfortable person to be with, by attempting to be cheerful, even if you don't feel cheerful.
5. When you are tempted to argue with other people, remind yourself that everyone looks at any person, object or situation in a different way. Give people the right to be different, because they are different.
6. Don't startle others or make them nervous by discussing topics which are depressing or make them feel threatened. Make it a habit to confine your remarks to topics which you can discuss with a reasonable degree of optimism.
7. Give people the benefit of doubt when your feelings have been hurt. It is rare for people to insult us deliberately. Actually they are merely trying to boost their ego and solve their own problems, and occasionally we happen to be in the way.

8. Be sensitive to the moods of other people. Choose what to do and say partly on the basis of the way you notice the other person is feeling at the moment.
9. Make people feel more capable and adequate by showing that you have full confidence in their ability.
10. Give the other person a good name to live up to. Never attribute an unworthy motive to another person. No one is perfect, but a very few people appreciate having their faults pointed out to them.
11. Go out of your way to be helpful to others.
12. Be certain to show your gratitude for anything which others do for you.
13. Greet people cordially. Act happy to see them.
14. Practise being a good listener.
15. Develop and exercise your sense of humour by seeing the amusing elements in an apparently serious situation and by learning to take a joke on yourself.
16. Keep confidential information to yourself.
17. Show respect for the peculiarities of other people; we all have a few.
18. Be tactful, sympathetic, and understanding with the person who looks up to you for help.
19. Suppress any feelings of irritability towards other people.
20. Be dependable. Never make a promise that you doubt you can fulfil.
21. Be generous in your recognition and praise of the accomplishments of others.

(Extracts from
The Art of Good Human Relations
by John M. Briggs)

Annexure IX

The Ten Commandments of Good Human Relations

1. Thou shalt love people, not just use them.
   (The greatest thing in the world is a person.)
2. Thou shalt develop thy understanding.
3. Thou shalt compliment more than criticize.
4. Thou shalt not get angry.
   (If you are right, you don't need to. If you are wrong you can't afford to.)
5. Thou shalt not argue.
   (It's no use to win an argument and lose a friend.)
6. Thou shalt be kind.
   (It's nice to be important, but it's important to be nice.)
7. Thou shalt have a sense of humour.
   (A sense of humour is to a man what springs are to a wagon—it saves him jolts.)
8. Thou shalt smile.
   (No man is ever fully dressed unless he wears a smile on his face.)
9. Thou shalt practise what thou preachest.
   (One example is worth one thousand arguments.)
10. Thou shalt go to school with the Headmaster of the Universe, the Master of men, the Secretary of Human Relations — namely God.

(Extract)

Annexure X

Desiderata

By Max Ehrmann

Go placidly amid the noise and the haste, and remember what peace there may be in silence.

As far as possible, without surrender, be on good terms with all persons. Speak your truth quietly and clearly; and listen to others, even to the dull and ignorant; they too have their story.

Avoid loud and aggressive persons; they are vexatious to the spirit.

If you compare yourself with others, you may become vain or bitter, for always there will be greater and lesser persons than yourself.

Enjoy your achievements as well as your plans.

Keep interest in your own career, however humble; it is a real possession in the changing fortunes of time.

Exercise caution in your business affairs, for the world is full of trickery. But let this not blind you to what virtue there is; many persons strive for high ideals, and everywhere life is full of heroism.

Be yourself. Especially do not feign affection. Neither be cynical about love; for in the face of all aridity and disenchantment, it is as perennial as the grass.

Take kindly the counsel of the years, gracefully surrendering the things of youth.

Nurture strength of spirit to shield you in sudden misfortune. But do not distress yourself with dark imaginings. Many fears are born of fatigue and loneliness.

Beyond a wholesome discipline, be gentle with yourself. You are a child of the universe no less than the trees and the stars; you have a right to be here. And whether or not it is clear to you, doubtless the universe is unfolding as it should.

Therefore be at peace with God, whatever you conceive Him to be. And whatever your labours and aspirations in the noisy confusion of life, keep peace in your soul. With all its sham, drudgery and broken dreams, it is still a beautiful world.

* आरती *

तूँ पार ब्रह्म परमेश्वर, तीन काल रछपाल ।
नित पाऊँ शरणागति, सत चरण कंवल दयाल ।।
तूँ नित पतित उद्धार है, पूरण प्रभ जगदीश ।
मोह माया संकट हरो, दीजो ज्ञान संदेश ।।
नित ही तेरे चरण की, मन में रहे प्रीत ।
तूँ दाता दातार है, पुरुषोत्तम सुखरीत ।।
पवन पानी बैसन्तर, धरती और आकाश ।
सबको सिरजनहार तूँ आदि पुरुष अविनाश ।।
घट-घट व्यापक तूँ परमेश्वर, सरब जियां आधार ।
अनमति कूकर को राख लें, किरपानिधि करतार ।।
काल करम जाए दूषणा, खल बुद्धि हरो अज्ञान ।
सत शरधा पाऊँ चरण की, अखण्ड प्रेम चित ध्यान ।।
दीनानाथ दयाल तूँ, पल पल होत सहाय ।
कीरत साचे नाम की, मन तन आए समाय ।।
अन्तर का सब खेद हरो, दीजो सत विश्वास ।
शरणागत हूँ मन्द मति घट अन्तर करो परकाश ।।
अन्तरगत सिमरण करूँ, निरन्तर धरूँ ध्यान ।
घट-घट में दर्शन करूँ, आदि पुरुष भगवान ।।
तूँ साचा साहिब सरब परकाशी, शब्द रूप आखन्ड ।
गुणी मुणी उस्तति करें, तन मन पाये आनन्द ।।
होवें दयाल तूँ सत परमेश्वर देवें धीर अपार ।
निमष निमष सिमरण करूँ चित चरण रहे आधार ।।
काया अन्तर प्रत्यक्ष होवे नाद रूप बिस्माद ।
पल पल कीजूँ आरती तन मन तजूं व्याध ।।
जग आवन सुफला होवे तेरी आज्ञा मन में ध्याऊं ।
अन्तरगति करूँ आरती भव दुस्तर तर जाऊं ।।

अन्धमति मूढ़ा नित प्रति तेरे चरणी करे पुकार ।
"मंगत" मांगे दीनता सत धरम सुख सार ।।

"समता मंगल"

समता धरम हिरदे रसे विष ममता होवे नास ।
सत सरूप परमात्मा जल थल पाऊँ प्रकाश ।।
सब जीवों से प्रेम हो तन मन सेवा धार ।
समता साधन पायके नित परसां जय जयकार ।।
सत करम सत निश्चय निर्मल पाऊँ विचार ।
"मंगत" समता धार के जीत चलो संसार ।।

ARATI: PRAYER AT END

1. You are the furthest limit of Brahma, Paramesvara;
Guardian of Time past, present and to be.
Forever I take shelter at your feet:
These clement Lotus feet of perfect Truth.
2. The fallen forever you retrieve,
You perfect father of us all, O Jagadish.
Errors, delusion and their anguish, strip down these.
Help us to understand.
3. Eternal always are your feet:
In my mind rest affectionately,
O Giver, you give so generously,
Purushottama — grant delight.
4. Wind, water, fire, earth, space:
All these you create, and uncreate,
You, the Adipurusa before all worlds began —
You stand indestructible after all worlds end.
5. Each life is filled with you, God, like waterjar.
Support of each and all that breathes.
Take this trembling hound into your keeping,
Maker, Unending Ocean of tenderness.

6. May it pass, this season of disgrace.
Foil cruel-minded ignorance
True faith is found firm only at your feet,
A perfect undivided love and pure contemplativeness.

7. You are Dinanath: pitying Protector of the poor,
Momently, in the closing and opening of an eye
You help where there is need.
By simply uttering your name,
Life-force returns again to body and mind.

8. Strip down my grieving. Give me faith that's firm.
Having sought refuge in you,
Slow of understanding as I am,
Light the inner lamp of this 'clayjar'.

9. In I go to remember you continually
To the inner household shrine of contemplativeness.
Show yourself to me in all your forms of living beings
O Bhagavan, first and primal Father of us all.

10. You, the true Master, Illuminating
The undivided primal Sound
Seers and sages sing your praises,
Finding in you, body and mind, the Ultimate Delight.

11. If you truly take pity on me Paramesvara,
Then give me steadiness of mind,
That moment to moment I remember you,
And my spirit dwell in the shelter of your feet.

12. Should you be perceptible within the body
As the awesome primal sound,
Each moment I'd offer you arati —
Bewilderments of body and mind instantly to renounce.

13. May my entry into this world be fruitful
Meditating your command
Performing the inner arati to you
I pass over this most impassable existence.

14. This unseeming fool yes, each and every day
implores help at your feet
"Mangat", the Mendicant begs
Humility and True Faith, O essence of delight.

SAMATA MANGAL
BENEVOLENT ONENESS

1. The essence of the way
of Samata
lies in this: at the heart's core
the poison of selfishness must go.
God's true likeness: Radiance
leaves its footprint on both land and sea.
2. All living beings loved
in mind and body served
and given support — if so,
the messengers of Samata are at work.
And for our daily sufficiency,
Let's all give thanks above.
3. Right action,
Right conviction,
A blameless steady mind
Upholding Samata
Let's leave worldliness
behind! says "Mangat".

(Translation by Priya Devi)

Epilogue

I hope you have enjoyed reading the book as much as I have enjoyed organising and presenting the material. I had undertaken this project primarily for my own education as stated in the Introduction. For me it has been mainly a revision of some of the lessons from my spiritual master. He was abundantly liberal and wished his disciples to study the writings of saints and founders of various religions and faiths. I have ventured to do this. The selection of the title of the book — 'Power Unlimited' — and the attempt to relate the concept to modern, practical life is my own initiative and responsibility.

Using words to express the inexpressible, employing finite to indicate the infinite, transforming ordinary into the extraordinary, is indeed a difficult task. Mine has been a modest effort. But for the tremendous inspiration drawn from Gurudeva and various supportive sources, I could not have ventured on this journey.

In this book we have met and journeyed together. We may now understand ourselves better and be inspired to help others. And indeed through the 'Power Unlimited', we truly are comrades, a fact to which we can hold fast as we move towards self-realization. For the lucky ones who have already achieved the goal, the book may serve more as a refresher reading.

D.N. Saraf

Glossary

In three parts:

I Sanskrit/Hindi, Urdu and other terms and names of some sacred books (also the Hindu Trinity)

II Prophets, men of God, saints, philosophers, writers etc. (from the East)

III Prophets, men of God, saints, philosophers, writers etc. (from the West)

(Note: Attempt has been made to cover as many as possible, not explained or sufficiently annotated in the book.)

I

Advait (also Advaita) — Non-dual, without a second. The word emphasizes the fact that Brahman is one, one only and indeed the Absolute.

Anhata (Anahad) — Mystical inner sound.

Atma (Atman) — Soul, spirit. As in Mahatma, meaning great soul. Maha = great, atma = soul.

Arati — Prayer at end. Ritual in which the seeker beseeches God to relieve him/her of the distress and afflictions of the world.

Avatar	Divine incarnation; God in human form.
Bible, The	Collection of 66 books divided into Old and New Testaments. The former may be described as the literary experience of the religious life of ancient Israel. The New Testament is about the coming of Christ and his teachings. The Bible, originally in Latin, was rendered into English by Wycliffe and his followers, 405 AD. King James-I got the Bible revised through 47 revisers in 1611. This is still considered authorised version of the Bible.
Brahma	Personification of God as Creator.
Brahman (Brahm)	God; the Absolute Lord, the Divine Essence; Imperishable Principle; Universal soul.
Chakra	'Wheel', energy centres within the body.
DNA (Deoxyribonucleic Acid)	Chemical compound of which genes are made.
Dhammapada	A canonical book. It forms part of Pali Buddhist canons. Contains a number of divine thoughts and sayings. Stated to belong to 328-380 BC though its exact place and date differ according to different records.
Dhyana	Inner contemplation; beatific vision.
Fakir or Faqir	An Urdu term for a saint, ascetic, mendicant.
Gita/Geeta (also Bhagavad or Bhagawad)	Gospel of Lord Krishna with 18 chapters (see against Krishna). Its message is timeless.

Guru or Gurudev (Gurudeva)	Literally one who gives light; Master; Spiritual preceptor. Satguru, Satgur or Sadguru: a true master or spiritual teacher.
Ishvara (Isvara)	Supreme Being, Parameshvar — the great God.
Jnana	Knowledge of Brahman.
Ka'bha	The shrine at Mecca, which houses the Black stone; the most sacred spot for Muslims.
Kal	Time, death.
Karma	Action, work, inescapable duty or obligation. The law of action and reaction.
Lakh	One hundred thousand.
Mahabharata	One of the two great epics of the Hindus, the other being the Ramayana. It is the story of the sons of Bharat, who was a great king of ancient India. India has for thousands of years been called Bharatvarsha or the land of Bharat, after the famous king. The Mahabharata tells of the great war between the Kauravas and the Pandavas, which took place in very ancient times and in which the latter were victorious.
Maharaj Ji	A term of great respect used to address saints and holy men. 'Maharaj' literally means 'great king'.
Mantra	That which liberates the mind from grief and sorrow; incantation; concentrated energy of certain sacred sound syllables — words purporting to have magical power.

Maya	Illusion, deception, unreality, phenomenal universe. The veil of illusion conceals the vision of God from our sight.
Moksha	Liberation, salvation.
Mukti	Final emancipation.
Muni	A silent monk, ascetic, an ecstatic.
Nad/Nada	Heavenly sound.
Nada Brahman	Vibrating with sound of the Ultimate.
Nadi	Nerve channel.
Nirvana	Dissolution of individual existence and re-union with the Supreme Spirit. Liberation.
Om Shanti	Let there be peace.
Pandit	Learned man. Hindu priest.
Paramhans (Paramahansa)	A highly evolved spiritual person.
Prana	Vital life force.
Pursha (Purusha, Purkha)	Primal being; Creator. In Vedanta, the real man or Self; the life — the Creative Source.
Purushottama	'The highest, the best, of Men'. Also the supreme being.
Qazi	Expounder of Muslim Law.
Quran, The	The Holy book in Arabic consists of 114 suras or chapters which are divided in *ayats* or verses. Most of them were revealed to Muhammad piecemeal (610 AD to 632 AD). The contents of the Quran comprise the dogma, body of narratives and moral and juridical injunctions. Central to the dogma is the belief that there is no god but God and that Muhammad is his Apostle and the last of prophets.
Ramayana	An allegory depicting the wander-

	ings of Rama. The oldest of the Sanskrit epics written by the sage Valmiki and rendered into Hindi verse by Tulsidas. The hero is Rama or Ramachandra, son of King Dasratha of Ayodhya in northern India. Rama is said to have been the seventh incarnation on earth of the god Vishnu. His exploits in rescuing Sita, his wife, from Ravana, the King of Lanka, who had abducted her, are well known all over. In India the name Ram or Rama is widely used as appellation for God.
Rishi	A sage, literally a singer. In the Vedic context, a singer of the Song of Eternal Life.
Sadhna	Spiritual practice for the purpose of upliftment.
Sadhu	A holy man following a path of spiritual discipline.
Samadhi	A state in which all consciousness of the outer world is transcended; the most purified and transcendental state.
Sant	An ascetic, a mendicant, a pious or religious person.
Sapanda	Divine creative pulsating, living, throbbing energy.
Saroop or Swaroop	Real form.
Shabd or Shabad	Word, Sound, Spiritual Sound. The same as the Word or Logos. As the soul manifests in the body as consciousness, so the Word of God can be heard as Inner, celestial music. Anahad Shabad — unstruck melody or sound, celestial symphony.

Shakta (Shakti)	Power, strength.
Shanti (Santi)	Patience, peace, tranquillity, quiescence.
Sheikh (Shaikh)	Chief; Muslim holy man; a descendant or any one of the disciples of the Prophet Muhammad. Also courtesy title among the Muslims.
Shiva or Siva	Third of the Hindu Trinity, consisting of Brahma, the Creator, Vishnu, the Preserver and Shiva, the Destroyer.
Sufi	The word mostly associated with Muslim mystics, ascetics and dervishes who have a profound esoteric, spiritual way of life.
Sunn	'Void', 'emptiness', 'vacuum'.
Surat	Reflection, memory, recollection, inner attention.
Swami or Svami or Soami	Literally Lord, the Supreme Lord or Supreme Creator. It is also a title given to religious teachers.
Taru Manjari	A source of 'eternal happiness'. Based on timeless wisdom of Vedas and Puranas.
Upanishads	Part of Vedas, their knowledge portion as opposed to their ritualistic part.
Vasnas	Tendencies, present knowledge derived from memory.
Vedanta	'End of Veda', i.e. the complete knowledge of the Veda; a re-interpretation of its basic truths in the light of upanishadic revelation.
Vedas	"Knowledge", revealed knowledge. Universally recognised as the earli-

	est spiritual revelations in the history of mankind. Four in number — Rig, Sama, Yajur and Atharva — they contain over 100,000 verses — *mantras* or inspired hymns — uttered by the great *rishis.*
Yogi or Yogni	One who practises Yoga.
Zen	A Japanese Buddhistic experimental philosophy, showing the way of enlightenment.

II

Abhinavagupta (AD 950-1025)	Grandson of a very learned Brahmin, Atrigupta who lived in the then Madhyadesh (modern UP) and was invited to Kashmir by King Lalitaditya, in the middle of eighth century. Highly learned, a profuse writer and a great sage, Abhinavagupta was regarded as Bhairva (Mahesvara incarnate). Contributed vastly to Kashmir Saivism.
Aurobindo Ghosh, Sri (1872-1950)	Born in Calcutta, educated in England from age of 7. Seeds of patriotism sown in his mind while still at Cambridge. On return to India in 1893 served for a while, and then entered politics. Later went into spiritual retreat at Pondicherry — a place he called 'my cave of *tapasya*'. Aurobindo is pre-eminent in more ways than one: poet, philosopher, interpreter of Indian culture and spirituality, patriot and revolutionary; but above all a supreme seer and Yogi.

	He has written about 100 books, including: 'Essays on Gita', 'The Life Divine', 'Savitri' (the epic poem), and 'The Ideal of Human Unity'.
Bhoomananda Tirtha, Swami	A contemporary saint, hailing from Kerala, took Sanyas at the age of 23. His life has been dedicated to propagating Brahma Vidya — Knowledge and Experience of the Self.
Buddha (the enlightened) (c. 563-c. 483BC)	The founder of Buddhism. Born as son of the Rajah of Sakian, Kapilavastu, Nepal. When about 30 years old he left the luxuries of the court, his beautiful wife and all earthly ambitions for the life of an ascetic. After six years of austerity and mortification under a banyan tree near Bodh Gaya, Bihar, he saw in the contemplative life the perfect way to self-enlightenment. The goal, according to Buddha, is *nirvana* which means the blowing out of the fire of all desires and the absorption of self into the infinite.
Bulleh Shah (1680-1758)	A Muslim saint of the Punjab, a disciple of Hazrat Inayat Shah, a Persian saint who lived in Lahore. His mystic hymns in Punjabi in the form of Kafian have gained unique popularity.
Chinmayananda, Swami (1916-93)	A modern sage, the seer and the saint, thinker and mighty preacher. Travelled all over the world spreading message of Gita and Vedanta. Established Mission for spread of education and spirituality.

Confucius (551-479 BC)
China's most famous teacher, philosopher and political theorist whose ideas have influenced the civilisation of all the Eastern Asia.

Dadu Sahib (1544-1603)
A saint of Rajputana (now in Rajasthan) well known for his boldness in defying the orthodox priests and for teaching Nam, the Word of God.

Gandhi, Mohandas Karamchand. Known as Mahatma Gandhi (1869-1948)
Born in Porbander, in Western India. Went to London at 19 to study law. Returned to India in 1891 as a barrister. Went to South Africa in 1893, where he launched himself as a tenacious political campaigner against the racial discrimination there. Returned to India in 1914, became a dominant influence in the National Congress movement. Rose to be an international political figure of his generation. Led India to freedom. Non-violence, non-cooperation had been his policy throughout the freedom struggle. Believer in hand-spinning, hand-weaving and other cottage industries. Life story: 'My Experiments with Truth'. (Killed at the hands of a Hindu fanatic.)

Inayat Khan, Hazrat Sufi (1882-1927)
Coming from a famous family of court musicians, became very well known as a singer and Saraswati Veena player. Left for the West when 28. He and his brothers performed music in the great concert halls of Europe and America for 10 years. Later worked for the Sufi Message of love, harmony and beauty.

Ibrahim — Abraham of the Bible. Was a man of truth and a prophet. He and his son Ismail are stated to have prayed to Allah for accepting their service to making Mecca a city of peace and security. Ibrahim proclaimed the Hajj (pilgrimage to Mecca).

Iqbal, Muhammed Dr. (Sir) (1876-1938) — Poet and philosopher, born in Sialkot, then in India, now in Pakistan. Studied at Lahore, Cambridge and Munich. One of the most serious philosophers, thinkers and Urdu poets of modern time — an extraordinary intellectual with genuinely perceptive mind. Achieved fame through his poetry full of mysticism and nationalism.

Ishwarananda Giri, Swami — A great living saint, exponent of 'Samvit'. Travelled widely in India and abroad. Headquarters at Mount Abu, Rajasthan. A scholar, a speaker and a writer, his works include: 'Bird Songs', 'Soul to Soul', 'Samvit Prayers', 'Vedanta and Vision of Life', among others.

Janaka (King) — An ancient king of saintly character; a just ruler and a man of great piety. He was the father of Sita, the consort of Rama, the hero of Ramayana.

Jyotirmayananda, Swami — A contemporary saint. Founder-President of Yoga Research Foundation, headquarters in Miami, Florida, USA, with Swami Lalitananda as Vice-President. Author: 'The Art of Positive Thinking'. His message is:

'When you succumb to the downward pull of *Rajas* and *Tamas* you follow the path of darkness; but when you continue to lift your mind through meditation, prayer, *japa*, good actions and good association, you are following the path of blessedness. Therefore, the Vedic Prayer: Tamso Ma Jyotirgamaya — "Lead me from darkness to Light".

Kabir Sahib (1398-1518) — A renowned and revered saint who lived in Varanasi, then called Kashi. He was a low caste weaver and a disciple of Ramanand. Innumerable number of spiritual compositions are to his credit.

Kahlil (generally spelled Khalil) Gibran (1883-1931) — Like those of many romantic poets of the East or the West, his youthful flights were away from the world that seemed largely in the hands of injustice and violence. Lebanon was his native country from which he took his reference. He became an exile; lived in Paris and finally settled in New York.

Gibran's figure of the poet stands at the top of his hierarchy. He rebelled against orthodoxy, against priesthood. Wrote in Arabic and English. Well-known books in English are: 'The Mad Man' (1918), 'The Prophet' (1923) and 'Jesus, the Son of Man' (1928).

Kripal Singh, Sant (1894-1974) — Pursued his spiritual development under Baba Sawan Singh (1858-

1948) — the great saint of Beas. Founded the World Federation of Religions and encouraged dialogue between believers of all faiths.

Krishna — Lord Krishna, held to be an incarnation of Vishnu. His celebrated Bhagavad Gita or Song Celestial which appears in the Mahabharata, contains the major teachings of Lord Krishna given in a dialogue between Krishna and Arjuna, one of the five Pandavas, just before the commencement of the great eighteen-day battle at Kurukshetra.

Krishnamurti, Jiddu (1895-1986) — Theosophist, born in Madras, India. Educated in England by Annie Besant, who in 1925 proclaimed him the Messiah. Later he rejected this persona, dissolved the World Order of the Star in the East (founded by Dr. Besant), and travelled the world teaching and advocating way of life and thought unconditioned by the narrowness of nationality, race and religion. Set up Krishnamurti Foundation. Wrote several books on philosophy and religion.

Laleshwari (Lalla, Lal Ded) — A mystic poetess of Kashmir — 14th century whose Lal 'Vakhs' (Sayings) are songs of spiritual bliss equally popular with Hindus and Muslims, in Kashmir.

Madhva (12th century) — While agreeing with Ramanuja's dualistic (*dvaita*) view, rejected any qualification of the uniqueness of *brahman*.

Mahesh Yogi, Maharishi	A famous living saint. Has popularised, especially in the West, what he calls 'Science of Creative Intelligence (SCI)' and 'Transcendental Meditation (TM)', through a wide network of training, research and publicity.
Mansoor-Al Hallaj (858-922)	Writer and teacher of Islamic mysticism (sufism). Defended Sufi movement against stiffening opposition. Finally arrested and crucified.
Manu	Considered to be the father of humanity; the Man par excellence; also the first priest who established the sacrifices.
Meera Bai (1498-1547)	Meera Bai — "the queen saint" — is India's most popular mystic and poet. Daughter of Rattan Singh Rathaur, prince of Merta, she was married to Bhojraj, the heir to the princely State of Chittaur. But unhappily, the young prince died about five years after her marriage. She then spent all her time in devotion (to Krishna) and in the society of holy men. Ravi Das, a cobbler, was her spiritual master.
Mother, The (1878-1973)	Mirra Alfansa (her childhood name) was born in Paris. Had deep and unusual spiritual experience from very early age. From eleven to thirteen, as she herself writes, a series of psychic and spiritual experiences revealed to her not only the existence of God but man's possibility of uniting with Him, of realizing Him integrally

in consciousness and action, of manifesting Him upon earth in a life divine.

A talented young lady having learnt painting, music and studied many museums, she came to India in 1914 with her husband Paul Richard, who was also interested in spirituality. They met Sri Aurobindo. The Mother was back to Pondicherry in 1920. Served/helped the Ashram and its inmates the rest of her life.

The spiritual significance of the meeting between Sri Aurobindo and the Mother is immeasurable. In later years it was a progressive and splendid development of integral yoga.

Muhammad (c. 570-c. 632) Born in Mecca, the son of Abdullah—a poor merchant. At the age of 25 he led the caravans of a rich widow, Khadija (age 40) who was so impressed by him that she offered him marriage and financial security.

While continuing as a merchant Muhammad became increasingly concerned about the polytheism and superstitions of the Meccans and other Arabs. He was deeply drawn to religious contemplation with growing conviction that there was only one true God. When he was 40 (c. 610) the angel Gabriel, it is believed, appeared to him on Mount Hira and told him he was the messenger of God. From then onward

	began the revelations to him by God. The teachings were collected and written down (c. 650) as the Quran (Recitation). Muhammad founded Islam, now a worldwide religion.
Nanak, Guru (1469-1539)	Born at Talwandi near Lahore (now in Pakistan). He condemned the orthodox creeds of the people with great vigour, and laid emphasis on the spiritual aspect of religion, and on love of God and man. He undertook four major tours to propagate his teachings. (There has been succession to the Mastership, the tenth, last one being Guru Gobind Singh—1666-1708.)
Nehru, Jawaharlal (1889-1964)	Born in Allahabad. Statesman and Prime Minister of India (1947-1964). Studied at Cambridge. Joined politics, became Secretary, the Indian National Congress Committee and later its President. As independent India's first Prime Minister he introduced a policy of industrialization, reorganized States on a linguistic basis and was one of the architects of Non-aligned group of Nations. Wrote several books of which 'Discovery of India' is most famous.
Nooruddin (1377-1438)	(Also known as Nund Rishi.) The patron saint of Kashmir. Greatly influenced by Laleshwari (Lal Ded), the well-known Hindu lady saint. Lived in a cave for 12 years practising penances. A strict vegetarian. Not literate himself, his beautiful sayings

	furnish Kashmiri literature with gems. He placed emphasis on moral values, discipline and love/affection among all sections of society. Revered equally by Hindus and Muslims. His 600 year old Charar-e-Sharief shrine — which attracted pilgrims from all religions — was unfortunately reduced to ashes on May 2, 1995.
Paltu Sahib (1710-80)	A famous Indian saint who lived in Ayodhya, U.P., most of his life. Noted for his bold and fearless exposition of the path to God-realization. Was burnt alive by priests and orthodox people who resented his bold teachings.
Patanjali	The foremost ancient exponent of Yoga. His eight-fold yoga is well known. His short and masterly work *Yoga Sutras* forms one of the six systems of Hindu philosophy. His date of birth is unknown though many scholars assign him to second century B.C.
Purna, Swami	A prince-turned spiritual master. Now a world teacher. President World Spiritual Society (India). Also of sister Societies in UK (Viswa Adhyatmik Sansthan) and in the USA (Adhyatmik Foundation Inc.). (Age estimated in eighties, looks in thirties.)
Rabiah Basri or Rabia of Basra (713-801)	A renowned Muslim mystic, and saintly woman, disciple of Hassan of Basra. She mostly remained ab-

	sorbed in love and longing for the Lord.
Radhakrishnan, Sarvapalli (Dr.) (1882-1975)	Scholar, statesman and philosopher. President of India (1962-67). Taught in India and abroad; was professor of Eastern Religions and Ethics at Oxford (1936-1952). Written a number of books: 'Indian Philosophy', 'Eastern Religions and Western Thoughts', 'East and West' etc. In his lectures and books he tried to interpret Indian thought for westerners.
Rajneesh, Bhagwan, Acharya (1931-90)	Graduated in Philosophy in 1956. Worked as a teacher/professor for ten years, whereafter he took to teaching 'the art of meditation', touring the length and breadth of India. In 1974 the Ashram in Poona opened which attracted people from abroad too. In 1981, a new phase — Rajneeshpuram, USA began at a 64,000 acre ranch in the Central Oregon desert. In 1985, problems began and Rajneesh had to leave USA, and go from place to place, finally back to Poona, where he breathed his last. Unhappily for him and his many disciples, an able speaker and writer (he has written over 500 books), Rajneesh was 'a controversial figure'.
Rama, Swami	A renowned exponent of holistic approach to life, spreading wisdom of the East to the West. Founder and spiritual head of the Himalayan International Institute of Yoga Sci-

	ence and Philosophy of the USA. The headquarters in the rolling hills of the Pucono Mountains, offer programs in education, research, awareness and self-directed change. Published number of books.
Ramakrishna Paramahansa (1836-86)	Born of poor Brahmin parents in one of the remote villages of Bengal. Had very little schooling. Became a temple priest near Calcutta. Worshipped an image of the "Blissful Mother". Day after day he would weep and implore 'the Mother' to speak to him. The 'Divine Mother', it is said, herself became the teacher and initiated him into the truths he sought. Later he underwent the disciplines of different religions, to experience and affirm that the goal of each religion was the same. To the world the unique gift of this great saint was his unique disciple — Vivekananda.
Ramanand (1340-1448)	An Indian saint, born near Madras. He was a disciple of Raghavananda, and the Guru of Kabir Sahib and Ravi Das. He came to northern India quite early in life and settled at Varanasi called Kashi in those days.
Ramanuja (10th century)	An expositor of Vedanta like Sankara, but against latter's *advait* doctrine. He contended that *atman* and *brahman* are relative terms — like part and whole — but not identical.
Ravidas (15th century)	Also Raidas. He was born at Benares and was a contemporary and friend

of Kabir Sahib. Though he belonged to a low caste — being a cobbler — many members of the highest caste became his disciples, notably Queen Meera Bai of Chittaur. Some of his hymns, full of love and devotion, are included in the Guru Granth (Sikh scripture).

Rumi (1207-1272) Thirteenth century Muslim saint, philosopher and greatest mystical poet of Islam. Born at Balkh, Persia (now Afghanistan). He was disciple of Shams-i-Tabriz, and the author of didactic epic Masnavi-ye Mar'fat (Spiritual Couplets).

Sadi or Saadi (1184-1292) Assumed name of Sheikh Muslih Addin. Poet, born in Iran. The catalogue of his works comprises 22 different kinds of writings in prose and verse. The most celebrated are a series of moral and religious works—Gulistan (Rose Garden), Bostan (Orchard) and Pand-Namah (Book of Instruction).

Shankaracharya (Sankara—short name) (AD 788-820) Born at Kaladi (Kerala), dedicated his life to God-realization. Every page of his life scintillates with spiritual wisdom, logical subtlety and philosophical profundity. He visited many holy places in India, held discussions with the learned leaders of various schools of thought, spreading the gospel of Unity in diversity. He wrote commentaries on ten Upanishads, the Bhagavad Gita and the Brahma

Sutra, established four principal monasteries (Maths) at the four cardinal points of India, assigning to each one of the 4 Vedas. The whole object of worship, he preached, is to 'become perfect, to become divine, to reach God and be God'. He passed away at the age of 32. This marvellous young Brahmin, it is stated, had completed all his writings at the age of sixteen.

Satya Sai Baba — Born in November, 1926 at Putaparthi (Andhra Pradesh) 1990 — Golden Jubilee Year of declaration of *Avatarhood* (status of prophet). Also 65th Birthday. His mission: 'to awaken in man the awareness of the Divinity inherent in him, by preaching the basic principles of *Satya* (Truth), *Dharma* (Righteousness), *Shanti* (Peace) and *Prema* (Love)'.

Shams-i-Tabriz (1206-48) — Shams-uddin Muhammad Tabriz, better known as Shams-i-Tabriz, a famous Muslim saint of Persia was born in Tabriz, Iran, later settled in Multan (now Pakistan). He was the Master of Maulana Rumi. He was assassinated by religious fanatics.

Sheikh Farid (1173-1265) — One of the most distinguished of Muslim mystics. Born near Multan in north western India (now Pakistan). His master was Khwaja Qutubuddin Bakhtiyar Kaki of Delhi. On his Master's death, he inherited his patched mantle. He was also called Ganj-i-Shakar (treasure of sugar), as

	in his childhood his mother used to tempt him with sugar while teaching and later performing prayer. The mother kindled that spark of Divine which later dominated Farid's entire being.
Shirdi Sai Baba	Birth shrouded in mystery. Said to have been born as Brahmin, nursed and brought up by a Muslim faqir. He had adopted Hindu-Muslim mixed ways of life and prayer to show that soul has no caste or race. Baba possessed supernatural powers, used them as 'God's gifts for God's purpose'. He was among rare saints, who having attained God-vision strove for welfare of people. 'Allah Malik' (God is Lord) was his pet remark by way of blessing whenever anybody approached him for anything. Died 1918.
Sivananda Sarasvati, Swami (1887-1963)	Founder of Divine Life Society, Rishikesh, India. Profound writer on spiritual subjects. Well-known works include 'Kundalini Yoga', 'Voice of Himalaya' and 'The Service of Pranayam'.
Surdas (16th century)	The blind poet, his poetry relates mostly to Krishna and Braj, the place where Krishna spent his early life, the unassuming role of a cowherd. Known for his devotional songs, Surdas even sang about Vedanta. He is said to have written 75,000 verses.
Tagore, Rabindranath	Poet and philosopher, born in Cal-

(1861-1941)	cutta, India. Best known for his poetic work, notably Gitanjali (1910—Song Offering) and his short stories. Founded Santiniketan — a school where Eastern and Western philosophical and educational systems are blended. Received Nobel Prize of Literature in 1913, the first Asian to do so.
Teresa, Mother	The simple, down to earth nun who was born in Agnes Bejaxhiv, to an Albanian middle class family in 1910, is now treated as a living saint. Her work among the wretched, the diseased and the dying, particularly the lepers, has won her world acclaim. The Missionaries of Charity, the order the mother founded in 1950, has been doing yeoman's service to the poor, the needy and the miserable. 'When I am cleansing the wounds of the poor, I am cleansing the wounds of Christ', says Mother Teresa. Winner of the Nobel Prize, this post-modern saint continues to work humbly, ceaselessly despite age and ailments, remaining beyond both eulogy and criticism to which she has been subjected.
Tuka Ram, Sant (1665-1706)	A prominent saint of west India. Was an embodiment of renunciation. Struggled very hard to march forward on the path of God realization despite innumerable worldly difficulties. His teaching was constant

	singing of God's name and keeping noble company.
Tulsi Das (1532-1632)	A famous North Indian saint author of the Ramayana based on the ancient epic. Born at Kashi, Varanasi in U.P. in a very poor family. He is regarded as one of the greatest medieval devotional poets of North India.
Vasisht	Was Rama's Guru. His teachings — mostly in the form of dialogue between him and Rama — are given in Yog Vasisht.
Vaswani, Sadhu T.L. (1879-1966)	This great modern sage believed in New Life, True Life — a life of fellowship, companionship with God. Beloved Dada as he was known, looked on all as his own. He gave profound talks on Yoga and allied subjects. Wrote many books. To mention a few: 'What is Yoga', 'Youth and the Coming Renaissance', 'In the Footsteps of Buddha', 'Awakeners of Humanity', 'Kindle the Light'.
Vyas, Ved, Rishi (3000 B.C.)	Son of great sage Parasara. His original name was Krishnadipayan. He is said to be author of the Mahabharata which includes the Bhagawad Gita of Lord Krishna.
Vivekananda (1863-1903)	Originally Narendranath, this youthful monk was initiated and tutored by Paramahansa Ramakrishna — the former being the stream and the latter was the spring. He startled the world with his most stimulating address at the first World Conference of

Religions held in Chicago in Aug-Sep 1983. In his own words his mission was: 'to preach unto mankind their divinity and how to make it manifest in every movement of life'. During his tours in the country itself (after returning in 1897) he endeavoured to bring life and vigour to the motherland. Being a capable organizer he founded the Ramakrishna Math and Mission.

Yogananda (1893-1952) Originally Mukunda Lal Ghosh, and a graduate of Calcutta University, this name was chosen in 1915 when he was admitted to the Giri Branch of the Swami Order by Sri Yukteswar, his guru, who sent him, in 1920, as his emissary to the West. Paramahansa Yogananda's 'Autobiography of a Yogi' gives detailed account of this great master. His Yoga lessons have won worldwide acclaim. They are 'valuable for daily physical, mental and spiritual welfare'. His non-sectarian and scientific instructions are based on original Raja ("Royal") Yoga of Lord Krishna.

III

Aristotle (384-322 BC) Born in Greece. First a pupil then a teacher in Plato's Academy at Athens. Remained there for 20 years and attained reputation in rhetoric. Was tutor for 3 years to the future Alexander the Great. Set up his own

	school. Aristotle's work represents an enormous encyclopaedic output over virtually every field of knowledge, logic, metaphysics, ethics, politics, rhetoric, poetry, biography, zoology, physics and psychology.
Brunton, Dr. Paul (1898-1981)	Born in London. Early in life he became interested in comparative religion, mysticism and philosophy. He travelled extensively in the Orient, investigating the ideas and practices of Yogis, mystics and holy men. His works include 'A Search in Secret India', 'Hermits in the Himalayas', 'The Quest of the Overself', 'The Spiritual Crisis of Man' etc.
Buck, Pearl (1892-1973)	The first American woman to win the Nobel Prize for Literature. Famous the world over for her magnificent novels of Chinese life. Translation of a Chinese classic — 'All Men are Brothers' very well known.
Camus, Albert (1613-60)	The French existentialist, writer. Born in Algeria. Actor, teacher, playwright and journalist. Received the Nobel Prize for Literature.
Christopher, Isherwood (1904-86)	Novelist. Born in Cheshire. Studied at Cambridge and London. Taught English in Germany for a while. Became US citizen in 1937 to work as scriptwriter.
Coleridge, Samuel Taylor (1875-1912)	Poet. Studied at Cambridge. Initiated revolutionary ideas. Rejected Wordsworth's animistic views of nature. Besides poetry, he is known for criti-

	cal writing and for theological and politico-sociological works.
David, Thomas Osborne (1814-45)	Writer and politician who was the chief organizer and poet of the young Ireland movement. His writings virtually became gospel of the Sinn Fein movement.
Emerson, Ralph Waldo (1803-82)	Poet and essayist. Born in Boston. Studied at Harvard. Known for 'The Conduct of Life'. A transcendentalist in philosophy, a rationalist in religion and a bold advocate of spiritual individualism.
Foster, E.M. (1879-1970)	Born in London. Studied at Cambridge. His works include: 'Where Angels Fear to Tread' (1905), 'The Longest Journey' (1967), 'Passage to India', 'A Room with a View to India'.
Francis of Assissi, Saint (1181-1226)	Confessor, founder of the Franciscan Order. Born in a wealthy family, he left it for service of the church. Worked among the poor and the sick, particularly lepers. Himself passed through conditions of extreme illness and discomfort; became blind in 1225, died aged only 45. Francis is considered as one of the most attractive and best loved saints of all time.
Goethe, J.W. (1749-1832)	Born in Frankfurt (Germany). A creative writer. Carried out scientific research in botany and comparative anatomy. A man of genius but at odds with society.
Hegel, George W.F. (1770-1830)	Born in Stuttgart, he worked at various German Universities, especially

	Berlin. Usually classified as an objective Idealist. His system is characterized by the use of dialectic of thesis, antithesis and synthesis. He influenced such widely diverse thinkers as Marx, Bradey and Crocs.
Heraclitus (536-470 BC)	("The Observer") of Epherms. A philosopher who held that there is nothing abiding in the world, only change is real.
Huxley, Aldous (1894-1968)	Novelist and essayist. Studied in Oxford, lived in Italy in 1920s, moved to California in 1937. Reputation made with his novels: Chrome Yellow (1921) & Antic Hay (1923). Best known works: 'Brave New World' (1932). Later writings became more mystical.
Jesus, Christ (c. 6/5 BC-c. AD 30/33)	The central figure of the Christian faith, he was the first born son of Virgin Mary. Born in Bethlehem. About 18 years passed in obscurity before baptism at the hands of his cousin, John the Baptist provided a public intimation of Jesus's mission. After 40 days in the wilderness, wrestling successfully with all sorts of temptations, Jesus gathered around him 12 disciples. Christ's flouting of traditional religious practices, the performance of miracles and the Sermon on the Mount are some of the milepoles of his history. Crucified on the hill of Calvary. (The year of death is uncertain but it is usually considered

as AD 30/33.) Stated to have reappeared before his Apostles. Christ's nature as 'son of God' and redemptive work are fundamental beliefs of adherents of Christianity.

Kant, Immanuel (1724-1804)	Born and died in Konisgberg (Germany). Scarcely travelled 40 miles away from his home. Philosophy was the subject of his study, also astronomy. Held classes of logic and metaphysics at the University of Konisgberg.
Kierkegaard, Soren (1813-55)	Danish religious thinker. He held: 'Sin is worse than suffering', 'Man is egotist and must experience despair', 'God is beyond reason and man'.
Laski, Harold J. (1893-1950)	Born in Manchester. Ranked as one of the outstanding political thinkers, educators and debaters of the English-speaking world. Some of his major publications: 'Foundations of Sovereignty' (1921); 'Liberty in Modern State' (1930); 'Democracy in Crisis' (1933); 'The Danger of Being a Gentleman' (1939); 'The American Presidency' (1940).
Locke, Johan (1612-1714)	The first great British empiricist. Was also a political, economic and religious thinker of note. An ardent defender of freedom of thought and speech.
Loon, Hendrik Willem van (1882-1944)	Popular historian born in Rotterdam, The Netherlands. Migrated to the USA in 1903 as journalist. In 1922 published the best-selling illustrated 'Story of Mankind'.

Lucretius, Carus (98-54 BC)	Noted Roman poet; author of the famous dialectic poem De' Natura Rerum, in six books which form an interesting exposition of Epicureanism.
Ludwig, Emil (1881-1948)	Born in Germany but for many years a Swiss citizen. Writer, biographer. His best books are noted for their dramatic power and vividness. Most enduring work — magnificent biography of river — "The Nile". Author controversial biography of Christ — 'The Son of Man' (1928).
Machado, Antonio (1875-1939)	Poet and playwright. Born in Spain. Became French teacher. Wrote lyrics, characterised by a nostalgic melancholy.
Maslow, Abraham (1908-70)	Psychologist. Born in Brooklyn, N.Y. A professor at Brooklyn College (1937-51) and Brandeis University (1951-61). Regarded as the founder of humanist psychology. His seminal: 'Motivation and Personality' (1954) explored the new humanistic model.
Morgan, Charles (1894-1958)	Writer. After serving Navy published 'Gunman' (1919) from Oxford University. Joined The Times in 1921. His novel 'Portrait of a Mirror' (1929) and other later well-known books are 'The Fountain' and 'The Voyage'.
Pascal, Blaise (1632-62)	French. Mathematician, physicist, theologian, man of letters. Wrote fragments about Christian truth, for a case book, discovered after his death.

Peale, Norman Vincent (1898-1994)	Christian Reformer, pastor and writer. Long ministry at Marble Collegiate Reformed Church. He wrote the best-seller 'The Power of Positive Thinking'. Was much in demand as a lecturer on public affairs.
Radha, Swami Sivananda	Founder and spiritual director of the Yasodhara Ashram, a yoga retreat and study centre located at Kootenay Bay, British Columbia, Canada. She is also the founder and president of the Association for the Development of Human Potential in the United States. Received her training at the Sivananda Ashram in Rishikesh, India. Returned to the West in 1956 to disseminate the yogic teachings and practice.
Romains, Jules (1875-1972)	Poet, dramatist, essayist and medical researcher. One of the world's leading French literary figures. Creator of masterly series of "Men of Good Will".
Russell, A.W. Bertrand (1872-1970)	Secured his early reputation as mathematician and symbolic logician. Developed it as educator, philosopher and writer of many popular works on science and related subjects. Had been lecturer and Fellow of Trinity College, Cambridge. Some of his books include: 'Mysticism and Logic' (1918); 'Roads to Freedom' (1918); 'Marriage & Morals' (1929); 'The Conquest of Happiness' (1930).
Sappho (c. 610-c. 580 BC)	Greek poet. The most celebrated female poet of antiquity. Wrote lyrics

	unsurpassed for depth of feeling, passion and grace.
Socrates (470-399 BC)	Was a great Greek philosopher. Mentor of Plato. Was mainly interested in ethics. Executed (committed suicide according to a version) after being charged as irreligious.
Spinoza, Benedict (1632-77)	Believed in Monism. His chief work 'Ethics, Philosophy and Science' expresses them as an integral system.
Voltaire, Francois (1694-1778)	Writer, dramatist and historian. Born in Paris. Embodiment of 18th century Enlightenment. He was quite against the bigotry of organized religions. His ideas were an important influence on the intellectual climate leading to the French Revolution.
Webb, Beatrice (1858-1943)	Collaborated with her husband Sidney Webb for 40 years in the production of many standard works on social problems, the most monumental of which was "Soviet Communism — A New Civilisation'. Has recorded her own development as a socialist in her book "My Apprenticeship" (1928).

Select Bibliography

Auden, W.H. "I Believe" — The personal philosophies of twenty-three men and women of our time. London: George Allen and Unwin, 1940.

Ashokananda, Swami. "The Soul's Journey to its Destination." Calcutta: Advaita Ashram.

Aurobindo Ghosh, Sri. "The Message & Mission of India." Bombay: Bharatiya Vidya Bhavan, 1964.

Aurobindo Ghosh, Sri. "Savitri." Pondicherry: Sri Aurobindo Society.

Azzan, Abdul Rahman. "Eternal Message of Muhammad." London: Quarter Books.

"The Bhagavad Gita." Gorakhpur: Gita Press.

Blavatsky, H.P. "The Voice of Silence." Madras: The Theosophical Publishing House, 1978.

Brelvi (Prof.). "Seeratul-Nabi." Pakistan: Institute of Sindhology, University of Sind, 1982.

"Bridging Science & Spirituality." Mount Abu, Rajasthan: Brahma Kumari World Spiritual University, 1984.

Bryant, (Dr.) M. Darrol. "Religion in a New Key." New Delhi: Wiley Eastern Ltd., 1992.

Budhananda, Swami. "Will Power and Development." Calcutta: Advaita Ashram.

Carothers, Merlin R. "Power in Praise." Plainfield, N.Y., USA: Logos International.

Charan Singh, Maharaj. "Die to Live." Beas, Punjab: Radha Soami Satsang, 1980.

Chawla, Navin. "Mother Teresa." Delhi: Gulmohar Press, 1992.

Chinmayananda, Swami. "A Sweeping Look at Vedanta." Bombay: Central Chinmaya Mission Trust, 1993.

Cohen, David. "The Circle of Life." New York: Harper Collins Publishers.

Collins, Mabel. "Light on the Path." Adyar, Madras: The Theosophical Publishing House, 1975.

Davidson. "The Web of Life." England: The C.W. Daniel Company Ltd., 1988.

Deshpande, G.T. "Abhinavagupta." New Delhi: Sahitya Akademi, 1992.

"Dissolving Doubts." Prasanthi Nilayam (A.P.): Sri Sathya Sai Books and Publications Trust, 1985.

Giri, Ishwarananda Swami. "Bird Songs", "Samvit Prayers", "Pearls of Wisdom". Mount Abu, Rajasthan: Samvit Sadhanayana, 1977.

Giri, Ishwarananda Swami. "Taru Manjari." Jodhpur: Ankuran Prakashan, 1981.

Giri, Ishwarananda Swami. "Vedanta and Vision of Life." Ahmedabad: Gujarat University, 1979.

Giri, Purna Swami. "Petals of Truth", "Seeking the Lotus Within", "Indra's Pearls", "The Fruit of Purity", "Maya's Play", "The Lost Necklace", "Poorn Yoga". USA: Adhyatmik Foundation Inc.

Gopi Krishna. "Higher Consciousness." Bombay: D.B. Taraporevala Sons & Co. Pvt. Ltd., 1984.

Gopi Krishna. (1) "The Dawn of a New Science" and (2) "Reason and Revelation". New Delhi: Kundalini Research & Publications Trust, 1979.

Goyandka, Jayadayal. "What is God." Gorakhpur: Gita Press, 1966.

"Granth Samata Prakash", "Granth Samata Vilas". Jagadhari, Haryana: Sangat Samatavad.

Gupta, Som Raj (Prof.). "Merey Gurudev." Jagadhari, Haryana: Sangat Samatavad.

Haryal, P.R. 1) "Samata Sadhan Saranksh"; 2) "Mortality to Immortality". Delhi: Con. International, 1989, 1992, respectively.

Jayakar, (Mrs.) Pupul. "J. Krishnamurti — A Biography." Delhi: Penguin Books, 1987.

"Jeevan Gatha (Life of Mahatma Mangat Ram)." Jagadhari, Haryana: Sangat Samatavad, 1993.

Jhabwala, S.H. "Geeta and its commentaries." Bombay: Dhawla Popular, 1961.

Jung, C.G. "The Undiscovered Self." USA: Little Brown Co.

Jyotirmayananda, Swami. "The Art of Positive Thinking." Miami Florida, USA: Yoga Research Foundation, 1988.

Kanal, S.P. "What can take the place of God in Religion?" Chandigarh: Dev Samaj.

Kasturi, N. "Sathyam-Sivam-Sundaram." Prasanthi Nilayam, Andhra Pradesh: Sri Sathya Sai Books and Publications Trust, 1981.

Kaul, B.N. Nazir. "Shaivic Thought Non-Meditational Meditation." Jammu (J&K State): Ram Shiva Gobind Ashram, 1993.

Khan, Altaf A. "A Complete Guide Book of Islam." Delhi: Adam Publishers & Distributers, 1994.

Khan, Hazrat Inayat. "Sufi Teachings." Delhi: Motilal Banarsidass Publishers Pvt. Ltd., 1990.

Khan, Hazrat Inayat. "The Radiance of Love, Harmony and Beauty." Delhi: Memorial Trust, 1988.

Kripal Singh. "Man Know Thyself." Delhi: Sawan Kripal Publications, 1980.

Mahesh Yogi, Maharishi. "Meditation of Maharishi Mahesh Yogi." New York: Bantam Books Inc., 1968.

Malaviya, Madan Mohan. "The Immanence of God." Gorakhpur: Gita Press, 1966.

"A Man of God (Mahatma Mangat Ram)." Naraina, New Delhi: Samata Yog Ashram, 1981.

Mandino, O.G. "The Greatest Salesman in the World." New York: Frederick Paul Publishers Inc.

Mittal, Rakesh K. "Dictionary of Positive Thoughts." Delhi: Sterling Publishers Pvt. Ltd., 1993.

Mumukshananda, Swami. 1) "The Message of Ramakrishna", 2) "The Message of Holy Mother", 3) "The Message of Vivekananda". Calcutta: Advaita Ashram, 1990, 1992, 1992, respectively.

Napoleon, Underhill. "Success through a Positive Mental Attitude." New York: Pocket Books.

Panarimalai, Swamigal, Sri La Sri. "The Holy Panchakshara." Bombay: A.V. Ramachandran, 1972.

Panikkar, Raimundo. "The Vedic Experience: Mantramanjari." London: Darton, Longman and Todd, 1977.

Paul Brunton (Dr.). "The Quest of the Overself." Calcutta, Delhi, Madras: B.I. Publications, 1975.

Peale, Norman Vincent. "Positive Imaging" and "The Power of Positive Thinking". N. York: Foundation for Christian Living.

Piel, (Dr.) Gerard. "Only One World our own to make and to keep." New York, USA: W.H. Freeman and Company, 1992.

Poddar, Hanuman Prasad. 1) "The Divine Message", 2) "How to Attain Eternal Happiness". Gorakhpur (U.P.): Gita Press.

Prabhananda, Swami and Christopher Isherwood. "Bhagwad Gita: Introduction by Aldous Huxley." Madras: Sri Ramakrishna Math, 1974.

Puri, J.R. "Guru Nanak — His Mystic Teachings." Beas, Punjab: Radha Soami Satsang, 1982.

"The Quran" (English Translation). Beirut: Dar-ul-Choura, 1980.

Radhakrishnan, S. (Dr.). "Bhagavadgita." Bombay: Blackie & Sons (India) Ltd., 1977.

Rajagopalachari, C. "Upanishads." Bombay: Bharatiya Vidya Bhavan, 1982.

Rajchandra. "Atma Siddhi." Bombay: Bharatiya Vidya Bhavan, 1976.

Rajneesh, Bhagwan Shree. "Death — the Greatest Fiction." GmbH, Cologne, Germany: The Rebel Publishing House.

Rama, Swami. 1) "Life Here and Hereafter", 2) "Wisdom of Ancient Sages". Honeysdale Pennsylvania: Himalayan International Institute of Yoga Science and Philosophy of the USA, 1983.

Schuller, Robert H. "Self Love — The Dynamic Force of Success." New York: Howthorn Books Inc.

Schuller, Robert H. "Move Ahead with Positive Thinking." New York: Guideposts Associates Inc., Carmel.

Schuon, F. "Spiritual Perspective and Human Feeling." London: Faber & Faber, 1964.

Sharief, M.M. "A History of Muslim Philosophy." Germany: Otto Harrassowitz, Wiesbaden, 1966.

"Sri Aurobindo — His Life & Teachings." Bombay: Popular Prakashan, 1965.

"Shri Sai Sat Chitra." Ahmednagar: Shri Sai Baba Sansthan Shirdi, 1991.

Sinha, (Dr.) Phulgenda. "Yoga for Mental Power." Delhi:

Oriental Publishers, 1978.

Sivananda, Swami. "Life is Yoga", "Yoga Asans". Rishikesh: Divine Life Society.

Sivananda Radha, Swami. "Kundalini Yoga." Delhi: Motilal Banarsidass Publishers Pvt. Ltd., 1992.

Smith, Huston. "Forgotten Truth — The Primordial Tradition." New York: Harper Row Publishers.

Smith, T.V. "Live Without Fear." New York: The New American Library of World Literature Inc.

Subramaniam, Kamala. "Mahabharata." Bombay: Bharatiya Vidya Bhavan, 1989.

Sulabh Devi. "Points to Ponder." Trichur, Kerala: Narayanasrama Thapovanam Parlam.

Swaminathan, K. "Ramana Maharishi." Delhi: National Book Trust, 1975.

Tapovan Prasad. "Chinmaya Lahri." Bombay: Central Chinmaya Mission Trust, 1987.

'Thoughts for Today." Mount Abu: Prajapita Brahma Kumari Ishwariya Vishwa Vidyalaya.

"Thus Spake Gurudev (Mahatma Mangat Ram)." Jagadhari (Haryana): Sangat Samatavad, 1993.

Thus Spake— "The Buddha", "Sri Sankara", "Guru Nanak", "Vivekananda", "The Vedas", "The Christ". Madras: Sri Ramakrishna Math.

Toffer, Alvin. "Powershift." London, New York: Bantam Books.

"Vachan Mala — Maan ka Kripa Prasad." Nagpur: Sai Publications.

Vaswani, J.P. "Prophets and Patriots." Poona: Mira Publications, Sadhu Vaswani Mission.

Vatsyayan, (Dr.) Kapila. "Concepts of Space: Ancient and

Modern." Delhi: Abhinav Publications, 1991.

Vivekananda, Swami. "My Master." Calcutta: Advaita Ashram, 1984.

Warner, Rex. "The Greek Philosophers." New York: The New American Library, 1958.

Wayne Dyer (Dr.). "The Sky's the Limit." New York: Pocket Books.

Wheeler, Elmer. "How to sell yourself to others." New York: Dell Publishing House.

"Words of Jesus and Satya Sai Baba." Accra (Ghana): Shri Sai Centre of Accra, 1986.

Yogananda, Paramahansa. "Autobiography of a Yogi." Delhi: Jaico Publishing House, 1980.

Yogananda, Paramahansa. 1) "Man's Greatest Adventures", 2) "Developing Dynamic Will". Calcutta: Yogoda Satsang Society of India, 1980, 1987, respectively.

Magazines

All India Magazine, Sri Aurobindo Society, Pondicherry
Ahana, Sri Aurobindo Centre, New Delhi
Chinmaya Mission News Bulletin, New Delhi
Kabir Jyoti, Kabir Peace Mission, Kanpur
Silent Logos (Publication since suspended), Sangat Samatavad, New Delhi

